AF271586

On this series

Towards the end of the 20th century, ethnic conflict has emerged as the pre-eminent expression of violent conflict. Before we can explore ways, means and prospects of preventing ethnic conflict, we need to analyse the causes, genesis, course and outcome of conflict. When groups in conflict are defined simultaneously by ethnicity and religion, the conflicts between them appear to be exceptionally bitter and destructive. At the same time, it has been observed that religiously based tolerance can reduce the readiness to resort to violence. Hence, it appears appropriate to examine the impact of religious teachings on religion in practice and how this influences conflict behaviour. As a rule, sustainable regulation of ethnic conflict requires the agreement of a majority of each of the population groups involved – in other words: democracy.

This series of publications is intended as a collection of analyses of ethnic and ethno-religious conflicts in different countries within their particular context. Accordingly, the series will focus above all on empirical surveys of attitudes towards ethnicity, religion and democracy conducted with instruments that facilitate comparison.

Studien zu Ethnizität, Religion und Demokratie

edited by
Theodor Hanf
Jakob Rösel

Volume 16

Theodor Hanf/Karim El Mufti (eds.)

Policies and Politics of Teaching Religion

Nomos

Die Deutsche Nationalbibliothek lists this publication in the
Deutsche Nationalbibliografie; detailed bibliographic data
is available in the Internet at http://dnb.d-nb.de.

ISBN 978-3-8487-0940-3

1. Edition 2014
© Nomos Verlagsgesellschaft, Baden-Baden 2014. Printed in Germany.

This work is subject to copyright. All rights are reserved, whether the whole or part of
the material is concerned, specifically those of translation, reprinting, re-use of
illustrations, broadcasting, reproduction by photocopying machine or similar means,
and storage in data banks. Under § 54 of the German Copyright Law where copies are
made for other than private use a fee is payable to »Verwertungsgesellschaft Wort«,
Munich.

Acknowledgements

This volume is the result of in particular the efforts of Dr Rüdiger Blumör. Drawing on his experience of working in Afghanistan, he proposed a deeper debate on the topic and arranged for the German Society for International Cooperation (Gesellschaft für Internationale Zusammenarbeit – GIZ) to fund the seminar in Byblos in November 2012 at which the papers were discussed in detail, including his own substantial contribution.

We are particularly grateful to Dr Patrick McGreevy, Dean of the Faculty of Arts and Sciences at the American University of Beirut (AUB), who opened the conference, and Dr Hisham Nashabe, President of the Makassed University of Beirut, whose key note speech provided the framework for the ensuing debates.

Thanks are due to Dr Adnan El Amine, Lebanese University, Dr Thomas William Haase, Chair, Department of Political Studies and Public Administration at the AUB, and Dr Jeremy Menchik, Boston University and Visiting Scholar at the AUB, for their confident moderation of the individual sessions.

Mr Paul Eddé kindly arranged the conference venue with its view from the birthplace of the first alphabet across to the mosques and churches of the city of Beirut in the distance.

John Richardson proofread the English texts and Angela Herrmann prepared them for publication. We thank them for their work.

Theodor Hanf and Karim El Mufti

Contents

Acknowledgements   5

Introduction   9
THEODOR HANF AND KARIM EL MUFTI

Teaching Religion, not Violence. Keynote   11
HISHAM NASHABE

Religious Education and/or the Making of a Citizen. The Case of Lebanon   13
KARIM EL MUFTI

Teaching Religion in Egypt and Tunisia. A Challenge to Citizenship Education   21
MUHAMMAD FAOUR

Capitalizing on Inequality? Religious Schools in Turkey and Israel   39
ANNALENA DI GIOVANNI

Teaching Religion in a Multinational State. The Case of Bosnia-Herzegovina   61
KARIM EL MUFTI

State-Building and Religious Education in the Former Yugoslav Republic of Macedonia   69
GIUDITTA FONTANA

A Review of Religion in the British Education System   89
KELSEY SHANKS

Teaching About Religion in a Spirit of Laïcité. The Case of France   101
ANNE FRANÇOISE WEBER

Teaching Religion in Germany   111
KARL SCHMITT

Madrasa Education in Afghanistan. Between Reform and Militancy   127
RÜDIGER BLUMÖR

Policies and Politics of Teaching Religion in India   145
SHREYA PARIKH

What We Know – and What We Don't. An Epilogue   153
THEODOR HANF

Authors   157

Introduction

States are under constant pressure to legitimise their actions. Any state's long-term stability depends on its reaching a fundamental consensus with its citizens. Although such a consensus does not exclude conflicts of interest, it does presuppose – as a necessary prerequisite for the peaceful regulation of conflicts of interest – the existence of shared values. Hence, as a rule, states act through their institutions to strengthen these values and in particular to ensure that they are handed down from one generation to the next.

In most states these basic values are defined in the constitution or by law, usually in the form of a list of human rights or by reference to the Universal Declaration of Human Rights. Accordingly, civic education at school focuses primarily on the constitution and the institutions of state.

In states with political systems that have strict separation of state and religion the communication of values is restricted to civic education, occasionally supplemented by the teaching of philosophy or ethics. However, today very few states maintain a strict separation of state and religion. Similarly, at the other end of the spectrum, few states define themselves as a theocracy. In the great majority of states the institutions of state enjoy some form of religious legitimacy; there is a degree of cooperation between state and religion; the consensus on values is influenced to varying degrees by religion; and religious instruction is an important instrument for communicating shared values – i.e., from a functional point of view, is intended as a vehicle for instilling society's value horizons in the collective unconscious.

In historically Christian states, religion has lost much of its relevance as a source of legitimacy for values. In any case, the relationship between state and religion is subject to general provisions governing the freedom of religion and equidistance between the state and all religious communities. In the European Constitutional Convention the heated debate about including a reference to God in the preamble to the constitution was ultimately decided in favour of a more reticent reference to Europe's *cultural, religious and humanistic heritage*. The preamble to the German constitution, by contrast, does include a direct reference to God and prescribes religious instruction as a compulsory subject in school.

In states with a predominantly Muslim population the relationship between the state and religion is much closer. Constitutional provisions vary from the recognition of all monotheistic religions, through a Moslem head of state or Islam as the official state religion, to Islamic law as one – or even the most important – source of legislation. Religious instruction in school, usually for Christian as well as Muslim communities, is compulsory in all states with a Muslim majority. Of particular interest is the importance accorded to specific religious communities, religious movements and religiously inspired political movements.

A comparison between different states can contribute more precise insights than studies of individual states into the role of religious and civic instruction in communicating a code of social values and, over and above this, into the goals of a state-defined "values policy" and whether this policy promotes social consensus or disagreement. To this end, it may be useful to compare case studies trying to answer similar questions.

The cases presented in this volume include Afghanistan, Bosnia-Herzegovina, Egypt, France, Germany, India, Indonesia, Israel, Lebanon, Macedonia, Tunisia, Turkey and the United Kingdom. The authors have been invited to address a number of issues, starting with the legal framework, such as the constitution and laws, which determines both the relationship between state and religion and the legal basis for religious and civic instruction. In the latter instance, particular attention will be given to whether religious instruction involves instruction *about* religion or *in* religion. Second, the studies examine the institutions in charge of religious and civic instruction – ministries, religious communities and state and non-state schools – so as to establish where responsibility for drawing up curricula and appointing teachers lies. Third, an analysis of curricula focuses on the value concepts of religion, state and society that they communicate. The fourth point is to determine whether data are available on the effectiveness of teaching as a means of socialisation in the case-study countries. The last point of investigation is whether religious instruction is a source of political conflict and, if so, what are the opposing positions and who represents them.

Finally, on the basis of these comparative case studies an attempt will be made to identify on the one hand similarities that suggest some tentative generalisations and on the other issues for which reliable empirical evidence is lacking – an invitation to further research.

Theodor Hanf and Karim El Mufti

Teaching Religion, not Violence
Keynote

HISHAM NASHABE

Religion is a difficult subject to teach. It becomes more so in a pluralistic society where several religions and sects live side by side. In such an environment sensitivities are heightened and the need for a common sense of belonging becomes a necessity for peaceful coexistence, cooperation and development.

Theoretically, you can avoid all the problems of teaching religion by abandoning religion altogether. But, whether we like it or not, the teaching of religion is a living concern in societies such as the Lebanese.

So, let us be realistic and accept religion as a major issue in the education of our people, both young and old. And, in dealing with this issue, let us "tread softly" because we are treading on holy ground; on peoples' hearts …

Fortunately, religion, all religions, seeks human happiness in this life and in the here-after. Peace, not violence; love, not enmity or animosity; justice, not oppression, are conducive to human happiness and well-being.

In this day and age religion as peace, love, justice, happiness and well-being must be easier to achieve, as people, all over the world, are seeking these ideals more fervently than at any other time in recorded history. The fact is, however, that today, wars and violence in various forms are more widespread in the world, and religion is being exploited to foment violence, create differences, and build walls of separation among peoples.

In this age where the "clash of civilizations" has become a theoretical basis for understanding history, the teaching of religion has become an ever more difficult task, but at the same time, an ever more urgent one.

In Islam, violence, and clashes among "peoples and tribes" are recognized as realities. In order to find for them a solution, peoples have "to know one another", and then, refer their differences to the principles of justice so that peace is established. War, in the Islamic perspective, is an aberration rather than the norm.

During my work in UNESCO as representative of Lebanon in various councils and committees, I have repeatedly called for the rewriting of the history curriculum in schools on the basis of "demilitarizing history". The curricula we now teach in our schools make wars the most important landmarks of history; our national heroes are in most cases military heroes who die in battle. Of course, we should not belittle the exploits and sacrifices of these heroes, but to teach our children that heroism is essentially gained on the battleground is not conducive to the renunciation of violence and the promotion of peace. Similarly, the heroes of the wars of religion should not take precedence over the heroes of piety, peace and justice.

In Lebanon, I was fortunate to be a friend of Sayyid Muhammad Husayn Fadlallah to whom I proposed that we rewrite history from a non-militaristic outlook. He agreed with me and called the person responsible in his party to cooperate with me on this project. Since the Sayyid passed away we made little progress on this project.

Religious reforms are needed at many other levels, intellectual, academic and institutional. These reforms are now on the table, in Lebanon and in many other countries. Hopefully, we will someday see these reforms applied, and witness the divorce between religion and violence as a new landmark in the history of humanity.

Religious Education and/or the Making of a Citizen
The Case of Lebanon[*]

KARIM EL MUFTI

The first panel of the Byblos Seminar on "Teaching Religion in Deeply Divided Societies" included almost all Lebanese religious educational institutions that focus on the different systems of religious education in Lebanon, alongside eminent educational experts. Dr Hassan Kobeissi from the Education Faculty of the Lebanese University offered a documented history of community-run schools in the country, which culminated in a legislative framework in Lebanon that permits self-determination for the different communities in Lebanon. As for the representatives of the different Lebanese communities, they affirmed their support for the right to administer their own affairs and explained the leading role they play in shaping the Lebanese citizen and society. But this vision was challenged by another school of thought that sees in religious education a potential threat to the idea of citizenship.

Consolidation of the communities' right to self-determination in Lebanon in exchange for preaching tolerance

Interestingly, the communities' representatives present at the seminar strongly supported their communities' substantial constitutional rights in all aspects of social life, including the strategically important educational sector.

In Lebanon, Article 10 of the Lebanese Constitution of 1943 as amended states that "education is free so long as it is not contrary to order and to good manners and does not touch the dignity of creeds. No derogation shall affect the right of communities to maintain their own schools, subject to the general prescriptions on public education laid down by the State". As a consequence, the right of the Lebanese communities to establish their private religious schools has been a constitutional right in the Land of the Cedars since the French Mandate, expressed in the Mandate Act of 1922 (Art. 8), the Constitution of 1926 (Art. 10) as amended in 1943 and 1989.

The roots of this policy date to before the French Mandate. The right to religious education was granted to non-Sunni sects when Ottoman rule was established in

---

[*] This is a summary of the discussions at the roundtable on the Lebanese case with the representatives of religious educational institutions and relevant scholars and experts, and moderated by Dr Adnan El Amine, head of the Lebanese Association of Education Studies. Participants included representatives from the *El Mabarrat Association* (Shi'a), the *Association of Evangelical Schools in Lebanon*, the *Joint Christian Education Committee in Lebanon* (Catholic and Orthodox) and the *Makassed Philanthropic Islamic Association* (Sunni) and a written contribution from the representative of the *Irfan Establishment* (Druze).

Lebanon in 1516, as "education was regarded entirely as a communal matter, whether local or foreign" by the authorities, who allowed each religious group to organize its own schools and foreign missionaries to teach in Mount Lebanon. A national effort to organize a common basic curriculum and educational system in Lebanon without challenging the right of the communities to run their own schools was initiated in 1846. (There has been only one – unsuccessful – attempt to interfere with this communal right, namely in 1973, when the Ministry of Education tried to remove religious courses from curricula.) The increase in the number of schools in the period between the Mandate and independence, both state- or community-run indicates the strength of this centuries-old system (see Table 1).

Table 1: Evolution of the number of private and public schools in Lebanon

Year	No. of private schools			No. of public schools
	Total	Local	Foreign	
1919	668	-	-	-
1920	820	-	-	-
1925	1037	578	459	131 or 133
1935	1201	845	413	149
1939	1338	797	361	180
1943	1279	953	326	304

Source: Hassan Kobeissi. *History of Private Schools in Lebanon*, International Research Seminar "Policies and Politics and Teaching Religion", Byblos, 10 November 2012

In 2009, the proportion of private schools (1442 schools) in Lebanon remains higher than that of public schools (1356 schools), or 51.4% vs 48.6%; 69.6% of Lebanese students attending private schools compared to the 31.4% in public schools, thereby perpetuating the long history of autonomous private establishments, namely those run by religious institutions.

Justifying the need for the constitutional arrangement favouring communal self-determination, the religious representatives were very expansive over the politically correct narrative of preaching tolerance, while acknowledging different religious beliefs; a very shaky concept, as many scholars have pointed out. Dr Hassan Kobeissi reminded the panel of Fouad Boustany's remark that "the history of education in Lebanon is Lebanon's history itself", which reflects the difficulty of simultaneously achieving two different educational goals: one social: "shaping individuals to be part of a specific and particular social tissue", the other religious: to "shape individuals to becoming believers in a specific cult".

Respecting the letter and spirit of the Lebanese constitution, all religious educational institutions represented at the seminar defended their right to run private religious schools. Sheikh Sami Abil Mona, the Secretary-General of the Irfan Establishment (Druze), expressed relief that the state supported the communities's right to run private schools:

"State involvement is a must", he stressed, voicing religious educators' unanimous approval of the Lebanese constitution. Yet, all representatives were eager to stress the fact that no element or method in their curriculum was aimed against other sects and communities in the country, thereby highlighting their will to respect public order in compliance with the constitution.

Alongside this, the representatives of the religious educational institutions emphasized the importance of spiritual guidance for children as part of their right to provide genuine religious education to the members of their respective communities, while at the same time teaching them tolerance and mutual respect.

As such, religious education (both Islamic and Christian in this case) is offered as a means to promote a sense of universality among all human beings, united in God's oneness. Hence, the message religion can offer is one of peace and respect. Sayyed Jaafar Fadlallah, the Religious Guide of El Mabarrat Association, stressed that the issue of violence and political tension in Lebanon "is not to be found in religion, we all believe in one God"; "we all believe in His guiding principles He has set for life", reminding those present that Islam preaches openness and respect towards all communities. Dr Amine Farshoukh, the Dean of the Faculty of Islamic Studies of the Makassed Philanthropic Islamic Association (founded in 1787), also praised the positive side of religious diversity in Lebanon and pointed out "how openness is necessary for knowledge" and called for a joint course on religions in both public and private schools. For the Muslim educators, the different Islamic rites have much in common. The believer's proximity to Allah means the believer need not be isolated in society or reject differences, since, as Sayyed Fadlallah states, "Allah teaches that difference is a fundamental value, like the distinction between man and woman and the diversity of cultures and different affiliations".

The representatives of Christian educational establishments also defended the idea that religious education is based on higher human values and principles of tolerance and respect. Nabil Costa, General Secretary of Association of Evangelical Schools in Lebanon, praised the Lebanese state for providing a social and religious mosaic in which "each religious group can teach its own religious beliefs to their children". In the Evangelical schools, students are provided with one hour of Christian religious teaching a week, in addition to another hour visiting the school's chapel. The main objective of religious education for M. Costa is "to empower each member of the community with the ability to respect one another and accept the members of different communities, helping them when needed"; "these are Christian principles and if we cannot transmit these values to our children, we could consider our mission failed", he remarked, stressing that many students attending the Evangelical schools come from other religious groups, which, in his view, "shows how open and tolerant our establishments are".

This specificity was also mentioned by Dr Amine Farshoukh. He reminded the panel that many Christian students attended and continue to attend the Islamic University run by the Makassed Philanthropic Islamic Association (founded in 1981). Another sign of tolerance mentioned by Dr Farshoukh is the fact that for decades one of the most important Islamic Makassed schools was run by a Christian teacher, and "the topics of the main religions are covered through a course on the culture of religions". On that note, Melhem Chaoul, the director of the Social Studies Institute at the Lebanese University, stressed the importance of distinguishing between religious teachings and the teaching of religion as a cultural and historical topic, as most of the religious institutions favour the first option over the second. Dr Ali Khalife, the director of the Formation des Maîtres at the Mission Laïque Française, made the same observation, reminding the group that although there is a joint school textbook on the culture of religions, "no religious education structure would want to rely on it in its curriculum".

Despite each having developed its own method and proudly regarding its work as the reference point, every religious community running private schools agrees on the importance of their social function: shaping the citizens of tomorrow and preparing for a strong nation.

A mutual understanding: religious education as portal in shaping Lebanese citizens and nation

Three elements are regularly highlighted as important beneficiaries of religious teaching by the communities' institutions. Religious education is presented as an important vector to instigate values of honesty and righteousness with the object of educating better *individuals*, preparing them to develop a sound *society* that together would build a unified *nation*. This core objective of religious education in Lebanese religious schools is a particular focus in the education of the future elites who will bear such responsibility. This trilogy constituting the fundamental elements of what is considered a *civilized world* holds a significant place in the pedagogical objectives of religious education in Lebanon as developed by the religious communities.

Thus, for the speakers, there can be no separation between religion and the social tissue. For Sheikh Sami Abil Mona, "teaching religion is the road towards a sane and healthy society, hence a message of integrity and knowledge". Moreover, the president of the Adyan Association, Father Fadi Daou, acknowledged that "it would be very difficult to suppress religious education in Lebanon". According to Hiba Nashabe, the director of the Khaled bin al Walid/Al Horj College Makassed, "religious education does not lead to religious extremism"; she suggests religious education be merged with civic education courses in an attempt to prepare righteous and virtuous citizens, open to all the different segments of the diverse Lebanese society.

Inter-faith cooperation in the education field was also suggested as an important path for encouraging a robust society. Dr Amine Farshoukh reminded the panel that the Makassed institution regularly holds exchange programmes and joint visits with Catholic schools in an effort to preach tolerance and respect among different communities in Lebanon.

A third important idea put forward by the religious communities was the shared belief of the Lebanese representatives of religious educational establishments that the teaching of religion constitutes a modern tool of education, in line with modern human rights (particularly freedom of religion and self-determination), to prepare future generations of Lebanese to understand and follow the human principles in each religious doctrine.

Sayyed Jaafar Fadlallah indicated that his institution was now modernizing its educational curriculum in line with the principles of tolerance and mutual respect in a diverse Lebanon. For her part, Hiba Nashabe defended the idea that the shaping of a citizen in Lebanon must go hand in hand with teaching the fundamentals of religious education. Hence, in the Makassed schools both Islamic and Christian teachings have been integrated into the educational curriculum (though in separate classes, each student learning his own religious dogma) in a modern approach to coexistence and multi-culturalism.

Father Boulos Wehbe and Dominique Labaki took the modernization process to another level by discussing the successful action of the Joint Christian Education Committee in Lebanon in producing a joint catechism textbook for Christian Schools. This step was the result of a series of decisions taken during the 1996 Religious Summit in Deir Shurfa between the Catholic and Orthodox patriarchs and archbishops to strengthen the cooperation and religious coordination among the different rites, such as organizing mixed inter-Christian marriages, holding joint religious ceremonies and, last but not least, producing a joint school manual for catechism. Father Wehbe pointed out that the project of a joint textbook for Christian education was approved by all Middle Eastern Churches in Lebanon – Catholic, Orthodox and Protestant – for all classes from Grade 1 to Grade 12, and successfully implemented, and that its content is constantly updated by the joint committee.

Representatives from Muslim educational institutions noted that a similar initiative was launched among different Islamic groups, but without any success, suggesting political factors – mainly between Sunni and Shi'a rites – were largely responsible for this failure to create an educational synergy for Islamic education textbooks.

In connection with this setback, the panel's debates outlined the contradictions and the sensitivity of the concept of tolerance. Jeremy Menchik from Boston University reminded the panel that scientific observations have shown that "people most of the time are intolerant; most people have a group that they dislike; most people deny another group in society the same rights they themselves enjoy, which also applies to the right to education, yet we don't have war all the time", raising the question of whether our pedagogical goal should "really be achieving tolerance; perhaps we should focus more on having a state and citizenship education that prevents attitudes of intolerance leading to the politicization of differences and the mobilization of tolerance into violence".

Scepticism towards religious education, the secular voice

A very similar narrative was outlined by the religious educators at the seminar, who praised the importance of defending the right of the communities to teach religion and at the same time preaching tolerance and respect for all segments of society. However, given the violent history of modern Lebanon and the on-going political tension based on sectarian differences and political confrontation, this discourse was faced with many voices of scepticism and defiance.

Many pro-secular participants denounced a "hidden agenda" or "hidden curriculum" in the religious schools, which produced radical sectarian members of society instead of creating citizens first. Dr Marlene Nasr pointed out that "an important issue in Lebanon lies in the 'other close-by', not the 'other far away'". All communities emphasized the importance of 'respecting the other', but can we build a society when each segment of it calls the rest of the population 'the other' asked Dr Nasr? Dr Dalal Bezri was even more critical of those in favour of pro-religious education: "Since these private schools run by religious communities praise tolerance and mutual respect to the utmost degree, what happens to the students who graduate from these schools that they become so sectarian and culturally intolerant? [...] Either schools are too weak and cannot counter the attraction towards political violence, or the problem lies in the educational content and methods of the schools". Dr Melhem Chaoul concurred with the observation that sectarianism was rampant in the country and informed the participants of a study conducted by his Institute in 2011 on the "perception of the students of the Islamic Institute in Saida on Shi'a in the South and the Bekaa"; he regretted that they could not publish the data of the research.

Indeed, the representatives of the religious educational establishments admitted that there is no turning away from this problem, but "we cannot blame the schools more than they deserve", stated Sayyed Fadlallah and Dr Costa. The latter remarked, "I don't think those who are bearing weapons come from our schools"; "mixed students from different religious backgrounds in our schools is a great indicator that we are not at war in Lebanon". As for Hiba Nashabe, she stressed her school was teaching children to respect not the "other" but the "partner in the nation".

Dr Ali Khalife challenged the educational methods of the religious groups, which he sees as hindering the formation of modern citizens in Lebanon. As such, he refuted any form of modernity in religious education, defining the latter as "purely politically motivated", a concept that relates more to "intellectual terrorism" than to spiritual enrichment. From a pedagogical point of view, Dr Khalife stressed that "no child can fully integrate the complexity of religious teachings" in an educational process that "amounts to no less than "brainwashing and exploitation, which goes against the education goals of developing the child's scientific approach and critical thinking". While acknowledging the diverse social and religious Lebanese tissue, Dr Khalife suggested "teaching religion should not be an independent course to achieve pedagogical goals for the sake of the student, but should be taught as part of history and culture".

Professor Theodor Hanf shared his impression that this high level of frustration with sectarianism in Lebanon does not need to be focused entirely on the issue of education: "If you want to change the political structure, change the political structure, don't try to do it through education". At the same time, he acknowledged that "Lebanon is a country that enjoys the principle of freedom of religion, but this principle should also include freedom *from* religion, which does not exist in Lebanon because you cannot 'drop out', you cannot exit your community affiliation". He suggested an important hypothesis that should be additionally tested, according to which "the more selfish people are and self-conscious about their identity, the easier it would be for them to be tolerant in their relationships with others".

Other recommendations of the panel include, for instance, the idea mentioned by Sayyed Fadlallah of producing genuinely unprecedented sociological studies of the generation of those in Lebanon who recently turned 50 and who graduated from the religious schools so as to determine their beliefs and values and how they have been managing identity issues related to their Lebanese citizenship and religious affiliation. Other participants suggested sociological studies to explore the interaction of Lebanese in mixed social spaces, be it the market place or civil society, in order to better understand whether sectarianism remains a fundamental variable in these interconnected areas.

*

The debate over the Lebanese case in religious education offered an interesting perspective on many of the contradictions in the outcome of religious education in a country capable of such levels of violence, despite the immense efforts religious educators themselves put into teaching the universal values of respect and tolerance, which are still waiting to be implemented in a sustainable political framework. Despite the different claims heard during the seminar, the degree of responsibility for the deterioration of inter-sectarian relations in the recent past cannot be determined and surely needs further research and study. That said, further understanding of the specific dynamics and impact of religious education on the entrapment of each community in its own self-interests would not replace the need for political will among sectarian leaders to tackle unresolved issues in Lebanon which education alone obviously cannot resolve.

Teaching Religion in Egypt and Tunisia
A Challenge to Citizenship Education[*]

MUHAMMAD FAOUR

Introduction

Fledgling democracies in the Arab world need to reform their educational systems in order to better prepare their youth for the challenges of a pluralistic society. Young Arabs should develop their capacity to think independently and creatively, communicate effectively, analyze change processes, and solve emerging problems. Such education reform requires education for citizenship in which schools have to develop and nurture an interactive, respectful, and culturally sensitive climate in classrooms. In such a climate, ample opportunities are presented for students to get involved in decision-making at school and in the community and to engage in national and global issues.[1]

However, there are several obstacles to education reform, such as weak governance in educational systems, inadequate preparation of teachers, and limited funding. But an even greater challenge is how to reconcile a curriculum directed at promoting pluralism and tolerance of different ideas and opinions with the teaching of religion in public schools. All religions uphold absolute values and defend what they believe is 'truth'. It is a dilemma all democratic countries struggle with. In Tunisia and Egypt, this dilemma is compounded by the rise of Islamist political parties, which are calling for a more prominent role for religion in society.

In order to understand the dilemmas Egypt and Tunisia face in moving toward education for citizenship, it is necessary to understand the role religion plays in their K-12 schools now and to analyze to what extent religion is taught in a manner that can advance civic and citizenship values. It is also necessary to understand the views and practices of the most powerful Islamist parties with regard to education, since they are likely to be in charge of the next round of education reforms. More particularly, what are the views of the Muslim Brotherhood parties in Egypt and Tunisia on the existing civic education programs and the role of Islam in civic and citizenship education? How compatible are their perspectives on religious education with the notions of pluralism and democracy? And what steps have they taken so far to translate their views into action?

The paper first presents an overview of the place of religion in the existing curricula and school climate of K-12 public education in the Arab countries, particularly in Egypt

---

[*] This paper is a revised and updated version of an earlier one by the author titled *Religious Education and Pluralism in Egypt and Tunisia*, Carnegie Endowment for International Peace (August 2012).

[1] Muhammad Faour and Marwan Muasher, *Education for Citizenship in the Arab World: Key to the Future*, Carnegie Endowment for International Peace (October 2011), 8, 9, 18.

and Tunisia. The Azharite religious schools in Egypt, which are supervised by Al-Azhar, are excluded as they represent a particular case for Egypt that has no counterpart in Tunisia or other Arab countries. Prominent features of religious education in Egypt and in Tunisia are highlighted as well as the respective relationship to civic or citizenship education. Subsequently, the views of the Islamists, the Freedom and Justice Party in Egypt and Ennahda Party in Tunisia, regarding religious and citizenship education and their expected impact on education in general are discussed. The paper presents some recent changes in the school curriculum in Egypt, and concludes with some thoughts on the prospects of religious and citizenship education in Egypt and Tunisia. The information and analysis in this paper are based on: (a) published and unpublished documents, research papers, articles and books; and (b) meetings with Arab education experts, representing both Islamist and secular viewpoints.

The History of Religious Education in the Arab countries

In the Arab world, the majority religion, Islam, shapes the very fabric of social life and is a central component of the legal system as well as economic, political and cultural life. It is also a key component of personal identity. Consequently, religion and education in the Arab world are strongly linked. Historically, education used to be undertaken in the places of worship and controlled by the clergy. In the traditional *kuttab* system, Muslim students learned the Qur'an and *hadith* (Prophet Muhammad's sayings) from religious scholars and received basic education in Arabic language and mathematics. The *kuttab* served a vital social function as the vehicle for formal public education for Muslim children and youth until the advent of Western models of instruction.

Under Ottoman rule in the nineteenth century, Christian missionaries from Europe and the United States established K-12 schools in what are now Lebanon, Syria, Egypt, Jordan, and Palestine. Subsequently, apprehensive of the proselytizing role of the Christian missionaries, Islamic associations, such as the Makassed Islamic Philanthropic Association in Lebanon and other Arab countries, established their own modern schools, which taught Islamic religion as well as basic subjects. They offered a more modern and better quality education to Muslims than did the *kuttab*.

Today, the teaching of Islamic religious education in schools in Arab countries differs by type of school, how religion is taught and represented in textbooks, and the time allocated for teaching it. In the public school system, it is a separate course of study. In most countries, Islamic religious education is also integrated into the Arabic language and social studies curriculum in the form of themes, topics, and values. In private Islamic schools in Arab countries and in public schools in several countries, notably the GCC countries, the entire school climate is characterized by Islamic norms and code of behavior. Students and staff are required to observe praying and fasting and other Islamic rituals. Girls have to wear the *hijab*, and all student activities enhance religious norms and values.

However, the place of religion in public education varies significantly from one Arab country to another. Although most Arab countries teach religion in their public schools, they do so in different ways. Religious education in some countries targets values that are antithetical to those set forth in the civics curriculum, while in other countries it is compatible with pluralistic values. In terms of time allocation, the number of study hours dedicated to religion in primary schools ranges from one or two in countries like Morocco, to three in Jordan, and up to six in Oman. In Saudi schools, the time allocated to Islamic studies at any school level is the highest among Arab countries. At the primary level, it is nine hours per week.[2]

Religious Education in Egypt

In Egypt, where ten percent of the population is Christian, Christian students in public schools are taught about Christianity by Christian teachers or priests and Muslims are taught about Islam by Muslim teachers or sheikhs. Courses include instruction in their respective religious dogmas, rites, and codes of behavior. Muslim students in public schools are taught about Christianity only through the perspective of the Qur'an and *hadith,* while Christian students do not learn about Islam in the Christian Religion course, as it post-dates their religious texts.

Egyptian students in public schools dedicate three out of 30 hours per week to religious study at the primary level and two hours at the higher levels. School textbooks for Islamic religious education use two contradictory approaches to Christianity and Judaism. One approach presents Christianity and Judaism as monotheistic religions that originated with Abraham, the 'first Muslim', and whose messengers – Jesus and Moses – are described as Muslims. The other approach considers the Torah and the Gospels as distorted versions of the true sacred books revealed to Moses and Jesus, teaching that only the Qur'an includes the correct content of these books.[3]

According to the Egyptian textbooks, there is only one true religion. It is Islam, which God revealed to Adam and all the prophets including Moses, Jesus and Muhammad. "And whoever desires other than Islam as religion – never will it be accepted from him, and he, in the Hereafter, will be among the losers."[4] Furthermore, the textbooks embrace the concept of Jihad or *shahadah* against the enemy. There are two categories of enemies: infidels and homeland's enemies.[5]

---

2   UNESCO, *World Data on Education* (August 2011) http://www.ibe.unesco.org/en/services/online-materials/world-data-on-education/seventh-edition-2010-11.html; Bradley James Cook, Egypt's National Education Debate, in *Comparative Education*, 36:4 (2000), 481.

3   For detailed statements from religion and social studies textbooks on these approaches, see Arnon Groiss, editor, compiler and translator, *Jews, Christians, War, and Peace in Egyptian School Textbooks*, report prepared by the Center for Monitoring the Impact of Peace (New York, 2004), 20–27; http://www.impact-se.org/research/reports.html.

4   Al-Imran sura, verse 85. This verse and others are explained in the Grade 8 textbook, part 1 (2010–2011), 22, and in a commentary in the Grade 11 textbook (2002), 167–168, as cited by Groiss 2004, 28–29; the same meaning appears in Islamic religion education textbooks for Grade 7, Part 1 (2002), 22, 25, and for Grade 11 (2002), 30.

5   Groiss, 2004, 9.

Several indicators show that the textbooks for the Islamic religious education course in Egypt do not target the development of students' analytical thinking. This is evident in the choice of method of presentation of material, assignments, and type of exercises. After each lesson is presented, there is a summary of the main points and a number of exercises. The summary section helps the students recall what they will later be quizzed on. The exercises tend to be of the type that requires memorization and recall of facts. This approach to education emphasizes rote learning.[6] Although teaching religion might unavoidably be about teaching absolute truths and indisputable matters in the eyes of the believers, there is a considerable difference between Egypt and Tunisia with regard to content, learning objectives, and teaching methods, as shall be elaborated on later.

Students in Egypt, both Muslim and Christian, are familiarized with many aspects of Islam when learning other subjects, notably Arabic language and social studies, which include history, geography, and civics. The study of Arabic has special significance for Muslims because it is the language of the Qur'an and the language used in prayers. Thus, high competence in it is a requirement for the advanced study of Islam, and basic competence is needed to practice Islam in a meaningful way. Arabic is also the official language in Egypt and all other member states of the Arab League, and all students must learn it at school. Integrating Islamic principles and values into the teaching of Arabic in public schools is an effective way of introducing Islam to children from various religions.

Studies that applied content analysis to Arabic language textbooks in Egypt[7] found numerous religious texts and themes that advocate piety and religious observance. The Arabic texts assigned for language study at the primary level in Egypt include selected verses from the Qur'an and quotations from the *hadith* relating to the Prophet Muhammad's life. At the secondary or high school level, Arabic language texts include essays that emphasize Islamic values and the tolerance of Islam towards other religions.[8]

Most of these selections are used to teach important universal social values like honesty, hospitality, charity, and kindness. Such values are not contradictory to the beliefs and traditions of other religions. For example, in "road to strength and success," an Arabic lesson for the sixth grade, the main idea/theme is based on two verses from the Qur'an that call for people to cling to religion's directives because religion is the force that binds people together in affection and brotherhood. In another lesson for eighth graders, the title *"the importance of maintaining kinship ties"* is lifted directly from the

---

6   This observation applies to all grades including the secondary grades. See, for example, the text-books for primary grades: http://manahg.moe.gov.eg/Prim_Book.aspx; textbooks for higher grades are also available on the Ministry of Education's website. See also Charlotte Neill, Islam in Egyptian Education: Grades K-12, in *Religious Education*, 101:4 (2006), 491; Elham Abdulhameed, *Egyptian Education and its Relationship to the Culture of Citizenship in Egypt: Current Status and Prospects*, (Arabic) paper prepared for Carnegie Middle East Center, May 2012, 15, 16.

7   See for example, Ahmad Youssof Saad, *The Concept and Issues of Citizenship in Educational Texts: Between the Approaches of Empowerment and Content of Mobilization*, no date (unpublished manu-script); Neill; Pakinaz Baraka, Citizenship Education in Egyptian Public Schools, What Values to Teach and in Which Administrative and Political Contexts, in *Journal of Education for International Development*, 3: 3 (2007); Arnon Groiss.

8   Egypt, Ministry of Education, *Arabic Language*, Third Secondary Class (2012–2013), Chapters 1–3.

Qur'an, and the text presents it as a custom of Egyptian people as well as an Islamic virtue.[9]

Yet there are also verses that challenge the beliefs of non-Muslims, such as those that preach God's absolute unity and that contradict the Christian belief in the Holy Trinity. And there are lessons that advocate gender inequality such as a lesson in Arabic language for Grade 8 on "men's and women's allocations/shares." The title is a phrase from the Qur'an, and the text explains verses from the Qur'an which state that people belong to different statuses or classes and that men's and women's shares of inheritance are not the same.[10] Some Muslim sects, notably Shiites, and non-Muslims do not endorse this belief.

When it comes to teaching history, which is part of the social studies course in Egyptian public schools, instruction tends to focus on the ancient period and on the period since the advent of Islam. There is a detailed description of the life of the Prophet Muhammad and of the first Islamic state, which he founded in Medina. The period of the four "rightly guided caliphs" is also presented in detail. By contrast, instruction in Coptic history is very brief and largely limited to economic and social dimensions of the Coptic community of today.[11] Perhaps more disturbing to Christian students is the textbook's negative presentation of 'Romans' (*al-roum*, i.e. eastern orthodox Christians) as people who 'deviated' from the Christian principles that were advocated by Jesus. This reinforces the belief of many Muslims that Christianity, as it is preached and practiced by Christians since the advent of Islam, is a distorted version of the authentic religion that has been integrated into Islam.

In the primary and middle public schools in Egypt, there is no separate course on civic or citizenship education.[12] Rather, the civic and citizenship concepts are integrated into the contents of social studies, Islamic or Christian education, and Arabic language. Thus, key civic concepts such as freedom, social justice, and equality of citizens are taught in the same course as religious concepts. One example is the textbook for Islamic religious education for the fifth grade in public schools. It contains a poem titled "My Country," whose theme, it is claimed, is about citizenship education. The tone of the poem and at least two of its verses highlight religious adherence to Islam, not equal citizenship for all religions:

> I swear by the Lord of the faith (i.e., Islam), you (i.e., my country) will not be vanquished. I swear by the Lord who perfected the religion for the Muslim. We will protect your soil and the roads, and hail victory to the believers (i.e., Muslims).[13]

---

9   Ahmad Youssof Saad, 33, 34.
10 See Neill, 496; and http://manahg.moe.gov.eg/Prep_Book.aspx.
11 In the history textbook for the first secondary class, there is a short section on the 'Coptic era of Egyptian history.'
12 The course on 'national education' in the third secondary class does not cover major issues in civics or citizenship. Rather, it deals with two main topics: the mutual impact between Arab-Islamic and European civilizations and Arab nationalism. For details on course content, see http://manahg.moe. gov.eg/Sec_Dis.aspx.
13 Verses translated from Arabic by the author. See Egypt, Ministry of Education, *Islamic Religious Education* (in Arabic), Fifth Elementary Grade, 51.

In secondary schools, civic education is offered as a separate subject called "national education." Since the January 2011 Revolution, the revised textbook for the third secondary class (Grade 12) includes large sections that promote Islamic perspectives, particularly that of the Muslim Brotherhood. In the chapter on democracy, a section titled 'democracy in Islamic thought – shura' discusses the concept of shura in detail, supported by several Qur'anic verses and *hadiths*. It is presented as a sacred, God-given concept that represents a form of government as well as a value system that encompasses features of a pluralistic society. This approach is likely to develop in the minds of Muslim students the conviction that shura is the best form of democracy that suits Egypt and all other Muslim-majority countries.[14]

The chapter on human rights in the national education textbook for Grade 12 dedicates a section to human rights in Islam. After presenting the Universal Declaration on Human Rights, the text argues that the Declaration is not legally binding on states and that other international, regional and national covenants on human rights have stronger legal weight. The text defends the cultural and political specificity of states which justify their refusal to strictly implement all the articles of the Universal Declaration. The Arab Charter on Human Rights of 2005 is highlighted as a document that satisfies the principles of Islam and of the other major religions and that affirms the belief in the unity of the Arab homeland.[15]

This selective endorsement of universal human rights relieves the new political regime in Egypt of the obligation to approve full gender equality and the right of people to change their religion. One recent illustration of the sensitivity of this issue is the Islamists' outrage over a statement in the national education textbook which asks students to respect those who change their religion. This matter was referred by the minister of education to Al-Azhar for expert advice. Al-Azhar recommended that the statement be deleted.[16]

Civic and citizenship education was recently enhanced by adding a new course, "citizenship and human rights" to the requirements of the second secondary class (Grade 11). The new course provides useful information on concepts relating to citizenship and human rights, including a historical overview that charts the development of these concepts. However, the textbook gives special attention to the perspective of Islamists, particularly the Muslim Brotherhood, in three sections titled "political awareness in Islam", "the concept of citizenship from the Islamic perspective," and "women's rights in Islam." The perspectives of other religious groups, notably Christians, are ignored.

According to the textbook *Citizenship and Human Rights*, political awareness in Islam is

> "based on the Islamic faith ... within the framework of the individual's commitment to Islam in thought, lifestyle, and behavior ... and aims at safeguarding the existence of

---

14   Egypt, Ministry of Education, *National Education*, Third Secondary Class (2012–2013), 11–16.

15   Ibid., 62–73.

16   As communicated by the Ministry of Education on its website http://portal.moe.gov.eg, accessed on November 4, 2012.

the nation (i.e. Islamic nation) … which is divided into small states and peoples who now care less about this nation than about the homeland and the small country."[17]

Which concept of nation, Egypt or the Islamic nation (*umma*), will the Egyptian student adopt?!

Students in public schools thus receive inconsistent messages regarding the concept of nation or what it means to be an Egyptian citizen. Large sections of the social studies textbooks subscribe to the principles of pluralism, national unity, acceptance of other beliefs and cultures, and equality between Muslims and non-Muslims. However, religious education in the same schools, whether Islamic or Christian, develops feelings of religious distinction and inequality. Similarly, gender equality is promoted in social studies textbooks, but not endorsed in the Islamic religious education textbooks, notably with regard to inheritance. When it comes to the practice of citizenship rights in the real world, Egyptian students are exposed to Islamic texts that imply that non-Muslims cannot hold senior administrative positions in the state, such as head of state or chief of the army.

Further complicating the matter is the role of teachers in imparting religious values and behavior, which is often overlooked, despite its critical significance. In Egypt, some scholars use the term 'hidden curriculum' to describe the impact of many Islamist teachers on students, whether positive or negative. These teachers impose their own thoughts and attitudes on students, a process that is affected by the prevailing culture within schools and made easier through the prevailing teacher-directed methods of instruction, rote learning, and the lack of open discourse and critical reasoning.[18] The role of teachers is similarly influential in other Arab countries.

The picture is somewhat different in private schools. In secular and international schools in Egypt there may be either no religious education or a social studies course that includes general information about various religions and the role of religion in society. A number of private schools in Egypt resort to a variety of extracurricular activities and community service internships to enrich their programs in religious education.

In private schools the school ethos or culture is marked by the religious values of the principal. A school that is run by a Christian order or an Islamic party/association will subject the students to the norms and values of the administration. Thus, in an Islamic school, Islamic culture and Islamic norms pervade the instructor's interaction with the students and their families. Such schools encourage and laud what they consider students' praiseworthy 'Islamic' behavior, such as performing religious rituals and honoring one's parents. They also criticize what they consider to be behavior incompatible with *sharia*, like consuming alcoholic beverages or, in the case of girls, failing to wear the headscarf or obey their legal guardians. In contrast, a Christian school would request the students to attend Sunday mass and exhibit other exemplary Christian behavior.

---

17 Egypt, Ministry of Education, *Citizenship and Human Rights*, Second Secondary Class (2012–2013), 33–34.

18 Bradley James Cook, Egypt's National Education Debate, in *Comparative Education*, 36:4 (2000), 484.

Religious Education in Tunisia

Tunisia presents a different case in religious education. The values and learning objectives of religious and civics studies are more compatible than in Egypt, and aim, more explicitly than in Egypt, at the promotion of pluralistic values and concepts such as equality, social justice, freedom, and mutual respect.

This liberal approach to religion is based on the Tunisian constitution, which was colored by the political and social vision of Habib Bourgiba, founder of the Republic of Tunisia. In 1989, then President Ben Ali appointed Mohamed Charfi, lawyer and long-time human rights activist and critic of the president, minister of education, perhaps as a way to keep an eye on him and/or to purge the educational system of anti-Western content. Charfi implemented important reforms that included scrutiny of all school textbooks. The purpose was to delete all statements that promoted intolerance between different religions and groups, while keeping the liberal aspects of Muslim thought in religious education. The science curriculum was revised to incorporate Darwinian evolution and the Big Bang Theory. These reforms were rejected by the Ennahda party, which accused Ben Ali of "de-Islamizing" the country.[19] Charfi's reforms may have contributed to the democratic and pluralistic worldview of the young generation of Tunisians who rebelled against the regime in December 2010.

As 98 percent of the Tunisian population is Sunni Muslim, with Jews and Christians comprising less than two percent, the only religion taught in public schools today is Islam. Yet public secondary schools teach the history of all three religions, Judaism, Christianity, and Islam, as part of social studies.

Tunisian students study Islamic religion for two hours a week in lower primary grades and 1.5 hours at all higher grades. In public primary schools, the textbooks for the Islamic education course emphasize the ethical and moral aspects of Islam and its main pillars, while at the same time training the child on how to perform religious rituals, notably praying and fasting. Religious tolerance towards Christians and Jews is highlighted as an Islamic value. Unlike other Arab countries, including Egypt, the Tunisian books go further to warn against exclusion of non-believers and enmity towards them, stressing pan-human solidarity. One telling example is Prophet Muhammad's show of respect for a Jew's funeral that passed by him in Medina. When asked why he stood up, he said: "Is it not a soul? Whenever you see a funeral procession, stand up."[20]

Tolerance is a recurrent theme in Tunisian school books. According to one text, tolerance defined in terms of respect for other religions and freedom of faith is found in 36 chapters (*sura*) and 125 verses of the Qur'an, thus representing the "basic idea in the Qur'an."[21] Dialogue with and acceptance of the 'other' is promoted, and the 'other' is regarded as having equal rights and duties with Muslims, irrespective of color, religion,

---

19   Mohamed Bechri, *Islamism without Sharia: The Tunisian Example*, May 21, 2012, 1; http://fikrafor um.org/?p=2260.
20   Islamic Education, Grade 9 (2007), 32.
21   (Literary) Texts, Grade 9 (2007), 159.

or education.[22] There is emphasis on the unity of mankind, peaceful coexistence between different races and religions, and the equality of all nations. The Islamic education course promotes peace, accepting war only in the case of aggression or oppression.[23] The definition of Jihad in Islam is that of a spiritual struggle against the moral deficiencies of the self. The concept of Jihad or *shahadah* against the enemy is not endorsed. Democratic values are adopted as a historical product of a universal culture.[24]

The Islamic education course for primary and middle schools in Tunisia presents the rituals as a personal affair and a religious duty that carries an individual responsibility towards God. There is no implied enforcement by society or the state.[25] At the secondary level, the Islamic education course in public schools is titled 'Islamic Thinking,' a reflection of the objective of the curriculum to foster analytical thinking that does not contradict the main pillars of Islam.

A Comparative Review

A comparison of the curriculum documents pertaining to Islamic education in public secondary schools in Tunisia and Egypt reveals the following: (a) the Tunisian curriculum follows international practices in presenting a reference framework, objectives, learning outcomes, and methods of learning and assessment, while the Egyptian curriculum document is a brief syllabus sheet displaying the contents of the course; (b) the selected topics in the Tunisian curriculum, such as man and monotheism and man and society, are amenable to more analysis and philosophical thinking than the topics selected in the Egyptian curriculum such as the lessons learned from the Prophet's battles, smoking, drinking, deviance and selected Islamic values; (c) there is more coverage in the Tunisian curriculum of a host of issues that relate to civilization, modernity, reform, and knowledge, and the approach to religion at this school level combines the existential meaning in religions with the realities of modern civilization; and (d) the objectives in the Tunisian curriculum explicitly endorse dialogue, flexibility and moderation, tolerance, and openness to global approaches and universal values, whereas the Egyptian curriculum document does not mention course objectives. In Tunisia, the universal values of Islamic religion are presented as consistent with life in a modern, free, and pluralistic society.[26]

---

22 (Literary) Texts, Grade 13-Sciences, as cited in Arnon Groiss, *The Attitude to the 'Other' and to Peace in Tunisian School Textbooks: A Preliminary Report*, report prepared by the Institute for Monitoring Peace and Cultural Tolerance in School Education (formerly CMIP), New York, October 2008, 10; http://www.impact-se.org/research/reports.html.

23 Islamic Education, Grade 9 (2007), 34.

24 As cited in Groiss, 2008, 11–12.

25 Naila Al-Silini and Ahmed Al-Hadhiri, *Citizenship Education in Tunisia, Morocco and Algeria*, (Arabic) paper prepared for Carnegie Middle East Center, June 2012, 16.

26 For the Egyptian curriculum documents, see http://manahg.moe.gov.eg/Sec_Dis.aspx; for the Tunisian curriculum document, see http://sakhana.com/index.php?option=com_content&view=article&id=270:2010-10-19-15-39-46&catid=78:2010-10-19-14-57-25&Itemid=197.

Apart from the differences in the school curriculum between Tunisia and Egypt, students in both countries under the now-deposed regimes experienced a huge gap between what they learned at school and what they saw practiced in everyday life. Young students were aware of abuses of political power, corruption, and violations of basic human rights of citizens. As a result, a report that assessed the extent of integration of human rights principles in the curricula of secondary schools in the Arab world described these students as having a state of 'schizophrenia in their academic formation' due in part to the contradiction between idealistic values learned and life experience.[27]

Comparison with other Arab countries reveals a number of similarities. As is the case of Egypt, the public schools in Jordan and the Palestinian Authority expose students, both Muslims and Christians, to Islamic beliefs and concepts through Arabic and Arab history. The Arabic language curriculum in these countries is rich in Islamic topics and values, many of which are shared by the Christian and other faiths, such as honesty, justice, and helping the needy. The history textbooks emphasize Islamic and Arab history. As in the Egyptian history curriculum, the period of Prophet Muhammad's rule over Medina is discussed at length, highlighting various aspects of his organization of the first Islamic state. Special attention is given to the city of Jerusalem due to its relevance to the conflicts between Israel and Jordan and between Israel and the Palestinians.

The civic and national education curriculum in Jordan presents the issues of freedom, human rights and rule of law, supported by examples and explanations that are predominantly Islamic, with little reference to the universality of these rights. Rights of women and children are also discussed, with emphasis on the religious dimension. The unit on citizenship in the civic education course includes components that are not found in similar courses in democratic societies, namely the idea of faith in God, sacred books and messengers. This approach might send a message that people who do not belong to the three major religions have no sense of belonging to their nations.[28]

It is worth noting that teaching students about the various sects that exist among Muslims is not part of public school curricula in Arab countries. Most of these countries either offer a general course in Islamic principles and morals or restrict their content to the beliefs and rituals of the dominant faith of their society. Only the Islamic perspective of other religions and beliefs is presented. Research into sources that present different points of view on this matter is not encouraged, nor is engagement in open discussions in the classroom.[29]

---

27   This general observation applies to all Arab countries, as was highlighted in the General Report on
     the seminar organized by the Arab Institute on Human Rights on *The Status of Human Rights in the
     Curricula and School Textbooks in Secondary Education*, (in Arabic) Beirut, 27 February–1 March,
     2003, p. 4, item 1–5; see also Al-Silini and Al-Hadhiri, 18.

28   Muhyieddeen Touq, *Citizenship Education in Jordan and Palestine*, (Arabic) paper prepared for
     Carnegie Middle East Center, March 2012, 31, 32, 33, 35, 56.

29   See also Neill, 491; Elham Abdulhameed, *Egyptian Education and its Relationship to the Culture of
     Citizenship in Egypt: Current Status and Prospects*, (Arabic) paper prepared for Carnegie Middle
     East Center, May 2012, 15, 16.

Religion and Education: The Views of the Islamists

For Islamists, education is a key component of creating a pious and good society. Rached al-Ghannoushi, leader of Ennahda Party in Tunisia, speaks of the totality of Islam and its guidance in all aspects of life, personal and public, including education.[30] He argues that people need religion and its spiritual and moral guidance in all walks of life, and that it is certainly a core part of education. The Muslim Brotherhood parties contend that Islam places a high value on education, ranking the learned people above the ignorant, and that religious education is an essential subject at schools.

Although the Freedom and Justice Party (FJP) in Egypt and Ennahda in Tunisia encourage reliance on modern methods of instruction in scientific subjects, such as critical thinking, dialogue, research, and open debate,[31] their approach to teaching religion is different. When it comes to teaching religion, the Muslim Brothers advocate a specific form of dialogue enjoined by various Qur'anic verses. Namely, they call for gentle persuasion and civil debate. But this form of dialogue does not permit any open contradiction of the Islamic faith, for instance in the form of atheism or agnosticism.

Egypt's Freedom and Justice Party

Egyptian Islamists regard religion as the most important component of their national character. Thus, public education should incorporate Islam, the religion of the majority of the people, to enhance the Islamic character of students. The published platform of the Freedom and Justice Party (FJP), which represents the Egyptian Muslim Brotherhood, declares its commitment to "deepen the Arab and Islamic identity" of Egyptians.[32] What they advocate is far more than teaching some chapters of the Qur'an and selected statements from the *hadith*. They would like to introduce comprehensive educational reform that creates an integrated curriculum with explicit Islamic themes across all subjects. The FJP aims to provide "a holistic education at all levels in a way that deepens religious values in students."[33] Although the FJP does not elaborate on how it intends to achieve this goal, one of its education experts highlighted the party's experience in running private schools that create a school climate representative of a true Islamic community.[34]

The Islamic school climate refers to the character of school life that reflects Islamic values, interpersonal relationships (among students and staff and between students and teachers), and teaching and learning practices based on Islamic principles and prac-

---

30 As cited in John Esposito and John Voll, *Makers of Contemporary Islam*, Oxford University Press, 2001, 105.
31 *The Program of the Freedom and Justice Party,* 31, where the Party states its intention to promote dialogue, forgiveness, and participation in order to build a good citizen and increase political participation. In addition, it plans to develop and modernize the curriculum to encourage analysis, dialogue, research and discussion (p. 52).
32 *The Program of the Freedom and Justice Party,* Cairo: Dar Al-Tawzi Wannashr, 2011 (in Arabic), 49, 50.
33 *The Program of the Freedom and Justice Party*, 53.
34 Ahmad Al-Halawany, meeting of experts, Carnegie Middle East Center, March 8, 2012.

tices.[35] An Islamic school climate is characterized by an Islamic code of conduct which includes dress, social behavior, and practice of Islamic rituals. Accordingly, girls cover their bodies and wear the *hijab*, and all members of the school community observe Islamic rituals, notably daily prayers and fasting in the month of Ramadan. The school should have either a mosque or a dedicated space for prayer. Food served on school premises should contain no pork and beverages no alcohol. Students are required to recite and memorize chapters of the Qur'an and the *hadith*. Where coeducation exists, interaction between males and females is carefully monitored by the school staff and violations are swiftly punished; most Islamic schools, however, practice gender segregation. Books and magazines that are accessible to students are censored to remove anti-Islamic material, and anti-Islamic content is deleted or erased from available learning resources. Teachers and administrators frequently refer to Islamic principles and practices to educate students about life and social behavior.

A variety of channels are used to communicate a school's Islamic ethos, such as school magazines, co-curricular and extra-curricular activities, and meetings with parents. Extra-curricular activities include trips to religious sites, visits to religious scholars, and the celebration of religious events and holidays. School magazines portray several aspects of the school climate. One telling example is the contents of *Ethraa* (trans. 'Enrichment'), the school magazine at Manarat al_Farouk Islamic School in Cairo, a well-known Islamic school. Each issue includes a number of sections that aim at indoctrinating the students in Sunni Islam. Most topics, even those that have no direct link with religion, include references to Islam. The school curriculum is explained from an 'Islamic perspective,' underscoring its distinction from the Western curriculum, primarily by targeting students' spiritual and moral development in addition to academic and physical aspects. The ultimate goal of Islamic education, according to *Ethraa*, is to promote social relations among members of society, and between them and God. In one of its issues, Shiites and their beliefs are presented in a negative way, with emphasis on their deviation from Orthodox Islam.[36] In another issue, Islamic fundamentalism is praised because one needs to build the present and the future on the past.[37]

The objectives of the current religious education program in public schools are, to a large extent, compatible with the political goals of the Muslim Brotherhood. The Ministry of Education pays considerable attention to religious instruction: "Religious and moral values should be deeply ingrained among our children."[38] Although the ultimate goal of the state under deposed President Mubarak was to combat Islamic extremism, it allowed more Islamic content in the curriculum to offset the Islamists' criticism that it intended to destroy culture and Islam through secularization. For example, Hussein Kamel Bahaedddin, Minister of Education in the 1990s, was decisively opposed to 'ter-

---

35 For a more comprehensive definition of school climate, see Jonathan Cohen, Terry Pickeral and Molly McCloskey, *The Challenge of Assessing School Climate*, Educational Leadership, 66:4, December 2008/January 2009, www.ascd.org/publications/educational-leadership/dec08/vol66/num04/The-Challenge-of-Assessing-School-Climate.aspx.

36 http://alfaroukschools.com/data/downloads/magazine/ethraa24.pdf, 7.

37 http://alfaroukschools.com/data/downloads/magazine/ethraa21.pdf, 11.

38 As cited from a Ministry of Education document titled *Implementing Egypt's Educational Reform Strategy* (1996) in Cook, 482.

rorism' in education, yet had to declare that the state's education policy enhances religious values and that the religious education curriculum was approved by Al-Azhar.[39] This educational policy, which was adopted by secular ministers of education, appeased public sentiment as the majority of Egyptians are religious Muslims. Ironically, it also concurs with the current policy of the FJP as described in their aforementioned platform.

Still, the FJP has started to impact public education in more ways than one. One way is to revise textbooks in order to align their contents better with the FJP's political and religious perspectives. The new editions of the national education textbooks and the new course on citizenship and human rights dedicate sections in each chapter to elaborating on the Islamic perspective. The FJP could also be using more subtle ways to enhance the Islamic orientation of the school curricula. The numerous Muslim Brotherhood teachers in public schools serve as an effective force to impart the Brotherhood's Islamic vision, values, and code of behavior. The FJP could restructure teacher pre-service and in-service training programs to include more Islamic orientation and to recruit Islamist teacher trainers. It might also try to add new co-curricular and extra-curricular activities modelled on the Muslim Brotherhood's private schools. These changes could be introduced gradually and discreetly without much resistance from secular politicians or education officers at the Ministry of Education. The goal, as stated by one of its education experts, is not to create a new curriculum in Islamic religious education. Rather, it is to change the school ethos and student behavior to accord with a true Islamic model.[40] The case of Manarat al_Farouk School presented above may serve as an illustration.

Nevertheless, the FJP does not intend to stop Christian students from studying their own religion in Egyptian public schools or to enforce the Islamic dress code on Christian students, notably the *hijab* for girls.[41] Muslim girls are also unlikely to be forced to wear the *hijab*. But should the FJP succeed in creating an Islamic climate at a school, most students would feel intimidated into compliance. This situation exists today in Islamic schools in Egypt and other Arab countries. Furthermore, the Islamic climate and culture in a school demands respect by non-Muslim members of the school community for Islamic rituals, symbols, and code of conduct. In the month of Ramadan, for example, non-Muslim students are expected not to eat or drink on campus in public. Nor may non-Muslims criticize Islamic scholars, principles, or practices.

Ennahda of Tunisia

The Ennahda's ability to impact the educational system is more challenging than that of their counterparts in Egypt. It will be more difficult for Ennahda to change the curricula of public schools, in particular the curriculum for Islamic religious education, for several reasons. First, the country has had a long history of secularization, and the liberal

---

39   See Cook, 483.
40   Ahmad Al-Halawany, meeting of experts, Carnegie Middle East Center.
41   Ibid.

interpretation of Islam has pervaded the school curriculum, particularly Islamic education, for many years. Second, civil society is strong and mainly secular; many associations are led by secular women, human rights groups and youth. Third, the Ministry of
Education, with Ennahda's approval, is in the hands of a secular party.

All the public statements and speeches of Ennahda leaders have so far indicated their
patience in introducing change in various aspects of life, including education, and their
taking into account the likely repercussions among substantial segments of the population. Furthermore, the position of Ennahda regarding the implementation of *sharia* is
more liberal than that of the FJP in Egypt. The writings and speeches of its leader
clearly express a tolerant position toward different viewpoints and the endorsement of
pluralistic values.[42] Thus, Ennahda is unlikely to apply the Islamic code of behavior in
public schools even to Muslim students, resorting instead to educating them about their
religious duties and the benefits of abiding by *sharia*. More importantly, if Ennahda
eventually succeeds in establishing an Islamic climate and culture in public schools, this
would make members of the school community feel uncomfortable if they do not comply with the prevailing Islamic norms and practices such as headscarves for girls, praying, and fasting during Ramadan. Even without coercion, most would be expected to
comply. In such a situation, Christians' and Jews' non-compliance would be tolerated,
but they would certainly feel out of place.

During the current transitional phase of regime change, further Islamization of education does not have priority over politics and the economy in Ennahda's agenda. It is
unlikely to introduce *sharia* to the educational system or impose an Islamic code of conduct on students, both Muslims and Christians. Civics and social studies curricula will
not be substantially revised to include dramatically more Islamic content. And Islamic
religion will continue to be offered as a separate course with limited revision, if any.

Islamists and Citizenship Education

The Muslim Brotherhood holds that religious identity is both more profound and more
comprehensive than national or citizenship identity. For them, religious identity derives
from a wider conceptualization of life, the world, and divinity, at the heart of which is
man. Al-Ghannoushi, leader of Ennahda, argues that the goal of *sharia* is realization of
the supreme interests of humanity, the most important of which is safeguarding religion.[43] Being more important than citizenship in any country, religion thus supersedes it
in any context including education. According to al-Ghannoushi, nationalism is a "component of Islamic universalism."[44] In Egypt, the Ministry of Education under Mubarak

---

42   See Rashed Al-Ghannoushi's speech titled *Secularism and Relation between Religion and the State
     from the Perspective of Ennahda Party*, CSID-Tunisia, March 2, 2012, in which he criticized the
     Saudi coercion of girls into veiling, considering coercion a failure of their educational system; see
     also his recent publication *Democracy and Human Rights in Islam*, Beirut, Addar al-Arabiya lil
     Ulum, (forthcoming), as cited in *Al-Hayat*, February 16, 2012, 9.
43   Al-Ghannoushi, 2012, 9.
44   As cited by Esposito and Voll, ibid., 105.

adopted this view, perhaps not deliberately, when placing citizenship education within religious education and social studies in primary and middle school.

Recently, however, the post-Mubarak Ministry of Education added a course on citizenship and human rights to the second and third secondary class curriculum as one of six new courses. The fact that it is a 'pass or fail' course taught only in the two highest secondary classes makes it much less important than the course on religious education which is taught in all grades. Still, the influence of the Muslim Brotherhood is evident in the contents of the textbook. As elaborated earlier, it underscores the Brotherhood's perspective on human rights.

Islamists in Egypt and Tunisia consider a course on civics or citizenship to be far less important than a course on Islam, as religion has priority over nationalism and citizenship. They will not accept, and neither will the general public, that Islamic education programs be marginalized or their contents diluted. Any new initiative in education reform that emphasizes education for citizenship would have to maintain religious education as part of the educational curriculum, but try to change it to make it more compatible with democratic values.

Education for citizenship in a democratic, pluralistic society encompasses three main aspects: (1) knowledge of civic concepts, systems, and processes of civic life; (2) skills in civic participation, problem solving, and negotiation; and (3) disposition, a sense of belonging, values, and ethics. The purpose of education for citizenship is to develop well-rounded, responsible citizens who know their legal rights and duties, and apply this knowledge to evaluate or justify government policies and practices. Thus, teachers of any subject and supervisors of any activity at school educate their students for citizenship when they impart values such as responsibility, cooperation, and respect for diversity. The entire school climate and culture can be structured to promote or hinder education for citizenship.

This definition of citizenship education is not adopted or applied fully in either Egypt or Tunisia. But the Islamists in those two countries are likely to endorse it on condition that it is subject to the barometer of *sharia* and placed within the context of an Islamic school culture. Put differently, from an Islamic perspective the mission of a school is to raise a devout Muslim who is also a responsible citizen of his/her country and who possesses the professional and social skills required to succeed in the twenty-first century. The dilemma, however, is that strict application of *sharia* is not compatible with all the articles of the Universal Declaration of Human Rightsor with pluralism as practiced in established democracies.

Despite their public endorsement of democracy and pluralism, neither the FJP nor Ennahda accepts full equality of all citizens, Muslims and non-Muslims. Al-Ghannoushi justifies this position by dividing citizenship into two categories: unqualified (*muwatana 'amma*) for Muslims and qualified (*muwatana khassa*) for non-Muslims. He approves the prohibition of non-Muslims from occupying senior government positions in a democratic state where Muslims comprise a majority.[45]

---

45   As cited in Esposito and Voll, 115.

Gender equity looms high in citizenship education, in the United Nations Declaration on Human Rights, and in all UN decisions and programs on women and empowerment. Yet the FJP and Ennahda concur with the mainstream Sunni Islamic position, which deviates from the international consensus. Their position endorses equal rights for women and men in pay for work, acquisitions, fair treatment, and religious obligations, but not in inheritance, where according to Islamic teaching females inherited half as much as their male siblings. The Muslim Brotherhood does not support the appointment of women to the highest political, religious, or judiciary offices, namely that of president, mufti, or supreme judge. Furthermore, Islamists are more likely to support the current policy in most Arab states under which women are denied the right to pass citizenship to their children.

Given these deviations of Islamists' positions from democratic values and pluralism, what are the prospects of reconciling education for democratic citizenship, as defined above, with the teaching of Islam in Egypt and Tunisia?

Islamic Education and Citizenship: The Way Forward

Despite the tyrannical nature of President Ben Ali's regime, the Tunisian experience in reforming school education, particularly the Islamic education curriculum, provides important lessons. As elaborated earlier, teaching Islam at Tunisian public schools aims at nurturing tolerance and respect for other religions and Islamic sects, accepting Western democratic values as universal values that transcend national and regional boundaries, and developing students' interest in profound thinking on issues relating to the meaning of life and the relationship between man and God and man and society. These teaching objectives are compatible with a modern democratic conception of education for citizenship and are far more advanced in promoting democratic values and pluralism than comparable objectives in Egypt. For this reason, one international study that analyzed the contents of school textbooks for several Arab countries praised the Tunisian educational system as the model for all Arab countries.[46] Therefore, a new initiative in education reform in Tunisia could keep the present Islamic education curriculum as the foundation for a more liberal Islamic orientation.

In Egypt, there was an attempt during Mubarak's rule to design a course that incorporated the common values and morals of Islam and Christianity; however, its syllabus, published as a textbook for the elementary level, has not been applied But recently in the post-Mubarak era, a new initiative was proposed by the Egyptian Family House, a national group comprised of Al-Azhar, churches from different Christian denominations, and a number of academics. The initiative calls for preparing a new religious education program by focusing on values that are common to Muslims and Christians. A special committee was formed to design this program and obtaingovernment approval.[47]

---

46   Groiss, 2008, 14.
47   As announced by Mahmoud Azab, Advisor to the Grand Imam of Al-Azhar, at the UNESCO
      meeting on inter-faith dialogue, Beirut, March 2012.

If this initiative passes, it will be a fundamental step in the right direction of democracy and pluralism in Egypt, and can serve as a model for other Arab countries. Any new education reform plan should include it as an integral part of its plan and render the curricula and programs for other subjects and activities compatible with it.

This new education initiative is based on the document of basic freedoms unveiled by Al-Azhar in 2012. The document is an effective, proactive measure by moderate political forces led by Ahmad Al-Tayyib, the Grand Imam of Al-Azhar, to prevent newly elected conservative members of parliament from rewriting the constitution to fit their restrictive interpretation of Islam. Supported by the Coptic Church and most political parties in Egypt, Al-Azhar's 'bill of rights', has four main chapters: (1) freedom of belief, (2) freedom of scientific research, (3) freedom of opinion and expression, and (4) freedom of literary and artistic creativity. Freedom of belief is a right for all citizens. It is based on explicit verses in the Qur'an. Not only does this bill of rights endorse freedom of belief, but it also prohibits any attempts to exclude others or label them infidels and rejects orientations that "denounce the beliefs of others".[48]

Religious education in Egypt today neither contributes to acceptance, respect, and mutual understanding between faiths, nor helps the students develop a more profound understanding of their own faith or their own selves. The new proposed course by the Egyptian Family House signals a promising change toward pluralism. A new course on the commonalities between Islam and Christianity which promotes diversity and respect for the different other would open up students' minds to a new perspective on their religion and themselves and embolden them to start questioning and investigating the issues they study. These are among the characteristics of education for citizenship that may also encourage future attempts at liberalizing the current religious offerings in both Islam and Christianity.

But much more than this new initiative is needed in Egypt. An overhaul of the entire educational system with all its components is imperative. All elements of the school climate should be reformed with emphasis on citizenship values and skills. Education for responsible citizenship offers a promising opportunity for the youth in Egypt and Tunisia: the opportunity to develop into responsible citizens equipped with the requisite civic and religious knowledge, skills and competencies to prosper in a free, pluralistic, and peaceful society.

---

48 Al-Azhar Ashareef, *Bayan Al-Azhar wal-Muthaqafeen 'an Mandhumat Alhurriyat al-Asasiyah* (The declaration of Al-Azhar and the intellectuals about the system of basic freedoms), mimeographed (January 2012), 2–3; Muhammad Faour, Education is key to avoiding religious tension in Egypt, *The National*, January 17, 2012.

Capitalizing on Inequality?
Religious Schools in Turkey and Israel

ANNALENA DI GIOVANNI

To any dispassionate observer, Turkey and Israel present many analogies. To start with, they are both young entities: the Republic of Turkey was declared in 1923 on the Anatolian remnants of the Ottoman Empire, while the State of Israel came into being in 1948 in part of what had been the British Mandate of Palestine. Both seemed a bet against all givens, a legacy that still affects nationalistic sentiments. The conquest of a common land for a common people was in the cases of Turkey and Israel not without hostilities and in fact involved the forced migration of many others – Greeks, Armenians, Arabs – and a mass of returnees who would carry with them their different backgrounds and expectations. In all of these lands a new common language was imposed in the space of a few years. Turkey "reinvented" Turkish from old Ottoman and popularized it among immigrants from Bulgaria, the Black Sea shores and Lower Anatolia; Israel rearranged and replenished biblical Hebrew, a language confined to religious literary use for at least two millennia, and ensured it gained the upper hand over Ladino, Yiddish, Polish, Arabic, German and Russian. This bet was won through education.

True, all these features are not unique to Turkey and Israel. The invention of linguistic, historical and even geographical narratives is nothing new per se, nor is the pivotal role of schooling for the assimilation of these values: most of the states now part of the European Union built their respective nations through the designation of a common destiny within a common land. Often, they did so by imposing a language. For example, literary Italian was promoted to the spoken idiom when the country gained independence in the early twentieth century, and Castilian was sanctioned as official Spanish. In many other instances nation-building was an antagonistic matter, and the borders of the common land triggered centuries of struggles over territory – one just has to think of France, Poland or Austria and the decades of war they experienced.

Yet there is an additional element that makes the case for a comparison between Turkey and Israel in matters of education: an ongoing conflict against the national religious confession. In other words, the fundamental division in their contemporary societies runs, at least formally, through the dichotomy between religious and non-religious citizens. In both countries devotional attitude is not a matter of private belief: it defines loyalty to the nation and it is perceived as being in conflict with democracy. Oddly enough, this conflict characterizes the two Middle Eastern republics which in the last decades have maintained the closest ties with Europe, a continent where private religious schools are found everywhere and grassroots religious organizations and political actors openly refer to religious values. But while no "threat to democracy" is associated with a self-defining Christian party governing in Germany, with a head of state – Queen Elizabeth II – as head of a church (Church of England), or with customary church attendance expected of politicians in Italy, such normality between citizenship and faith is not the case in Turkish and Israeli society. The two segments of the population, the religious and the secular, do not meet and do not want to, even at the risk of a ruptured national identity. Both withdraw into their own networks, their political affiliations, their lifestyle and their aesthetics, depending on which side of the barricade they are on. Seculars perceive the religious as a menace to the very foundations of their country, while the religious perceive the seculars' fears as persecution, and consequently seek revenge through communal bracing. Between minority complexes and secular fears the education of young citizens in Turkey and Israel serves, not surprisingly, indeed perpetuates, the harshest of social divisions.

Given this very particular polarization, this study aims to offer a brief comparison of the private religious education systems in Turkey and Israel. They provide a service to roughly 5% of pupils in Turkey, and 20% in Israel. Despite relatively small figures, their impact on public debate and politics is formidable.

Efforts to implement a basic state curriculum in these independent schools have met with different fates in the two countries. In Turkey, Islamic schools not only teach the full state curriculum, but compete with top-level public schools to prepare students for university examinations. The opposite is true in Israel, where the state comptroller has never been allowed to know what is being taught in private ultra-Orthodox schools.

The opposite is true in respect of state funding: whereas Imam Hatip schools rely heavily on private sponsors in Turkey, Israel devotes a considerable percentage of the annual budget to private religious schools.

Both countries also have extensive public education systems intended to strengthen secular national values among pupils. In fact, they entrench pre-existing inequalities to the advantage of well-established sectors of the population and wealthy urban areas. As we shall see, this factor is a major determinant in the success of private education and the success of confessional parties that provide it.

Finally, the two case studies inherited an Ottoman tradition of confessional autonomy which grants the right to special institutes for their recognized minorities (Greeks, Jews and Armenians in Turkey; Christians, Muslim and Druze in Israel; Turkish Alevis, as a non-recognized minority, do not enjoy autonomous schooling), an aspect that unfortunately goes beyond the bounds of this article.

Background: Secularism in Arms?

Judaism in Israel and Sunni Islam in Turkey seem to represent defining identity markers for these countries. Yet a scroll through the biographies of both founding fathers will show that David Ben Gurion was as secular as Mustafa Kemal Ataturk was, and that both opposed handing land and social control to networks which were in fact pre-existing and well established, and therefore – at least to their eyes – probably capable of delegitimizing the modern state each was striving to build. These networks were the *ulema* in Ottoman Turkey and the different rabbinates and Talmudic schools in Palestine.

The first victim of a Jew in the struggle for Palestine was not an Arab, or even a British officer: he was Yaakov Israel De Haan, a religious Jew. His murderer was also a Jew, and, unlike De Haan, a Zionist. That is to say, in 1924, almost 25 years before the creation of any state, the seeds of the Israeli *Kulturkampf* between the religious and the secular fronts were already sown.

This appears to be the case in Turkey, too, where the first constitutional experiment in Ottoman Istanbul in 1908 was defeated not by the sultan and his administration, but by the Islamist unions that led the 1909 counter-revolution. Thus, it is not surprising that right after the declaration of the Turkish Republic, in 1924, a Ministry of Religious Affairs was created with the sole purpose of "preventing non-state and anti-Kemalist circles from using religion for political mobilization against the state"[1].

Prominent historian Erik Zürcher has defined the Turkish Republic as "a paradox", where Turkishness was built up as the basic identity and "historiography and linguistics played a key role, as did suppression of alternative or even sub-identities"[2]. Islam can be listed as one of these sub-identities, sacrificed in the name of a state which more than once resorted to massive ethnic cleansings against its non-Muslim elements. One of the main preoccupations of the fragile, "paradoxical" republic was with the expulsion of most of its non-Muslim population, thus blurring the lines of Kemal Ataturk's secularism. Zürcher stressed how the rejection of Islam as an ethnic marker was a practical, rather than an ideological choice:

"... the predominant concern of the Young Turks was to save and strengthen the State, (...) the same underlying logic that of saving and strengthening the State, in the eyes of the Kemalists imposed the need for radical modernization and secularization"[3].

Thanks to this top-to-bottom survival strategy, secularism – meaning the positivist separation between state and religion – was one of the six guiding principles of the founding ideology of the Turkish Republic, Kemalism, while at the same time, the very identity of this state was built on the opposition between Muslim and non-Muslim[4].

The contradictions of a state apparatus struggling for a homogeneous, Sunni Muslim majority, while preaching that any Islamic marker was a threat to the national identity are still visible in contemporary Turkey, where the ruling Islamist party still adopts defensive rhetoric in its public discourse, and a secularist intellectual elite and the military apparatus feel constantly threatened by any public display of religiosity. Needless to say, religious schools are the battleground in the feud between secularists and Islamists.

Unlike Turkey, Israel came into being having to bridge the further contradiction of being a secular state for a people in a land with which the connection had, for millennia,

---

1   Dede, A.Y. (2008), *Islamism, state control over religion and social identity: Turkey and Egypt*, PhD thesis, Western Michigan University, 2008, 81.

2   Zürcher, E.J. (2010). *The Young Turk legacy and nation building: From the Ottoman Empire to Atatürk's Turkey*, London: I.B. Tauris, 211.

3   *Ibid.*

4   *Ibid.* p. 195.

been only through religious templates based on the transmission of sacred knowledge and of the rituals associated with it.

Such transmission instructed the learned ones on how to interpret the Scriptures on matters of purity and impurity; it was what kept the Scriptures alive after the disappearance of ancient Hebrew; it sanctioned the way the community regulated itself, and how social practices were elaborated and legitimized; finally, transmission of knowledge – passing on the memory of persecutions and migrations, but also *halakhic* rules on how to behave with strangers – assigned meanings to the segregation between Jews and gentiles.

The first Zionists who resolved to leave the old world behind them and settle in Palestine during the earlier *aliyot* were the children of this tradition, and its discontents who aimed at using education to pass on a different kind of knowledge. Schools, to them, were to be the *mizzug galuyot*, the melting pot where newcomers from all European countries would be cleansed of their past and molded into Hebrew-speaking New Jews, proud, secular and independent. By turning into reality the utopia of a Jewish homeland, they would never again seek safety and rights in a gentile country at the risk of another pogrom, nor wait for a Messiah to return to Palestine in order to establish the kingdom of God at the end of times.

Given the Zionist ethos of a "break with both the gentile and the rabbi" in the middle of a land held sacred by Judaism, the tension over opposite narratives explains the ongoing division between religious and secular Israelis. Till this day, the two sides do not compromise: religious gangs attack mixed-gender buses and people walking on Saturday, while the secular refuse to have their neighbourhoods "invaded" by ultra-Orthodox families. There still people between the two fronts who engage in active citizenship, while maintaining religious practice; there are the non-haredi congregations like the Reformed or the Zionist religious, affiliated with the National Religious Party; but since the 1970s the Chief Rabbinate has left all *halakhic* authority in the hands of the ultra-Orthodox, giving huge political and economic leverage to the most intransigent expression of Judaism.

The secular descendants of this *Kulturkampf* represent about 40% of the Jewish population in modern Israel and, one may reasonably say, the majority of key governmental, intellectual and military institutions. Yet, religion is only the most evident division within Israel, and limited to a specific segment of the Israeli population, the Ashkenazi, i.e., European, Jews.

The second cleavage in the Land of Milk and Honey is ethnic. With the creation of the State of Israel, hundreds of thousands of Sephardi or "Mizrahi"[5] Jews found

---

5   Philologists have traced the cultural and ethnic roots of followers of the Sephardi rite to the early communities of Spain, Portugal, parts of Italy (where the Italian rite is also followed), Greece and Ottoman Turkey. Many of those forced to leave Catholic Spain moved to Morocco, Bulgaria, the Netherlands and France. In Israel the term Sephardi is currently interchangeable with Mizrahi, coined to describe "Oriental" Jews who arrived from North Africa, the Middle East, the Caucasus, Iran and Kurdish areas and also Ethiopia and Yemen. Because of their traditional outlook and conservative lifestyle, they are also called Masortim. Huge numbers of Mizrahi Jews were forced to move to Israel after 1948 as a result of their countries' response to the Palestinian Nakba. The camps

themselves forced to leave the Middle Eastern countries where they had lived for centuries. To the Zionist leadership, this wave of newcomers came as an unexpected blow: these communities had a different history, a different experience of their identity, and above all a much more conservative set of values. Confined to "development towns" on the outskirts of the urban centres, Mizrahim were estranged from an Ashkenazi leadership that despised them, kept the best jobs for themselves and dictated the national culture. Today these dismayed immigrants, including more recent waves of Ethiopian and Yemeni Jews, make up 60% of the Israeli Jewish population and the greater part of its lower class, many of them settled in the illegal colonies outside Jerusalem or on the West Bank.

Oriental – Mizrahi – Jews are too conservative to be welcomed in secular state schools, where well-off Ashkenazi parents do not want them mixing with their children, yet not religious enough to join the ultra-Orthodox Ashkenazi ranks. Furthermore, coming from the Middle East, they lack a knowledge of Yiddish – still a language of instruction in rabbinical schools – necessary for a religious education. For them, education marks the earliest stage of their continued discrimination. Secular academic careers are hardly possible for children that grow up in Oriental Jewish suburbs, badly serviced by overcrowded state schools in which underpaid Ashkenazi teachers, themselves products of a more elitist education, do not hide their contempt for their pupils with a Mizrahi background[6].

Hence, through schooling, separated systems nurture highly contrasting values. At the top of the ladder are those students who fulfil all the criteria of the model Israeli citizen: upper-middle class, secular, resident in well-off districts of Jerusalem or in kibbutzim, and descendants of one or more generations of European immigrants. Higher education is the most likely goal for this type of graduate, and a closer look at electoral maps[7] in Israel will show that this student is more than likely to vote for the centre-left, engage in civil society campaigns and advocate dialogue with Palestinians. But this secular, well-educated, open-minded youngster is also part of an elite whose political power is decreasing.

Lower down the ladder are the religious Jews who, despite widespread poverty and a faulty autonomous education system that barely enables them to master Hebrew, enjoy huge political leverage and veto power. For example, marriage is still conducted exclusively through religious institutions in Israel, and food requires the approval of *kashrut* authorities through the chief rabbinates (of which there are two, Ashkenazi and Sephardi) and the ministry of religion. More interestingly, the ultra-Orthodox are the

---

where the Zionist leadership accommodated them upon their arrival subsequently became the development towns where they and their descendants now live. Ben Gurion used to refer to them simply as "Arabs", despising their lack of Zionist indoctrination. Religious circles rejected them because of their different rite; it is extremely unlikely for a Sephardi student to be accepted by any Ashkenazi Talmud Torah school. They represent a good 60% of the Israeli Jews. Following Israeli practice, in this paper both "Mizrahi" and "Sephardi" are used.

6   See: Swirsky, S. and N. Dagan-Buzaglo (2009), *Separation, Inequality and Loosening Control: The State of State Education in Israel*, Tel Aviv: ADVA Center.

7   See http://www.electoralgeography.com/new/en/countries/i/israel/israel-legislative-election-2009.ht ml retrieved on 8 February 2013.

faster growing part of the population, yet are the least active in the public service, starting with the army.

Mizrahi Jews are at the bottom of the ladder, just above Arab Palestinians. Ethnically discriminated and socially marginalized, their only political strength is the Mizrahi party, Shas, which has further undermined the public image of the Mizrahi through several cases of corruption and racist statements by its religious leader, Rav Ovadia Youssef.

Religiousness, ethnicity, family background: the three deeply intertwined strands are perpetuated through education. With the effort of gathering a universal Jewry into one land for one people, discrepancies between different cultures, values, histories and even customs have matured into hostility. As education perpetuates inequalities, the Israeli schooling system can be confidently identified as a kingpin of social conflict in a deeply divided Jewish society.

Education in Turkey and Israel: An Overview

The most outstanding characteristic of contemporary education in Israel has been defined (Swisky, 2009) as: "separation – on the basis of ethnicity, degree of religiosity, and class."[8] Turkey fares no better. Later OECD reports point to the hugely unequal opportunities provided by the state schooling system, in which, according to PISA data, it is virtually impossible to choose a middle path:

> "... schools are segregated by socio-economic background, which further deepens the gap between students' achievements. (...) According to the ESCS index, while 64 percent of the children from the bottom quartile attend disadvantaged schools, only seven percent are able to attend advantaged schools"[9].

These figures mirror widespread social, ethnic and economic divisions, of which religiosity is only the most visible and polarizing factor. Far from offering equal opportunities, both educational systems – the Turkish and the Israeli – function like segmenting machines in which vested gains are carved out of divisions and political forces nurture their constituencies along this cleavage by openly supporting – financially as well as proactively – opposing principles of education.

Turkey: Education for the Better Educated

Through the years and the many military coups d'état, the education system of the Republic of Turkey has been reorganized in accordance with different yardsticks. The latest reform passed by the Grand National Assembly in March 2012 raised compulsory

---

8   See Swirsky, S. and N. Dagan-Buzaglo (2009), *Separation, Inequality and Loosening Control: The State of State Education in Israel*, Tel Aviv: ADVA Center, 7.

9   Köseleci Blanchy, N. and A. Şaşmaz (2011), PISA 2009: Where does Turkey stand? *Turkish Policy Quarterly*, 10(2), 7.

education to 14 years of age, endorsing a 4+4+4 system in which children are enrolled in primary school at the age of six, ideally switch to secondary school in the fifth year, and enter high school or vocational high school at 15. Primary school is centralized; all children are enrolled in state schools notionally based on the six main principles of Kemalism – republicanism, populism, secularism, revolutionism, nationalism and statism. The basic curriculum includes Turkish, mathematics, general knowledge, and two hours of "religions" (a course supposed to discuss Islam as well as the main world beliefs). Another four years of secondary school follow that include an introduction to foreign languages and the humanities. In the last four years a student supposedly has the choice between a general high school and a specialized track that emphasizes arts, pedagogy or social studies. If particularly gifted in mathematics, a student can apply for a scientific high school. Members of recognized minorities can go to community high schools that teach extra-curricular subjects such as Armenian, Jewish culture or Greek. In addition to general or specialized high schools there is also the vocational high school, where the focus is on technical skills and school-directed working internships.

In theory, students in all high school tracks can take the university entrance; but in practice, the Turkish system relies heavily on performance measurement records drafted on a nationwide scale. This means that although 1.6 million high-school graduates on average are eligible for higher education each year, only a quarter of them will get one of the 450,000 available university places.

They are allocated on the basis of the results of High School/Undergraduate Placement Examination, now abbreviated as YGS-LYS, but still known by its previous acronym ÖSS. This is a three-hour national multiple-choice test that examines a pupil's ability to quickly answer questions on a variety of subjects. The results, in conjunction with a pupil's school marks, determine who can go where. Since high-school education alone is not enough to obtain the high average marks needed to pass the placement test, cram schools, so-called *dershane*s, prepare pupils for the 195-minute test. *Dershane*s are private, and not every family can afford the cost. Only particularly gifted pupils who might bring prestige to a *dershane* receive scholarships. Each year, the ÖSS is a veritable national drama, filling newspapers and television programmes with endless accounts of anticipations. But this is not the only selection a Turkish student has to pass. The first, and most decisive choice, had already been made a few years earlier, in the sixth, seventh and eighth-year nationwide examinations called the Level Assessment Examination (generally shortened to SBS), when children are grouped according to their preparation and talent. Successful pupils can take the Anatolian High School entrance examination.

These elite schools guarantee university entrance and better training in basic curricular subjects and foreign languages. Competition is fierce. It is enough to mention the case of the most famous Anatolian High School, the Turco-French Galatasaray Lisesi in the heart of Beyoglu area of Istanbul. Each year more than a million children compete to be admitted to the entrance examination. Of the successful 500, just 100 are accepted to study and live on the premises of this prestigious institute, where they receive tuition in both French and Turkish and additional training in other foreign languages such as English or Italian. Graduation from the Galataseray Lisesi grants admission to any university course in Turkey and effectively grants access to key positions in the civil service. Secular prime ministers, ambassadors and top-ranking civil servants have graduated from here for centuries. Despite its almost mystical aura, the Galataseray Lisesi is open to everyone, regardless of economic standing. However, it is clear that ordinary primary school preparation is not enough to pass its entrance requirements.

Generally children need to be enrolled from the primary level in afternoon schools that prepare them to pass the national entry with a score that will ensure entrance to Anatolian High Schools and, thus, a bright future at the best universities and access to courses difficult to get into, such as medicine, law and international relations. Children of upper-class families with the means to invest in them from the age of their eight are the ones who will fill the few hundred posts at the best universities and benefit from the career options this leads to.

Solving problems, though, is not the only skill required to ensure a better future at such an early age. During the SBS exams children are also "measured" in the form of their teacher's feedback on efficacy, perception[10], school behaviour and attitude. It has already been pointed out that Level One school is public and compulsory. Teachers are trained to be the first upholders of Kemalist values, which are not always shared by large segments of the population served by such schools.

Geography is a determining factor as well as class: well-off areas and industrial cities benefit from a virtuous circle of better schools and more highly motivated teachers who interact for the most part with the children of an elite who can understand and reciprocate their codes and standards. This is not the case in rural areas (especially in the Kurdish southeast), the *gecekondu*[11] of Istanbul, and the more conservative neighbourhoods into which rural immigrants moved a generation or two ago, for example

---

10 See Altun, S. and D. Canca, D (2011), A Model Study on the Explanation of the Centralized High School Entrance Examination in Turkey, *World Applied Science Journal*, 15, 1253–1259.

11 It is safe to claim that Imam Hatip schools cannot be studied separately from the phenomena of the *gecekondu*, both being an expression of the desire *"... to achieve success (which) contributed to the growing spirit of entrepreneurship in Turkey"* (Karpat, 2004), and both a reflection of the average Istanbouli AKP voters. *Gecekondus* are literally the temporary night-time dwellings built by rural immigrants crowding into the outskirts of cities, in particular Istanbul, in the 1960s and 1970s. *Generally speaking, the gecekonducu* population shared a non-urban identity and a conservative background, and thus were looked down upon by well-established inner city residents. To quote prominent Turkish historian Kemal H. Karpat, who studied *gecekondus* in 1976:

"... The term gecekondu represented the city's traditional sense of superiority towards the village and the urbanites' alarm that peasants aspired to share the civilization and benefits of the city life, and possibly then to claim to be their equals. In the end, this is exactly what came to pass in politics, education and living standards without causing the collapse of the social order. (...) Coined by city residents, the term reflected almost exclusively their negative reaction to the influx of the villagers who defied established urban norms. It is in essence a legal definition that describes a makeshift, uncomfortable hut erected overnight on land owned by the state, municipality or individuals in defiance of the building codes and property rights. The definition is limited strictly to the urban space and the building itself and disregards entirely the complex human factors of which the dwelling is just a symptom." (Karpat 2004).

Underserved by public schooling and thus denied any chance of higher education, *gecekondu* dwellers have been the principal beneficiaries of Imam Hatip schools and scholarship programmes. See Karpat, Kemal H. (2004) *The Genesis of the Gecekondu: Rural Migration and Urbanization* (1976), in *European Journal of Turkish Studies*, Thematic Issue N°1, Gecekondu.

Kasimpasha, Recep Tayyip Erdoğan's quarter in Istanbul. Cultural unease, a sense of inadequacy and educational gaps are the most likely legacy of schools servicing these areas, thereby alienating students whose chances in life are frustrated by an educational deficit.

In conclusion, despite, or perhaps because of, the fiercely competitive nature of the schooling system, each year 40% of Turkish high school graduates fail to achieve basic mathematical literacy,[12] while only a few hundred can aspire to enter the most influential university networks, thanks mainly to their family background. An additional issue is female attendance after compulsory schooling. Because of the ban on the veil and fears of promiscuity (students are often boarded away from the family, especially if from under-served rural areas), the withdrawal of girls from school upon reaching puberty has further undermined education in Turkey. In short, opportunities offered by state schools are decidedly unequal. Imam Hatip religious high schools have worked on this cleavage, offering competitive preparation to those sectors of the population who, for reasons of background or geography, would have no chance of success in the conventional state education system.

Israel: Equal for the More Equal

Figures can sometimes be misleading and that is certainly the case with Israeli education. While boasting annual expenditure on education of at least one tenth of its budget,[13] Israel fails to graduate at least half of its high school students each year. Data from the 2011 *bagrut*, the 12th Grade psychometric university examination show that only an average of 48.8% of 18 year olds passed. Third-generation children of Ashkenazi descent located in better served urban areas and fully integrated in a country where they fit the citizenship paradigm have a better chance of entering higher education, with average graduation success of 64.4%. Figures are as high as 77.9% among the better educated elites living in the kibbutzim. But this is not the case among students of Mizrahi descent in overcrowded schools in suburban or development areas, whose success rate is at least ten points lower than that of their Ashkenazi peers. The percentage of Arab pupils gaining university entrance is as low as 38.2%; figures are even lower for students of private religious Jewish schools, of whom only 22.5% were eligible for matriculation in 2010 and just 5% passed.[14]

Surprisingly, this last group of students receives particularly lavish state support. In the past 20 years, the allocation of public funding to private religious education has steadily grown by between 367% for Ashkenazi ultra-Orthodox institutes and 973% for Mizrahi schools,[15] while parents who send their children to public secular schools are

---

12   OECD (2010) *PISA 2009: Overcoming Social Background,* Vol. II, 34.
13   See Hemmings, P. (2010), *Israeli Education Policy: How to Move Ahead in Reform.* OECD: Economics Department Working Paper No. 781, retrieved from http://www.oecd.org/eco/Working papers on 26/01/2013.
14   Israeli Central Bureau of Statistics, *CBS, Statistical Abstract of Israel 2010, Section 8.23.*
15   See Knesset Budget records for the years 2000–2010; Swirsky S. (1998), *Government Allocations,* Tel Aviv: ADVA Center.

asked to cover as much as 20% of tuition costs out of their own pocket. Whether tax money is well invested or not is hard to determine because so far the Israeli state has never provided comprehensive data on the curricula actually taught in private religious schools; some of them even refuse to teach in the official language, using Yiddish instead of modern Hebrew.

The corpus of basic literacy and values endorsed is as diverse as the funding. To quote Shlomo Swirsky (2009),

> "The official curriculum primarily addresses the third of the student population who do meet normative standards. These students attend schools that, for years, have served as the main pool for the future leadership in the state, society, and economy – the leaders, commanders, scientists, and managers. These schools are almost certainly the only ones in which the full official curriculum – and more – is taught."[16]

In fact, it seems very unlikely that education promotes social mobility in contemporary Israel. It can be inferred that behind the very encouraging figures of high performance in terms of university research and public expenditure, the Israeli education system is – to paraphrase George Orwell – equal only for the more equal among its Jewish citizens.

The Israeli compulsory education system currently consists of elementary school from six to 12 years of age, junior-high school until 15 years and an optional two years of senior high school. These last two years are preparation for the national matriculation exam, the *bagrut*, after which a student can go on to higher education. A 1968 reform, which has so far been only partially implemented, offers a choice in junior high school between a vocational track for non-academic employment and an academic track leading to university. As the pupils have to make a choice at an early age, parents' and teachers' recommendations are the decisive factors. Non-Jewish children follow a similar pattern but, as under the old Ottoman model, they are referred to a separate schooling system.

The above-mentioned 1968 reform was supposed to mend the gap between oriental and western Jews, but ended up sanctioning all inequalities, so that today most universities are populated by students of Ashkenazi descent, while Mizrahim, most of whom come from areas serviced mainly by vocational schools, have relatively little chance of going on to higher education and generally finish their education at sixteen years old.

To further complicate matters, the Israeli education system is governed by the 1953 State Education Act. Seeking to mediate between opposing political factions – secular, religious, and Zionist-religious – and at the same time to impose a certain degree of control on what is taught in the various schooling systems, it divided education into four parallel tracks: a "minority" system for non-Jews; a national-secular, a national-religious and a private religious system.[17] The latter is by far the most problematic of the four, as the teaching services it provides are, to quote the OECD, "unconventional".[18]

---

16   ADVA REPORT N.
17   This fourth tier is in fact more articulate, as private schools include not only the Haredi, but also international foreign institutes and private mixed schools where Jewish and Arab children are taught

Every year, each six-year-old student is enrolled in a specific schooling system with a different set of values and skills. Compulsory teaching continues for the following 12 years through an exclusive pattern which will eventually produce a member of a distinct community, a member who will behave, vote, find a job, participate in public life and even choose his or her residential area depending on which the educational stream has been initially chosen for him or her.

The national-secular school system is officially public, but parents are requested to contribute financially in order to cover tuition costs. This is a direct source of inequality, in which wealthy parents can afford better education for their children. This compounds the fact that the quality of schools is already higher in well-off areas, where class numbers are smaller and children from development towns are not welcome.

In mixed areas where both children of Ashkenazi and Mizrahi descent are enrolled the differentiation is of another sort. Because of the pressure put on teachers by output evaluation,[19] pupils are "grouped" according to their performance, which, once again, is heavily influenced by their background. Grouping affects their further education, as less-skilled students are prompted to enrol in technical and vocational schools. Hence, public schools can be said to reinforce class and ethnic divisions.

The same can be said about national religious schools, which are in fact even more demanding. This separate track was introduced in the late 1950s in response to parents' complaints that their children were leaving public school completely ignorant of their Jewish roots. Following the Orthodox Jewish American school model, these institutes teach the regular curriculum in the morning and run Torah and Talmudic studies in the afternoon. Because of the long teaching days, their courses are both competitive and demanding. Moreover, because for decades their administration was in the hands of the National Religious Party, a party of the religious minority in Zionist ranks founded before Israeli independence, the Judaism they teach follows the Ashkenazi rite and not the Sephardi one. An interesting feature of these very elitist schools is that lately they have had to compete with private Haredi schools. Since the ultra-Orthodox schools subject their pupils to a harsher Talmudic education, the national-religious schools have been drawn into imitating them.

A curious aspect of the competition between national religious schools and Haredi private schools is as the latter gain students at the expanse of the former, teaching habits are also changing. Some national religious schools have adopted the Zielberman teaching method, which emphasizes memorization of the sacred scriptures rather than exegesis. Da'ath Torah, which is the ultra-Orthodox literal interpretation of the Torah, is also increasingly being enforced in accordance with Haredi habits. National religious schools are also beginning to deny extended summer holidays and expecting their students' parents to meet far stricter standards of behaviour, for example expelling students whose mothers are divorced or do not cover their heads. Once again, discrimin-

---

together in the same classes. In the interests of simplification, this study will deal only with private religious Jewish schools.

18 See OECD (2009), *Economic Survey of Israel – Policy Brief.* Paris: Organization for Economic Co-operation and Development, 2009. Retrieved from: www.oecd.org.

19 Cf. Swirsky, *ibid.*

ation works to the disadvantage of Mizrahim, who are known to be both very conservative on moral issues and lenient on religious restriction.

Before delving into the utterly complex realm of private Haredi schools it should be noted that all systems have their political mentors, who follow their constituencies from the cradle to the grave, but above all to the ballot box. While, until its dissolution, the NRP used to protect the interests of its voters through the national-religious track, the best public schools, created in the tradition of Ben Gurion's Mapai, cater to open-minded, well-educated children who become centre-left voters; middle to low-rank public schools, by contrast, are more likely to produce students with sympathies for the center-right Likud or for ethnic secular parties like those representing immigrants from Soviet Russia, for example Avigdor's Lieberman's Israel Beitenu.

Private Religious Schools: Capitalizing On Inequality?

Imam Hatip Schools in Turkey

"Teachers are the only people who save nations", runs a Kemalist slogan. Ataturk saw the nation to be saved as a secular one, rooted in the principles of reason and science. But when the 1924 Education Reunification Act was passed in order to endorse a secular nationwide schooling system, Turkey was emerging from decades of confessional education in which, apart from a few prestigious secular schools dedicated to the training of public servants and urban elites, each confessional community was autonomous and Muslims relied on the *madrasahs*, schools administered by the *Waqf* and dedicated to passing on religious learning.[20] As the new Kemalist state defined itself through a unifying ethos of progress that allowed the past and its superstitions, as religion was labelled,[21] no space, a rather contradictory paradigm existed in which private Christian and Jewish institutions were more or less allowed to operate under alternative rules, while Islamic education disappeared.

A faculty of theology initially survived at Istanbul University in order to continue and possibly control the training of Islamic preachers, was then abolished in 1933 and subsequently reinstated in 1948. That meant that in order to be ordained an imam, a student would first have to undergo 12 years of secular public schooling.

---

20   See Gökçe, F. and O. Nilüfer (2010), *Minority and Foreign Schools on the Ottoman Education System*. Istanbul: *Uluslararası Eğitim Araştırmaları Dergisi* 1.1 (Summer 2010).

21   The following quote from Kemal Ataturk's 1927 *Nutuk,* (literally "speech") can be used to define secularism according to Republican standards:

   "My people are going to learn the principles of democracy, the dictates of truth and the teachings of science. Superstition must go. Let them worship as they will, every man can follow his own conscience provided it does not interfere with sane reason or bid him act against the liberty of his fellow men".

   See: Atatürk, K., D. Küçük, H. Aslan, Frankfurter Buchmesse, (2008), *Selected parts of speech (Nutuk)*. Istanbul: Profil Yayıncılık.

It was with the first electoral defeat of the Kemalist Republican Party in 1950 and the relatively[22] more tolerant approach under Adnan Menderes' Democratic Party that the first Imam Hatip courses were introduced, originally to train students for the Islamic Institutes opened in 1959. For the next two decades Imam Hatips were alternatively treated as official schools or else threatened with closure. In 1973, under the National Education Basic Law, they were finally registered as vocational high schools whose graduates could compete for general mainstream university entrance like any regular secular school graduate. From then on, Imam Hatips taught the state curriculum in the morning and Islamic knowledge in the afternoon for four years, after which young males could be ordained imam and seek employment in local mosques.

Today, of the roughly 235,000 Imam Hatip students attending one of the 490 Imam Hatip high schools, each year, just 15% of graduates seek to continue towards a religious career.[23] The rest has regularly enrolled in law, engineering or medicine. While the number of Imam Hatips has remained stable over the decades, they have considerably expanded their premises, investing consistently high private donations in boarding facilities, which are still free of charge, and improving the student-teacher ratio.

This phenomenon has been accompanied by more than one attempt on behalf of the secular camp to limit access by religious students to university premises for fear that this might enable an increasing number of Islamic graduates to fill key administrative positions. The main effort in this respect was the 1997 decree barring Imam Hatip graduates from university and lifting the minimum age for choosing religious schooling to 15. This had the effct of discouraging conservative families from keeping their daughters in school, as this would mean an extra four years of secular training first.

Such hostility is not without grounds: no more that 5% of the national school population may be enrolled in Imam Hatips, but a look at the present Turkish government reveals that the majority of sitting parliamentarians are Imam Hatip graduates, starting with Prime Minister Recep Tayyip Erdoğan, a former student of the Fatih Imam Hatip Lisesi. To this extent, Imam Hatip schools have had a considerable impact. As for the widespread accusation made by the secular camp that Imam Hatip will end up "Islamizing" Turkey, it is worth mentioning that they serve an already conservative community which was badly provided for by secular state schooling It is true that Imam Hatip students do not start their classes quoting Kemal Ataturk each morning, but they do receive a solid education in all scientific disciplines. Religion represents 40% of their courses; the remaining 60% is the full basic curriculum defined by law. The emphasis may be on morals, with teachers dealing at length with conservative values such as modesty, respect for elders, sexual abstinence and segregation between the sexes (schools are mixed by law, but pupils are discouraged from inter-

---

22 The adjective needs to be put in perspective, since Adnan Menderes has also been blamed for the pogroms against Greek and Armenian citizens in 1955. Although recent historical perspectives shifts responsibility for the pogroms onto the National Security Council and the Gladio organization, it is worth pointing out that the Democrats' lenient attitude towards Islamic traditions was matched by harsher policies against other communities.

23 See Ozgur, I. (2012). *Islamic schools in modern Turkey: Faith, politics, and education.* Cambridge : Cambridge University Press, 2012, p. I

acting; nonetheless, a good half of the students in Imam Hatip seem to have affairs and relationships like any teenagers). It is just such attitudes that appeal to parents who enrol their children in Imam Hatip schools.

The fact that from 1976 onwards hundreds, today thousands, of girls have enrolled in Imam Hatips adds to the unclear vocational connotation of these schools, as women are not supposed to officiate in mosques. This is particularly relevant for girls from middle-class families of traders and craftsmen who migrated from the countryside to the *gecekondu*, and from there to better-off areas. Their parents are more comfortable sending their girls to Imam Hatips then to regular public schools, which can raise question marks about a girl's honour.

At the same time, Imam Hatips have been credited with a softer attitude to religion compared to completely religious institutions.[24] In her study on Imam Hatip schools, Akpınar even reports a female teacher commenting on her students that due to the encompassing changes in contemporary society through television and social media "... the only difference between an ordinary public school student and Imam Hatip school student today is her wearing the turban[25]". Akpınar also quotes nationwide survey data[26] to show that opinions in Imam Hatip schools are, all said and done, no more conservative than those of the vast majority of Turkish citizens, regardless of their attitudes towards religion or of where their children are sent to study.

As for Imam Hatip students, it is interesting to note a wide margin of difference among opinions of girls and boys: according to a study by TESEV[27], girls attending Imam Hatip tend to be more open-minded than their male counterparts. In a survey of attitudes towards female emancipation, more than 86% of girls, a percentage higher than recorded in state schools, expressed a positive stance towards women working fulltime, in sharp contrast to the opposition expressed by their male classmates. TESEV suggests that the split could be due to the different backgrounds of Imam Hatip students: whereas girls come from the urbanized, but conservative, middle classes seeking basic education for their daughters, boys are boarding students from rural areas who attend Imam Hatip for social advancement.

Although a blend of the rural and urban, the open-minded and conservative Imam Hatip groups are closely knit. Classes are small, social rituals are strong, and a sense of moral superiority is widespread. Students keep within Imam Hatip circles even when at-

---

24 Akpınar, A. (2007), The Making of a Good Citizen and Conscious Muslim through Public Education: The Case of Imam Hatip schools, in Carlson, M., A. Rabo and F. Gök (2007), *Education in 'Multicultural' Societies – Turkish and Swedish Perspectives*, Stockholm: Swedish Research Institute in Istanbul, Transactions, 18, 166.

25 Ibid., 167.

26 See Yılmaz, H. (2006), *'Türkiye'de Muhafazakarlık Aile, Din, Batı: Ilk Sonuçlar Üzerine Genel Değerlendirme'* (Conservatism in the Turkish Family, Religion, the West: General Evaluation of Preliminary Results) Unpublished Research Report, Project Support: Open Society Institute and Boğaziçi University, Public Opinion Research: Infakto Research Workshop, January 2006, supervisors: Erdoğan, Emre and Güçlü Atılgan, research assistants: Başer, Bahar and Ak, Ömer, date of public research: January 2006; quoted by Akpınar in her study.

27 Hazırlayan, Y. et al. (2004), *Imam Hatip Liserleri: Efsaneler ve Gerçekler*. Istanbul: TESEV YAYINLARI, 2004.

tending university; they stick together and remain detached from fellow students with a state school background. In this sense, Irene Ozgur[28] has suggested viewing Imam Hatips as self-help functional communities[29] that are high-achieving in politics and economics, while maintaining a compact through mutual expectations and reciprocal scrutiny.

Ultra-Orthodox Schools in Israel

While Imam Hatips are, for the present, limited to high school and, since March 2012, secondary school, much of the Israeli debate on religious or non-religious schooling revolves around primary schools. Thanks to social divisions and also to the lack of control over the curriculum taught in each system, any ten-year-old pupil attending a primary school of a given kind (state-religious, secular or private) is already considered to be marked with a certain blend of education, community affiliation, and moral values that will determine subsequent tuition and, later, job opportunities. If successful in the national system, whether secular or state-religious, he/she will continue on to university; if in a private religious system, the future holds little besides a *kollel*[30] and life in a newly built block in a settlement near Jerusalem or on the West Bank, all free of charge. This is also thanks to the rule of *torato omanuto*. Based on an understanding that the study of the Scriptures is itself a job, *torato omanuto* grants religious students state support and exemption from military service. This lifetime assistance is funded by the taxpayers and is likely to become an increasing burden for Israel, considering that Haredim are a fast-growing community. They have jumped from 4% to 10% of the population in two decades and each household has on average six children. Two thirds of the Haredim are under 18 years of age, and they are expected to account for 30% of the Israeli population by 2020.

Unwelcome in middle-class urban areas and often housed in ever-expanding colonies in Palestinian territories, state-supported and not initiated in national values because of their religious schooling, while at the same time fighting fiercely to maintain their privileges, Haredim are likely to be an unruly, yet decisive factor in Middle Eastern politics in the coming decades. The power of their community is rooted in their religious primary school services, which are private and free of any state control.

As mentioned above, the state of Israel already offers some intensive religious training in the public track. This creates, though, a black-and-white division inasmuch as any family willing to raise its child "within the faith" has to accept strict scrutiny of parental mores and rabbinical training for the child in the afternoon, training that is increasingly subject to ultra-Orthodox influences. Families willing to accept such a radical choice are increasingly inclined to choose a Haredi school, where there is more extensive rabbinical education and fees are lower. This is particularly true of less wealthy families from poorer neighbourhoods. Accordingly, these schools have been losing ground in recent decades to ultra-Orthodox, private schooling. Today they

---

28 Ibid., 10.
29 Coleman, J., S. Kilgore, and T. Hoffer (1982), Cognitive Outcomes in Public and Private Schools, *Sociology of Education*, 55 (1982), 65–76.
30 Talmudic school for adults.

account for no more than 13% of the school population, compared with 20% enrolled in Haredi schools. The figures were the reverse just 20 years ago.

The issue of fees and costs is a byzantine feature of Israeli education: public schools are more expensive because they get less funding than private schools.

State funding is secured by an amendment to Section 11 of the 1953 Education Act, the so-called Nahari Law of 2007, under which the local authorities provide an amount for Haredi school expenses equal to 75% of the state education budget, regardless of the curriculum followed. It is a legacy of the early 1980s, when Likud leader Menachem Begin managed to outmanoeuvre the Labour establishment through a compromise with Orthodox parties. Today this compromise costs enormous sums. State-religious schools offer fewer hours of tuition compared, for example, to any Mizrahi school[31] of the *Ma'ayan ha Chinukh haTorani* system: the latter can pay a teacher as little as 300 dollars per month – knowledge transmission is after all part of the duties of a religious scholar – and still have almost all of its costs covered by either the national or municipal budget.

The strict proportionality of the Israeli parliamentary system makes it impossible to form a government without including at least one Haredi party in the coalition, regularly on the condition of leaving the unconditional funding of private religious schools untouched. While the State Comptroller has regularly questioned the lack of supervision of what exactly is taught in private religious schools, Haredi political parties more often than not tie their agreement to the position of minister of education, de facto "supervising supervision" as suits their needs.

Two years ago a detailed investigation commissioned by the newspaper Yediohot Aharonot[32] found out that science, history, Jewish literature and English as prescribed by the basic curriculum were not being taught in Haredi schools because they were considered "Zionist" and therefore incompatible with Judaism. Teaching was limited to Talmud memorization. Some schools had not even acquired the books prescribed by the ministry of education, while others would devote just an hour a day to teaching basic national subjects. Despite this, the state inspector reported that these schools were teaching the full curriculum and even awarded institutes extra funding. Unsurprisingly, the inspector was a Mizrahi who actively supported the oriental Haredi party, Shas. Yediohot calculated that the inspector's zeal cost the state around seven million US dollars a year, money denied to public schools.

The case of the *Ma'ayan haKhinukh haTorani* schools, created by the Shas party, may serve as representative of this phenomenon. This low-cost teaching service was created in the mid-1980s to meet the needs of conservative and historically disregarded communities such as the Mizrahi in development towns. Although Mizrahim in Israel would generally follow a conservative, but not orthodox religious ethos, the Ma'ayan schools succeeded in endorsing a Mizrahi version of Haredi Judaism (an interesting contradiction, considering that ethnic Mizrahim had never been welcomed in Haredi

---

31　See below.
32　Amir, Shoan, Haredi Teachers Fail General Knowledge Test, *Yediohot Aharonot*, 27 July 2010, and Amir, Shoan, The Haredi School Scam, *Yediohot aharonot*, 12 July 2010.

schools) and proselytized entire families through cheap tuition and longer school hours, which effectively relieved hard-working families of the worry of how to take care of their children. Like the Imam Hatip[33] schools, Ma'ayan stresses the moral superiority of its students compared to the rest of the population, inculcating in them a mixture of moral superiority, a sense of belonging and pride in community. Unlike the Turkish case, though, Israeli religious parties have been using private schools to nurture their constituencies by positively reinforcing a fragmentation bordering on hatred. Their sense of communal belonging is difficult to square with active citizenship. It is enough to quote the speech made by Rav Aryeh Deri at a rally of his party in 1997, after he was indicted for bribery involving the funding of Ma'ayan schools:

> "Zionism is a heretical movement that wants to create a new Judaism. Zionism tried to get rid of the Torah, tried to get rid of the Sephardic (i.e. Mizrahi) culture. It is clear to me why it is this holy movement in particular they are persecuting. This is not political persecution. This is religious and ethnic persecution. They are afraid that the Shasnik will change the secular character of the State if Israel, after they saw that with all their great vision they were unable to wipe us out. The true Zionists, that is us – the Sephardi observant Jews, which the establishment calls Primitives. They treated us like we were from outer space, but the more they humiliated us the more our power grew. You may break us physically but you may never break our spirit. For every indictment and every enquiry we will build more Talmud Torah schools and more synagogues".[34]

Fully dependent on political parties' support, private religious schools in Israel profit from encouraging an antagonistic stance against the state and its institutions and promoting themselves as an alternative service provider. This stance defines an identity, a sense of belonging and a resourceful community for students, for the modest price of casting the right ballot on election day. Moreover, this mechanism inevitably assigns legislative authority to religious leaders. Haredim follow the Daath Torah ideology, which is a total view of religion based on a literal reading of the sacred texts as law governing every aspect of everyday life. *Halakhic* authorities, i.e., the most erudite in the literary interpretation of the *Da'ath Torah* (literally: opinion of the Torah) are considered to be above officers of the state. Yet *halakhic* authorities are not necessarily enlightened champions of civic coexistence. A telling example is the chief rabbi of the Mizrahi community, Rav Ovadia Youssef, worshipped as a living authority of religious laws and spiritual leader of both the Shas party and its private religious schools, the above-mentioned Ma'ayan. In his untouchable position, Rabbi Youssef has declared that Ashkenazi Jews murdered in the Holocaust were being punished by God for sins committed in their previous life; that non-Jews were created to serve Jews; that sending missiles to exterminate Arabs is a religious duty; and that Hurricane Katrina was God's way of getting rid of an impure black race naturally unable to study the Torah.[35] Rabbi Youssef is presented as a role model in the Ma'ayan school system, and can be singled out as a

---

33   *cita* Sarfati
34   Dayan, A. (2008), Arye Deri's Speech of 23rd April 1997, in Rabinovich, I. (2008) *Israel in the Middle East: documents and readings on society, politics, and foreign relations pre-1948 to the present*, London: University Press of England.
35   All expressed in 1999, except for Hurricane Katrina, expressed in a 2010 sermon.

primary factor in the slow shift of the Mizrahi community towards an intransigent Haredi Judaism. Daily occurrences of Haredi students – both Ashkenazi and Mizrahi – attacking non-religious Jews on mixed-sex buses, setting cars on fire during Shabbat and randomly shooting at Palestinians are constantly in the news in Israel, contribute to further weakening the fabric of Israeli society. This is a direct result of class cleavage in which lower income categories of the Israeli school population are increasingly aware to the advantages offered by private religious schools and their mentors.

Conclusions

During the Conference Seminar on Teaching Religion in Divided Societies held in Byblos on the 10 November 2011, Professor Theodor Hanf suggested that "(...) It is not possible to resolve political problems through education engineering". In the case of religious schools in Turkey and Israel, though, the question is whether educational problems are caused by political engineering.

Recep Tayyip Erdoğan, a self-defining "Muslim and a Turk" and a representative of the conservative urbanized class of tradesmen and craftsmen from a rural background who initially settled on the outskirts of Istanbul and whom the secular republican establishment neither acknowledged nor engaged with, has been prime minister of Turkey since 2003. Erdoğan is an alumnus and staunch supporter of the Fatih Imam Hatip. Had it not been for his religious school, Erdoğan would never have received the preparation necessary to gain entrance to the prestigious Marmara University and eventually achieve his current position. Through Imam Hatip, Erdoğan gained an identity, a confidence, a sense of belonging and a respect for his own background. The state schools in his neighbourhood would not have provided this.

Although his economic policies might eventually tarnish his rising star, Erdoğan is both a religious student and a Turkish citizen. He does not appear to see a conflict between these aspects, despite the allegations to the contrary in the press and academic circles. Turkey is still coming out from numerous military coups which left a harrowing record in terms of human right violations and oppression of public intellectual discourse. Normalization after military rule continues. Although difficult to prove, it surely coincides with the rise to power of the religious AKP in the early 2000s. Therefore, while it would be inaccurate to credit the conservative Islamists with this improvement, it is important to evaluate criticisms carefully. AKP has no squeaky clean record, and is indeed investing a great deal of energy in "Islamizing" Turkey. However, its critics, whether in parliament or academia, are often likely to be representatives of a battered republican elite tackling its political foe over an issue as highly emotional as religion is in Turkey.

At the same time, as a student of Imam Hatip, Recep Tayyip Erdoğan serves a functional community, viz. the one which provided him an education. He identifies himself with the values of his group, defends its interests and does not hide contempt for public secular education. He enforces laws, like that of March 2012, which benefit[36] religious education instead of restructuring mixed state secular schools, and he expresses and understands an aesthetic which is shared and internalized by every Imam Hatip pupil, together with the rest of his/her family. In this sense, the role model he provides, that of the self-made pious businessman, addresses a precise constituency which remains misunderstood and under-serviced by secular Turkey. Citizenship values do not mean integration. Imam Hatip students will continue mingling within their own circles just as secular youth will. But this segmentation – a class rather than a religious cleavage – has not yet lead to conflict, and probably will not in the near future. Moreover, it is in keeping with the history of Imam Hatip schools.

Time will tell whether the growing number of Imam Hatip students will result in the replacement of Kemalist values by Islamic or, as they are now called, "neo-Ottoman" values. The functional community created by and for religious students is expanding at a formidable pace. Nowadays, most of the parliamentarians have studied at Imam Hatip, and draw on the same loyalty mechanisms which bind Imam Hatip to voters of Recep Tayyip Erdoğan's party, the ruling Justice and Development Party (AKP).

The same blend of identity, clientelism and estrangement towards secular markings binds together the students of private Israeli religious schools. Once again, the outcome is political since the support mechanisms of their community come through the ballot box. Each year the government coalition strives for survival and eventually compromises with all sorts of smaller parties and movements in order to obtain the 61% of votes needed to approve its state budget. Yet a quick glance at the Knesset records shows that this struggle for survival is never focused on the issue of settlements and illegal outposts mushrooming outside the 1967 borders, or on the Palestinian issue, and even less on normalizing relations with neighbouring countries. Instead the focus is on budgeting provisions for religious school networks and the corresponding electoral pool. In exchange for additional funding to buy yes votes, children coming out of these schools will never participate to Israeli public life or feel represented by national narratives. They will be increasingly marginalized by their countrymen on religious, ethnic, parental or class grounds. Whether conservative instead of ultra-Orthodox, Sephardi instead of Ashkenazi, poorer or simply not sufficiently educated in non-religious matters, they will be tied for life to their schooling community and the religious identity it forces on them. The violent outcome of this fragmentation can be read in the newspapers every day.

That conservative political parties are providers of confessional schooling in Turkey and Israel is a fact. But it is in the depth of the social divisions in Turkey and Israel that religious schools lead their secular counterparts: they offer a youth excluded by class, national narratives and geography a better self-image. Far from reinforcing already prominent beliefs and attitudes, Imam Hatip and ultra-Orthodox Jewish schools redress traditions and backgrounds, creating patterns of reciprocity and mutual solidarity and,

---

36 In March 2012 Erdogan hastily pushed passed a law through Parliament which reorganized schooling on the basis of three four-year cycles, and pupils could choose their track of study at the age of 10 instead of 14. Since the law was passed at the same time as Imam Hatips were granted permission to start operating at second level primary school, it appears clear that the law was intended to advance Imam Hatip education.

ultimately, capitalizing on pre-existing divisions that have never been addressed by the secular camp.

Apart from ensuring electoral gains, private religious education has also achieved one surprising result in both Israel and Turkey, viz. building self-respect among culturally conservative, economically disadvantaged and ethnically marked sectors of the population which in the images and markers of a secular nationalist elite remained marginalized.

Bibliography

Akpınar, A. (2007), The Making of a Good Citizen and Conscious Muslim through Public Education: The Case of Imam Hatip schools, in Carlson, M., A. Rabo and F. Gök (eds) (2007), *Education in 'Multicultural' Societies: Turkish and Swedish Perspectives*, Stockholm: Swedish Research Institute in Istanbul, Transactions, Vol. 18, 161–178.

Altun, S. and D. Canca (2011), A Model Study on the Explanation of the Centralized High School Entrance Examination in Turkey, *World Applied Science Journal*, 15, 1253–1259.

Atatürk, K., D. Küçük, H. Aslan and Frankfurter Buchmesse (2008), *Selected Parts of speech (Nutuk)*, Istanbul: Profil Yayıncılık.

Bar-Lev, M. (1984), Cultural Characteristics and Group Image of Religious Youth, *Youth and Society*, 16, 153–70.

Bar-Lev, M. (1988), The 'Hesder Yeshiva' as an Agent of Social Change in Israel, *British Journal of Religious Education*, 11, 38–46.

Bar-Lev, M. and P. Kedem (1983), Is Giving up Traditional Religious Culture Part of the Price to Be Paid for Acquiring Higher Education? *Higher Education*, 12, 373–388.

Bar-Lev, M. (1991), Politicization and Depoliticization of Jewish Religious Education in Israel, *Religious Education*, 86:4.

BenDavid-Hadar, I. and A. Ziderman (2011), A new model for equitable and efficient resource allocation to schools: The Israeli case, *Education Economics*, 19, 341–362.

Coleman, J., S. Kilgore and T. Hoffer (1982), Cognitive Outcomes in Public and Private Schools, *Sociology of Education*, 55, 65–76.

Dede, A.Y. (2008), *Islamism, state control over religion and social identity: Turkey and Egypt*, PhD Thesis, Western Michigan University, 2008.

Deshen, S.A. (1970), *Immigrant voters in Israel: Parties and congregations in a local election campaign*, Manchester: Manchester University Press.

Gökçe, F. and O. Nilüfer (2010), Minority and Foreign Schools on the Ottoman Education System, *Uluslararası Eğitim Araştırmaları Dergisi*, 1.1 (Summer 2010).

Hazırlayan, Y. et al. (2004), *Imam Hatip Liserleri: Efsaneler ve Gerçekler*, Istanbul: TESEV YAYINLARI, 2004.

Hemmings, P. (2010), *Israeli Education Policy: How to Move Ahead in Reform*. OECD: Economics Department Working Paper No. 781.

Kamil, O. (2001), The Synagogue, Civil Society, and Israel's Shas party, *Middle East Critique*, 10, 18, 47–66.

Karpat, Kemal H. (2004), The Genesis of the Gecekondu: Rural Migration and Urbanization (1976), in *European Journal of Turkish Studies*, Thematic Issue N°1, Gecekondu.

Kimmerling, B. (1998), Between hegemony and dormant Kulturkampf in Israel, *Israel Affairs*, 4, 3–4.

Köseleci Blanchy, N. and A. Sasmaz (2011), PISA 2009: Where does Turkey stand? *Turkish Policy Quarterly*, 10:2.

Leslau, A., M. Bar-Lev and Bar Ilan University (1994), *Religiosity among Oriental youth in Israel,* Ramat-Gan: Sociological Institute for Community Studies, Bar-Ilan University.

Leon, N. (2010), The transformation of Israel's religious-Zionist middle class, *Journal of Israeli History*, 29, 1, 61–78.

Maoz, A. (2007), *Religious Education in Israel*, Tel Aviv: Tel Aviv University, Buchmann Faculty of Law.

OECD (2010), *PISA 2009: OVERCOMING SOCIAL BACKGROUND*, Vol. II.

Ozgur, I. (2012), *Islamic schools in modern Turkey: Faith, politics, and education*, Cambridge: Cambridge University Press.

Rabinovich, I. and J. Reinharz (2008), *Israel in the Middle East: Documents and readings on society, politics, and foreign relations, pre-1948 to the present,* Waltham, Mass: Brandeis University Press.

Sarfati, Y. (2009), *The rise of religious parties in Israel and Turkey: A Comparative Study.* Columbus, Ohio: Ohio State University.

Spolsky, B. and E.G. Shohamy (1999), *The Languages of Israel: Policy, ideology, and practice,* Clevedon: Multilingual Matters.

Swirsky, S. and N. Dagan-Buzaglo (2009), *Separation, Inequality and Loosening Control: The State of State Education in Israel,* Tel Aviv: ADVA Center.

Taub, D. and J. Klein (2000), State Religious Education – Religion vs. State, *Journal of Church and State*, 42, 345–366.

Yonah, Y. (2000), Parental Choice in Israel's Educational System: Theory vs. Praxis, *Studies in Philosophy and Education*, 19, 445–464.

Zarembski, L. (2005), *Refracted vision: An analysis of religious-secular tensions in Israel,* Jerusalem: The Floersheimer Institute for Policy Studies.

Zürcher, E.J. (2010), *The Young Turk legacy and nation building: From the Ottoman Empire to Atatürk's Turkey,* London: I.B. Tauris.

Teaching Religion in a Multinational State
The Case of Bosnia-Herzegovina

KARIM EL MUFTI

More than 17 years after the adoption of the Dayton-Paris Agreement of November-December 1995, which ended the war in Bosnia-Herzegovina, the former Yugoslav Republic continues to present the archetype of a deeply divided society. As such, Bosnia-Herzegovina is still a fragmented country on many levels, socially, territorially, and politically.

The Fragmented Nature of the Bosnian Context

From a social perspective, the fabric of Bosnia is burdened with strong self-conscious group differences along ethnic lines, a cleavage that, according to Theodor Hanf,

> "incorporates not only common origins but also common language, religion or other features of ethnic identity. In this sense, 'ethnic groups' may be people, national groups or religious communities, groups distinguishable from one another by one or more cultural markers."[1]

In the case of Bosnia-Herzegovina, the cleavage is highlighted by religious and cultural factors, with the presence of three communities, three religions and two alphabets separating what the political system in the country constitutionally defines as "constituent peoples,[2]" i.e. the Bosniaks (the Muslim population which forms the majority with 52%[3]), the Serbs (35.1% of the population[4], who are Orthodox and use the Cyrillic alphabet), and the Croats (who are Catholic and constitute the smallest of the three groups with 12.3% of the population[5]). Given the intense nature of the respective "ethnonational[6]" efforts within each "people" to develop a separate identity, Bosnia-Herzegovina was constructed as a general socio-political entity that is similar to the

---

1 Hanf, Theodor. *Coexistence in Wartime Lebanon: Decline of a State and Rise of a Nation*, Oxford, Centre for Lebanese Studies, London, Tauris, 1993, p. 14.
2 Preamble to the Dayton-Paris Peace Accords.
3 UNDP estimate from 2002, www.undp.ba
4 *Idem.*
5 *Idem.*
6 A notion developed by Walker Connor. Cf. Connor, Walker. *Ethnonationalism: The Quest for Understanding*, Princeton, Princeton University Press, 1994.

multinational state former Yugoslavia used to be,[7] which is why Bosnia is sometimes called "Smaller Yugoslavia."[8]

Although confirming Bosnia-Herzegovina as a single independent state, the power-sharing arrangements of the Dayton-Paris peace accords territorially engineered the country into what Florian Bieber calls a "multinational asymmetric federation,"[9] divided into two highly autonomous entities, the predominantly Bosniak and Croat Federation of Bosnia-Herzegovina (FBiH) and the predominantly Bosnian Serb Republika Srpska (RS).[10] For years the district of Brcko, located on the the country's northern border at the junction of the two entities, endured a political and legal struggle between nationalist entrepreneurs, until it was recently declared an autonomous district beyond the control of both entities, adding yet another layer to the highly federalized and decentralized Bosnian state.

The fragmentation of the multiple layers of the Bosnian component is concomitant with a political landscape and institutions often paralyzed by nationalist leaderships from different communities as the latter maneuver to impose a nationalist agenda. Seventeen years into an invasive state-building and institution-building, spearheaded by international structures and organizations such as the Office of the High Representative,[11] Bosnia has yet to establish the foundations of political stability, as different local political formations continue to strongly diverge over the type, nature, and fate of the Bosnian state. In her last visit to Sarajevo, Secretary of State Hilary Clinton "urged Bosnian leaders to work together[12]" to end separatist speech and defend the integrity of Bosnia-Herzegovina, which came under renewed threat during the municipal elections of October 2012, which were won by the nationalist parties that control most of the power leverages in Bosnia. This paralysis of the political process in Bosnia is not something new: regular institutional deadlocks have led the High Representative to step in on numerous occasions and take national decisions, such as on the country's flag, anthem, and currency, and even the political agenda by engaging local politicians in reforming and unifying the army (achieved in July 2005) and the police forces (agreed in April 2008, yet to be implemented).

---

7   Fisher, Jack C. *Yugoslavia: A Multi-National State*, San Francisco, 1968; Rusinow, Denison. *The Yugoslav Experiment 1948–1974*, University of California Press, Berkeley, 1977; Ra'anan, Uri, Maria Mesner, Keith Armes and Kate Martin (eds). *State and Nation in Multi-Ethnic Societies: The Break-up of Multinational States*, Manchester: Manchester University Press, 1991; Pavkovic, Aleksandar. *Fragmentation of Yugoslav Nationalism in a Multinational State*, Macmillan, London, 1997.

8   Garde, Paul. *Vie et mort de la Yougoslavie*, second edition, Fayard, 2000.

9   Bieber, Florian. Bosnia-Herzegovina: Developments towards a more integrated State, in *Journal of Muslim Minority Affairs*, 22:1 (2002), p. 326.

10 The Federation consists of ten cantons, a sublevel of government holding an important number of prerogatives; the RS has a more centralized system divided into seven regions and municipalities.

11 The OHR is an international appointee of the Peace Implementation Council, which includes all the international countries involved in ensuring a sustainable and lasting peace in Bosnia-Herzegovina. He holds significant political prerogatives (also called the Bonn Powers) within the Bosnian institutions as he can legislate, nominate, and dismiss elected officials and civil servants.

12 *New York Times*, October 30, 2012, available at http://www.nytimes.com/2012/10/31/world/ europe/ clinton-urges-bosnias-leaders-to-work-together.html?_r=0

This forceful state-building slowed down when the European Representative (who took over the OHR) decided to stop using the Bonn Powers. However, it did not contribute to bring conflicting agendas of different nationalist parties closer together. The Republika Srpska political establishment, led today by Milorad Dodik and his SNSD party,[13] continues to use the threat of secession from the rest of the country as a tool of pressure if the other nationalist parties keep up their claims that the Serb entity is "the product of genocide" and "destined to disappear," a red line for all Serb nationalists in Bosnia-Herzegovina. Bosniak leaders are among those supporting these accusations, such as Bosnia's Grand Mufti, Mustafa Ceric, and political figures like SBiH[14] party chief Haris Silajdzic, Bosniak member of the Presidential Cabinet (2006–2010), who, when representing Bosnia at one of the UN General Assembly sessions, called on the rest of the world "not to legally acknowledge any situation that occurred as a result of genocide and crimes against humanity.[15]" On the same note, the (interim) Croat member of the Presidential Cabinet (2005–2006), Miro Jovic promoted the idea of "no third entity, no RS,"[16] meaning that if the Bosnian Croats were not to obtain an autonomous federal entity such as the Serbs have, then the Republika Srpska should be dissolved.

In response to these positions, Milorad Dodik regularly warns the other political groups:

> "If Sarajevo constantly sends us the same message, based on which the RS shouldn't exist because it is an entity born from a genocide, we will answer back with something called 'the people' and 'referendum',"[17]

an indication of a possible secession on the part of the authorities in RS. For the past decade, Bosnian Serb nationalists have been very vocal against the rest of the political elite and the international representatives in the country, using this Sword of Damocles whenever the debate over political reforms touches on the issue of the existence of RS. For instance, speaking of the date that is supposed to celebrate Bosnia-Herzegovina's independence, Dodik stresses that "the first of March does not coincide with the independence day of the country, (we) will never recognize it."[18]

On the other hand, nationalist formations in Bosnia are in agreement when it comes to the idea of defending the principle of self-determination entrenched in the different constitutions of the country (at the state and entity levels). This trend goes back to the war era when in 1993 the Serb-controlled part of Bosnia introduced religious education in schools, followed by the two other communities in 1994, which reversed Tito's policy of separation of church and state, introduced in Yugoslavia in 1946 and tightened from 1953 onward, when religious education was completely removed from school

---

13   Savez nezavisnih socijaldemokrata, Social National Democratic Party.
14   Stranka za Bosnu i Hercegovinu, Party for Bosnia-Herzegovina.
15   Speech at the General Assembly of the United Nations, September 23, 2008, *Oslobodjenje*, September 25, 2008.
16   Miro Jovic's speech at the Summit of the Central European Initiative, Zagreb, *Nezavisne Novine*, October 14, 2005.
17   *Dnevni Avaz*, June 7, 2006.
18   *Oslobodjenje*, March 2, 2008.

curricula.[19] The Dayton Agreement of 1995 maintained this policy by granting all three peoples the right to education, thereby allowing the three communities to self-regulate this sector.

As assessed by Adila Pasalic-Kreso, "the education system in BiH (...) resembles a broken glass that nationalist divisive politics is attempting to break into even smaller pieces. This does not lead to stabilizing BiH as a unified country.[20]" In fact, the education sector in Bosnia is highly decentralized: there are 13 ministries of education (one in each of the Federation's ten cantons, one at the level of each of the two entities and one at the level of the central state). Each level within the Federation decides the curriculum and school structure independently from one another, whereas the system is a bit more centralized in the Republika Srpska with Orthodox and Serb oriented teaching in schools. But the central state level has little ability to interfere or even coordinate the different curricula, leaving the education sector under the tight control of each community, all of which have integrated educational policy into their ethno-national strategy for greater nation-building.

Religious Education in Bosnia, a Strategic Nation-Building Tool

Given its plural context, education is inextricably linked to the right to express, promote and protect one's identity: "next to the family, (education) is the single most important agency for cultural reproduction, socialization and identity formation.[21]" As mentioned above, in post-Dayton Bosnia, education is in the hands of the entities, thus leaving very little margin of action by the central state. For instance, Section III, Article 4(b) of the Constitution of the Federation grants all responsibilities not expressly granted to the Federation government to the Cantons, including "making education policy, including decisions concerning the regulation and provision of education." Article 38 of the RS Constitution states that: "everyone shall be entitled to education under equal conditions," that "primary schooling shall be compulsory and free," and "everyone shall have access, under the same conditions, to secondary and higher education."

However, these provisions are not fully implemented in RS, despite the constitutional framework, as RS authorities retain centralized control over education through the ministry of education. The latter limited religious instruction exclusively to Orthodox Christianity, which was available to all students, and made it difficult for other com-

19 For more on education in Former Yugoslavia, cf. Russo, Charles J., Religion and Education in Bosnia: Integration not Segregation? *Brigham Young University Law Review*, September 2000, pp. 950–952.

20 Pasalic-Kreso, Adila. Education in Bosnia and Herzegovina: Minority Inclusion and Majority Rules – the system of education in BiH as a paradigm of political violence on education, *Current Issues in Comparative Education*, 2:1 (2002).

21 Williams, C.H. The Cultural Rights of Minorities: Recognition and Implementation, in Plitchtova, J. (ed.), *Minorities in Politics: Cultural and Language Rights,* Bratislava, 1992, cited in Henrard, Kristin. Education and Multiculturalism, *International Journal on Minority and Group Rights,* 7 (2000), pp. 393–410.

munities to obtain religious instruction for their own group[22] – until the High Representative stepped in and forced all implementing authorities to introduce non-discriminatory provisions under the Framework Law of 2004. As a result, religious instruction was to be made available to minorities living in their place of residence.

The OSCE in *Bosnia* has regularly reported on how "politicized schools have become,"[23] as they symbolize the "battlefield for ethno-linguistic dominance and control. The result is a system where children are taught in segregated schools and classrooms, according to ethnically specific curricula and textbooks."[24] These "textbooks contain both subtle and blatant hate speech, and schools display religious symbols of the majority prevalently in schools."[25] This assessment is largely based on the fact that schools in multi-ethnic parts of the Muslim-Croat Federation set up a "one roof two schools" system, where Croat and Muslim (Bosniak) students would attend different classes at separate schedules under the same roof; Croats would go in the morning and the Muslims in the afternoon.

Ironically, this system started as a "temporary" initiative of the international community, more specifically the OSCE, in 2000, because the World Bank had rebuilt schools in some cantons of the Federation, from which only the Croat majority was benefiting. This led the High Representative to order that these schools also be opened to Muslim students. As a consequence, local authorities implemented this decision in their own way: allowing Muslims to use the schools but at different times. Hence, what started as a "temporary measure" has become a permanent structure in three different cantons so far, creating a system that tends to have "religious education taught only to the children of the majority national/religious group."[26] The OSCE recognized its mistake and promised to learn from "an instructive lesson of unintended consequences," as claimed by Ambassador Davidson[27], adding that this phenomenon

> "also offer(ed) an object lesson in how a purely educational issue can unfortunately metamorphose into a political one. It is a perfect example of why politics does not belong in the classroom. It is now time for these schools to be unified. It is also time that all parties understand that, by saying this, we are speaking only of legal and administrative unification of schools. We are not speaking about unifying languages or curricula."[28]

This situation illustrates how sensitive the issue of education is in the country, despite the efforts of the international community to counter the ethnic politics fueling the nationalist agendas in this particular sector.

---

22 For instance, by setting 30 as the minimum number of students required for religious instruction for other religious communities, RS Ministry of Education 1998 Directive.

23 *Background of the Education Sector in Bosnia and Herzegovina*, OSCE Office in Bosnia-Herzegovina, available at www.oscebih.org/education/?d=2

24 *Idem.*

25 *Idem.*

26 Popov, Zlatiborka, Ofstad, Anne Mette. Religious Education in Bosnia and Herzegovina, In
, Zorica and Moe, Christian. *Religion and Pluralism in Education, Comparative Approaches in the Western Balkans*, Centre for Empirical Researches on Religion, Novi Sad, 2006, p. 74.

27 Statement of OSCE Ambassador Douglas Davidson, March 24, 2005.

28 *Idem.*

Moreover, the linguistic cleavage (in which teaching took place in each community's language), coupled with the history component in which each community developed its own war and peace narrative,[29] quickly acquired a religious dimension, as each community introduced pro-religious instruction policies to teach its own faith and transmit its heritage and teachings to future generations in accordance with its right to self-determination . This "desecularization of Bosnia," to quote Dzemal Sokolovic,[30] led to the integration of the religious curricula into the respective nation-building processes of the three constituent communities, thereby aligning faith with a specific history, nation, and language.

This trend has been consolidated in the country's legislation. Article 4 of the "Law on freedom of religion and the legal position of churches and religious communities in Bosnia and Herzegovina" (2004), which applies to both entities and the Brcko district, reads that

> "everyone shall have the right to religious education, which shall be provided solely by persons appointed so to do by an official representative of his Church or religious community, whether in religious institutions or in public and private pre-school institutions, primary schools and higher education."

In addition to the issue of limiting minorities' access to religious instruction in different parts of the country, the content of the religious curricula also presented nation-building agendas, aligning faith with a particular history and a particular nation with the aim at constructing "a shared perception"[31] among a group of people "who think of themselves as collectively possessing a separate identity based on (…) shared cultural characteristics."[32] For instance, an Islamic third grade textbook displays an attachment to "my homeland, Bosnia and Herzegovina;" an Orthodox third grade textbook sheds light on the history of the Serbian Orthodox Church through the anthem of Saint Sava, the thirteenth-century Serbian prince and Orthodox monk who founded the Serbian Church.[33] In Bosno-Croats Catholic third grade textbook, the students are taught to identify with the Croatian nation through the story of Marko, who was born during the "war in Croatia", with no mention of the fighting in Bosnia.[34]

Despite its wide presence in the country in the post-war period, the international community was slow to react to the consolidation of ethnonational religious education in the individual communities. Only in 2003 did it initiate a course entitled "Culture of Religions" to try to integrate curricula at all levels. Following the introduction of a unitary flag, currency, border police, and army, this quickly became a strategic item on the international state-builders' agenda in Bosnia. According to the OSCE, the

---

29 Cf. Baranovic, Branislava, History Textbooks in Post-War Bosnia and Herzegovina, *Intercultural Education*, 12:1 (2001).

30 Sokolovic, Dzemal, *Nation vs People: Bosnia is just a case*, Cambridge Scholar Publishing, 2006.

31 Kasfir, Nelson, Explaining Ethnic Political Participation, *World Politics*, 31:3 (1979), p. 366.

32 Van Dyke, Vernon, The Individual, the State and Ethnic Communities in Political Theory, *World Politics*, 29:3 (1977), p. 344.

33 Saint Sava Day is celebrated throughout Republika Srpska, but not Bosnia's Independence Day.

34 For content analysis of third year textbooks in Bosnia, cf. Marusic, Lana, *Religious Education in Bosnia and Herzegovina*, master's thesis, University of Oslo, 2011, pp. 79–94.

"'Culture of Religions'" is a subject designed to teach students about the four major religions[35] practiced in Bosnia and Herzegovina. Rather than teaching about religion from a doctrinal point of view, as in traditional religion classes for students of a particular faith, it teaches and invites all students to explore the four religions through the lenses of history, culture and society. This approach is inclusive and it serves as a confidence-building measure that seeks to advance inter-religious tolerance and understanding. Its aim is to reduce potential misunderstandings and conflicts arising from a lack of knowledge of other peoples' faiths and cultures by providing the next generation with a basic knowledge of the culture and history of the religions of others. While implemented differently in different parts of the country, this program could ultimately serve as an important part of the curriculum for all students."[36]

So far, the effect of this measure in fighting discrimination in Bosnia has proved very limited and the political efforts to bring communities closer through education have remained extremely short-sighted. For instance, the National Strategy document for 2012–2015 released by the Bosnian State contains no reference to reforming religious instruction, thereby indicating a political decision to leave these matters in the hands of the different communities.

However, nationalist policies in the country are being contested by Bosnia's own judicial bodies, whether the Constitutional Court (at its central and entity levels), which through the years has ruled against a number of constitutional provisions of a nationalist nature in both entities, or, more recently, the action of a local court in Mostar, which actually ruled against the "one roof two schools" system in the towns of Stolac and Capljina in April 2012.[37] Even though the decision was not implemented in full, this judgment consolidates the judicial tools in the Bosnian context to try and ensure a balance between freedom of religion on one hand and self-determination on the other.

---

35   The fourth religion is the Jewish faith, taught by the Jewish minority in BiH.
36   *Toledo Guiding Principles on Teaching about Religions and Beliefs in Public Schools*, Office for Democratic Institutions and Human Rights (ODIH), OSCE, 2007, available at http://www.osce.org/odihr/29154
37   *Bosnian Court Rules Against Ethnic Segregation in Schools*, RFE/RL, April 30, 2012, available at http://www.rferl.org/content/bosnian_court_rules_against_ethnic_segregation_schools/24565464.html

State-Building and Religious Education in the Former Yugoslav Republic of Macedonia

GIUDITTA FONTANA

Decisions about education in the Former Yugoslav Republic of Macedonia (hereafter, Macedonia) generally follow political, rather than educational, deliberations. The decision to introduce religious education in elementary schools is no exception.

A decade of increasingly violent arguments over the introduction of religious education in public schools, and over the form this subject should take culminated in 2008–2009. In April 2009, the Macedonian Constitutional Court suspended the recently introduced confessional religious education, arguing it violated the constitutional principle of separation between church and state.

When citizens, politicians and clergymen protested against the court's decision, they did not do so on educational grounds. Rather, they called for an end to Macedonia's 'atheist dictatorship'.[1] They did it so forcefully that Asma Jahangir, the UN Special Rapporteur for Religious Freedom, argued that 'it is vital that the independence of the judiciary is fully respected', and specified that the 'judgment does not in any way impinge upon the freedom to receive religious instruction outside of primary school teachings'.[2]

This paper will show that Macedonia is far from being an atheist dictatorship. Indeed, this hyperbolical slogan illustrates that the debate over religious education spilled over into what the US Embassy termed a 'culture war'.[3]

Rather than remaining confined to the realms of education policy, discussions about denominational religion in public schools added to arguments over the identity of the Macedonian people. Such arguments revolved around one fundamental issue: is religion a fundamental building block in the identity of the citizens of Macedonia? Is it a building block for the state?

Answers to these questions cannot but be contested in a multi-ethnic, multi-religious, multi-national society, and Macedonia is the epitome of a heterogeneous society.[4] The majority Slav Macedonians account for less than 65% of the population and the largest ethnic minority, the Albanians, account for about 25%. The smaller Turk, Roma and Serb minorities make up about 3.8%, 2.7% and 1.8% of the population, respectively; there are also smaller communities of Vlachs, Bulgarians, Montenegrins, Croats and

---

1   Risto Karajkov, The Government vs. the Court, *Osservatorio Balcani e Caucaso*, 24 April 2009.
2   Asma Jahangir quoted in Former Yugoslav Republic of Macedonia: UN Expert Speaks out on Religious Intolerance, *UN News Centre*, 30 April 2009.
3   US Embassy Skopje, Macedonia's Culture Wars, 8 May 2009.
4   So much so that 'Macédonie' in French and 'Macedonia' in Italian mean fruit salad.

Bosniaks.[5] Religious composition is similarly mixed, with about 65% Orthodox Christians, 33% Muslims, and smaller percentages of Catholics, Protestants and Jews.[6]

Identity-building is further problematised by the contested nature of the Macedonian state itself. Macedonia's neighbours deny the legitimacy of the Republic of Macedonia. Greece refuses to recognise the country by its constitutional name. As a consequence, Macedonia is recognised at the international level with the more convoluted but less controversial compromise name of The Former Yugoslav Republic of Macedonia. Bulgaria denies the existence of a Macedonian people, and Serbia has long viewed Macedonia as Southern Serbia.

An initial attempt at creating 'a national state of the Macedonian people'[7] failed within a decade of independence. In 2001 a violent conflict between the Macedonian army and an Albanian armed group, the National Liberation Army (NLA), threatened to spill over into civil war. The conflict ended with the externally mediated Ohrid Framework Agreement (OFA) which, by defining Macedonia as a plural society, established consociational power-sharing in the Republic.

The OFA itself highlights the intimate connection between state-building and education policy in Macedonia. Beyond reforming the constitution, the agreement also tackled the education system, reaffirming the rights of ethnic communities to mother tongue education and permitting the opening of a state-funded Albanian-language university. In the religious realm, Article 19 of the constitution was amended to endow Islamic, Catholic, Jewish and Methodist religious institutions with the same official position as the Macedonian Orthodox Church. However, no mention was made of religious education in state schools.[8]

The OFA undoubtedly contributed to the inclusion of Albanians and other minorities in state institutions and in the decision-making process. Parties representative of each community sit in parliament, and government is generally a coalition between a Slav Macedonian and an Albanian party. That said, the OFA failed to settle, or even tackle, the fundamental debates over the identity and legitimacy of the state. These debates would be played out in the following decade, through, among other things, discussions over the introduction of religious education in public schools.

---

5   Republic of Macedonia State Statistical Office, *Census of Population, Households and Dwellings 2002. Book XIII: Total Population, Households and Dwellings According to the Territorial Organisation of the Republic of Macedonia.* (Skopje: State Statistical Office, 2002).

6   Republic of Macedonia State Statistical Office, *Census of Population, Households and Dwellings 2002. Book X: Total Population According to Ethnic Affiliation, Mother Tongue and Religion.* (Skopje: State Statistical Office, 2002).

7   Preamble, *Constitution of the Republic of Macedonia,* 1992.

8   *Ohrid Framework Agreement* 2001.

Religion, Identity and Education before and after Independence

In the Yugoslav era, schools provided instruction in 'socialist morality', but not religious education. Religion did not even appear as part of the curricula of other subjects, such as history, art, music or language.[9]

In contrast to many Yugoslav successor states, Macedonia did not introduce religious education at independence.[10] No proposals for its introduction were made for the seven years following the declaration of independence. It was only in the late 1990s that calls for religious education, spearheaded by an alliance of religious institutions and the Slav Macedonian 'demo-Christian'[11] party VMRO-DPMNE[12], were made.

In fact, the 1999 coalition government of VMRO-DPMNE and the Albanian DPA[13] decreed without public or parliamentary consultation that religious education would be introduced in state schools.[14]

Catechism, the name given to the new subject, was introduced as optional in Grades 3 and 4 of primary school. The curriculum was theological and dogmatic; it referred to either Islam or Christian Orthodoxy, and children explored only their own religion. The teachers were priests from the Macedonian Orthodox Church or hocas from the Islamic Community.[15]

Within a year, the Constitutional Court of Macedonia had suspended catechism because it ran contrary to Article 13 of the Law on Primary Education, which banned all religious organisations from carrying out activities in schools. Article 24 of the Law on Religious Communities also stated that religious education could ake place only within an officially designated place of worship.[16] The ruling was met with silence and public indifference.

Such indifference can only be explained by the general irrelevance of religion in defining group identity in Macedonia in the late 1990s. While constraints on providing instruction in the languages of minorities had been met with vocal, and at times violent, protests, the marginalisation of catechism from state schools was ignored.

---

9   Zoran Matevski, The Religious Education in the Pedagogical System in the Republic of Macedonia, in *Kotor Network Conference "Religion in Schools: Problems of Pluralism in the Public Sphere"* (Kotor: 2005), 3; Zoran Matevski, Etem Aziri, and Goce Velichkovski, Introducing Religious Education in Macedonia, in Zorica Kuburić and Christian Moe *(eds), Religion and Pluralism in Education Comparative Approaches in the Western Balkans*, Novi Sad: CEIR in cooperation with the Kotor Network, 2006, 139.

10   Zoric Kuburić and Christian Moe, Introduction, in Zoric Kuburić and Christian Moe (eds), *Religion and Pluralism in Education Comparative Approaches in the Western Balkans*, Novi Sad: CEIR in cooperation with the Kotor Network, 2006, 1.

11   Dushka Matevska, The Relationship between the Political and Religious Elite in Contemporary Macedonian Society, *Politics and Religion* 5:1 (2011): 135.

12   The acronym stands for Internal Macedonian Revolutionary Organisation – Democratic Party for Macedonian National Unity.

13   The acronym stands for Democratic Party of Albanians.

14   Matevski et al., 141.

15   Matevski et al., 140.

16   Matevski et al., 141.

The irrelevance of religion in the definition of identity is not sufficiently explained by Macedonia's socialist past. First, a socialist past does not necessarily mean a secular or atheist future. This is particularly the case in the realm of religious education. Indeed, several Yugoslav successor states introduced religious education in their curricula immediately after independence. Croatia introduced it in 1991 and Bosnia followed suit in 1993.[17]

Second, not even in the Yugoslav era was the Republic of Macedonia particularly averse to religion or religious institutions. Certainly, Belgrade propagated a vision of religion as the opium of the people, seriously limited the scope for religious activities and encouraged the emergence of Titoism as a secular cult.[18] Yet, the Yugoslav authorities recognised the value of religion, and especially of indigenous religious institutions for state- and nation-building in Macedonia. Indeed, the League of Communists acted to gain the churches' unconditional support rather than to eliminate them.[19] It even supported the creation of the Macedonian Orthodox Church in 1967 despite the strenuous opposition of the Serbian Patriarchate.[20] As Quercia points out, the priority of the Yugoslav regime was to strengthen the newly created Macedonian nation at the expense of Bulgarian and Greek influences.[21] Thus, after creating a Republic in Macedonia in 1945 and endowing it with a codified language in 1953, the Titoist authorities provided it with a spiritual, religious voice. Far from being born atheist, the Republic of Macedonia was born as the home of an autocephalous Orthodox Church. This church remains unrecognised by other Orthodox Churches: Constantinople and Belgrade still view it as an illegitimate schismatic church.

More convincing is the argument that no group called for religious education because religion did not provide a fundamental marker of identity for any of Macedonia's ethnic communities at independence.[22] Indeed, Albanian identity, even before Communism, had been articulated as secular, defined to encompass Albanian-speaking Muslims (the overwhelming majority in Kosovo and Macedonia) as well as Christians (about one-third of the inhabitants of modern-day Albania).[23] In independent Macedonia, Albanian parties have consciously marginalised the religious component of identity, wary of pro-

---

17 Kuburić and Moe, 1.
18 Klaus Buchenau, What Went Wrong? Church-State Relations in Socialist Yugoslavia, *Nationalities Papers: The Journal of Nationalism and Ethnicity* 33:4 (2005), 550, 559; Matevska, The Relationship between the Political and Religious Elite in Contemporary Macedonian Society, 130.
19 Buchenau, What Went Wrong? Church-State Relations in Socialist Yugoslavia, 556.
20 Buchenau, What Went Wrong? Church-State Relations in Socialist Yugoslavia, 557; Paolo Quercia, Borderline Religion: The Role of Churches in Balkan Nation Building, *CeMiSS Quarterly* II:1 (2004), 25.
21 Quercia also points to Tito's long-standing design to reduce the demographic weight of Serbs in the Yugoslav federation. Quercia, Borderline Religion: The Role of Churches in Balkan Nation Building, 24, 26.
22 Ivan Ivekovic, Nationalism and the Political Use and Abuse of Religion: The Politicisation of Orthodoxy, Catholicism and Islam in Yugoslav Successor States, *Social Compass* 49:4 (2002), 523.
23 Ivan Ivekovic, Nationalism and the Political Use and Abuse of Religion: The Politicisation of Orthodoxy, Catholicism and Islam in Yugoslav Successor States, *Social Compass* 49:4 (2002), 532.

voking aggressive reactions from Serbs, Macedonians and Greeks against a potential 'Islamic danger'.[24]

For its part, Orthodox Christianity directly links Slav Macedonians to their predatory neighbours: Bulgaria, Greece and Serbia. This is demonstrated by the fact that the Macedonian Orthodox Church has never been recognised by Constantinople or by Belgrade. Thus, an emphasis on religion as a component of identity has always been a dangerous double-edged sword in the Slav Macedonian quest to define and project their distinctive ethno-national identity. Lack of recognition for their autocephalous church also contributes to a more generalised crisis of identity and legitimacy among Slav Macedonians.[25]

Religion is not a useful marker of group affiliation for smaller communities, either. For example, Turks point to their linguistic distinctiveness and complain about Albanian attempts to assimilate them through Islam. Romas belong to different religions, and base their collective identity on a common ethno-cultural heritage.

Even this brief overview clearly explains why, in the first years of independence, religion was a marginal factor in defining group affiliation and identity in Macedonia. It also contributes to explaining why there were no calls for the introduction of religious education in Macedonia until almost a decade after independence, and why the failure of the first attempt to introduce catechism in public schools was met with general indifference.

Indeed, in Macedonia, as elsewhere, schools reflected the fundamental cleavages in society. If religion was still marginal in the 1990s, language was not. Even in Yugoslavia education in the mother tongue was an inalienable right and Macedonia's education system mirrored its fundamental linguistic cleavage. Whereas in other education systems separation runs along religious lines, in Macedonia it runs along linguistic lines and language still provides the main organisingprinciple for the whole education system. In the decade after the OFA religious cleavages emerged to compound the linguistic ones, both in school and in society.

The 2008–2009 Debate over Introducing Religious Education

The defeat of its first initiative did not discourage the VMRO-DPMNE party. Returned to office in 2007 in coalition with the Albanian DUI, VMRO-DPMNE once again promoted the introduction of religious education. Once again, the education ministry, with little public or parliamentary consultation, decreed that two hours a week of religious education would be offered in schools in the 2008–2009 school year.[26] The Constitutional Court suspended it in April 2009. In its ruling, the court argued that confessional religious education, and the involvement of religious institutions in the drafting and de-

---

24 Ibid.
25 Risto Karajkov, Church, Mosque, Nato, Macedonian Parliament, *Osservatorio Balcani e Caucaso*, 14 August 2007.
26 Matevski et al., 141.

livery of the curriculum, directly contradicted the constitutional separation between church and state in Macedonia.[27]

What differed from 1999–2001 was the public reaction to the Constitutional Court's ruling. In contrast to the silence a decade earlier, in April 2009 citizens took the streets calling for an end to the 'atheist dictatorship'. Prominent politicians openly attacked the court while members of the clergy declared their determination to lobby for 'all obstacles standing in the way of the religious classes to be removed'.[28]

To some extent, such vocal opposition may be explained by the nature of the subject. Religious education was still optional and was now offered in Grade 6 of primary school, an age deemed more appropriate to critical reflection than to indoctrination.[29]

Moreover, in 2008–2009 parents could choose between the confessional Religious Education and the non-confessional Introduction to Religions.[30] The curriculum for Religious Education was drafted by representatives of the Orthodox, Islamic, Catholic, Jewish and Protestant religious institutions in cooperation with the Bureau for Educational Development.[31] The subject was to be taught by members of the major religious institutions. In contrast, Introduction to Religions was to be taught by a social science graduate following a curriculum based on what the then Education Minister Suleiman Rushiti labelled as 'something off the shelf' from abroad.[32] Rather than education *in* religion, Introduction to Religions was designed as pure education *about* religion. Although accurate data is unavailable, the press reported that in 2008–2009 just over 60% of pupils chose the confessional Religious Education. [33]

Only Religious Education was suspended by the Constitutional Court ruling. Introduction to Religions is still offered in Macedonian schools in accordance with the 2008–2009 curriculum. However, protesters did not seem to notice that education *about* religions was still available in Macedonia's primary schools. This debate, or rather 'venom sputtering'[34] as the US Embassy saw it, did not even touch on the pedagogical merits of Religious Education as suspended by the court.

Indeed, the camp attacking the Constitutional Court's ruling was an unlikely, but very vocal, coalition of the VMRO-DPMNE, the biggest party in government, the major religious institutions in the Republic and the majority of Albanian public opinion. It argued that religious education alone could provide moral and ethical values for youth and that only through knowledge about religions could relations between different eth-

---

27 Human Rights Council, *Report of the Special Rapporteur on Freedom of Religion or Belief, Asma Jahangir. Mission to the Former Yugoslav Republic of Macedonia,* Geneva: United Nations General Assembly, 2009, 6.
28 UN: Secularism in Macedonia at Risk, *Balkan Insight,* 30 April 2009.
29 Matevski et al., 150.
30 Religion Classes for Macedonian Pupils, *Balkan Insight,* 1 September 2008.; Karajkov, The Government vs. the Court.
31 US Embassy Skopje, *Macedonia: Implementing New Religious Freedom Law While Blurring Church-State Separation,* 18 April 2008.
32 Ibid.
33 Karajkov, The Government vs. the Court.
34 US Embassy Skopje, *Macedonia's Culture Wars,* 8 May 2009.

nic communities be improved.[35] The VMRO-DPMNE was particularly emphatic on this point: introduction of religious education was to be the flagship government initiative for improving inter-ethnic relations in 2006–2010.[36]

For their part, representatives of the Muslim, Orthodox, Catholic, Methodist and Jewish clergies called for confessional religious education that adopted an 'advocacy, not comparative, approach'.[37] They argued that before studying other religions it is crucial for pupils to acquire an understanding of their own religion,[38] and that teaching should be imparted by members of the clergy who 'believe in what they say'.[39]

On a more prosaic note, the VMRO-DPMNE party accused the Constitutional Court of making a 'political decision' in support of opposition parties.[40] Religious Education teachers took the streets to protest against their imminent unemployment and religious institutions advocated that, as taxpayers, parents have the right to religious instruction in state schools.[41]

The equally unusual coalition supporting the Constitutional Court's ruling maintained that Introduction to Religions was still available in public schools and asked why, given the fact that catechism was available in mosques and churches, it should also be introduced into public schools.[42] The Slav Macedonian opposition parties, part of the Slav Macedonian population and the major Albanian political parties (including the DUI, VMRO-DPMNE's government coalition partner), also pointed to the lack of state control over the contents of confessional religious education. They argued that clergy members, having studied in faculties outside state universities, do not hold teaching qualifications; nor are they regulated by the state.[43]

They also questioned whether confessional religious education can encourage understanding and tolerance among pupils of different religions. As mentioned, Macedonia's children are separated along linguistic lines in school. Supporters of the Constitutional Court's ruling argued that separating children by religious denomination, even if only for two hours a week, would only increase physical and psychological distance between members of different religions.[44] Moreover, if confessional religious education further fragments an education system already divided by language, then the choice between a non-confessional Introduction to Religions and the confessional Religious Education

35 Karajkov, The Government vs. the Court.
36 UNICEF Country Office Skopje, *Study on Multiculturalism and Inter-Ethnic Relations in Education,* Skopje: UNICEF, 2009, 17; Biljana Stavrova, All God's Children?, *Transitions Online,* 16 January 2007.
37 Stavrova.
38 Matevski et al., 153, 154.
39 Archbishop Stefan, quoted in Stavrova; the same point was made by Hadzi Jakup Selimovski, the director of the education department of the Islamic Community.
40 UN: Secularism in Macedonia at Risk, *Balkan Insight,* 30 April 2009.
41 Karajkov, The Government vs. the Court; Matevski et al., 150, 158.
42 Matevski et al., 146.; Macedonia Plea for Religion in Schools, *Balkan Insight,* 20 May 2009.
43 No Religion in Macedonian Schools, *Balkan Insight,* 27 August 2009; Stavrova.; US Embassy Skopje, *Macedonia's Culture Wars.*
44 UNICEF Country Office Skopje, 21; United Nations Development Programme, *People Centered Analyses Report,* Skopje: UNDP, 2008, 57; Macedonia Religious Classes 'Uncostitutional', *Balkan Insight,* 15 April 2009; Matevski et al., 153.

adds to fragmentation. Indeed, anecdotal evidence suggests that Muslim parents tended to choose denominational religious instruction, while Christian parents opted more frequently for Introduction to Religions.[45] Thus it was feared that, as high school and university student leaders put it, religious education would add 'another layer of academic separation, beyond the existing linguistic barrier'.[46]

In 2008–2009 religious education emerged as a rare cross-cutting issue in Macedonia's increasingly fragmented society. It placed the VMRO-DPMNE against its government coalition partner, the Albanian DUI, separated the ethnic parties from their electorates as Albanians supported the VMRO-DPMNE positions while Slav Macedonians leaned towards supporting the Constitutional Court's decision. It also encouraged the alliance of all major religious institutions. The debate was so incendiary that it appeared to threaten the independence of Macedonia's judiciary. Such vehemence cannot be explained solely by reference to the educational merits and demerits of Religious Education as introduced in 2008–2009. In fact, no voice objected to Introduction to Religions: this proves that neither of the two camps opposed the introduction of education *about* religions in Macedonia's public schools. Therefore, the events of April 2009 were not the attack of an 'atheist dictatorship' against its people.

In fact, as early as 2006, Matevski, Aziri and Velichkovski had legitimately concluded that the 'question about religious education is no longer whether it will be introduced, but in what form, for whom, and when'.[47] What changed after 2001, when religious education was so low on the public agenda that no one seemed to notice that it had been suspended from schools? A survey of popular attitudes to the introduction of religious education may provide a key.

Religious Education and the Evolving Role of Religion in Macedonia's Plural State

In 2006, the Skopje Centre for Research and Policy Making carried out an extensive survey to determine the attitudes of Macedonia's citizens to the introduction of religious education in public schools.[48]

The large majority of the population favoured the introduction of 'Religious Teaching' (see Figure 1). A breakdown of responses by ethnicity (Table 1) and by religion (Table 2) shows that the percentage of those in favour of religious education was particularly high among Albanians and Muslims. Yet, those against the introduction of religious teaching outnumbered those in favour only in the 'other' religious and ethnic

---

45 Author's Interview with Ljubica Grodzanovska, journalist, 9 September 2012.
46 US Embassy Skopje, *Macedonia: Implementing New Religious Freedom Law While Blurring Church-State Separation*; US Embassy Skopje, *Macedonia's Culture Wars*.
47 Matevski et al., 144.
48 Center for Research and Policymaking, *Introducing Religious Teaching in the Public Education System of the Republic of Macedonia. A Blueprint for a Programmatic Framework*, Skopje: Center for Research and Policymaking, 2006.

category. In other words, the majority of people belonging to every major religious and ethnic group in Macedonia in 2006 favoured the introduction of religious education.

This new support for the introduction of religious education could in and of itself explain the violent popular reaction to the 2009 Constitutional Court's ruling suspending Religious Education. Yet, a closer look at the survey questions this view.

Figure 1: Should Religious Teaching be Introduced in the Public Education System of the Republic of Macedonia?[49]

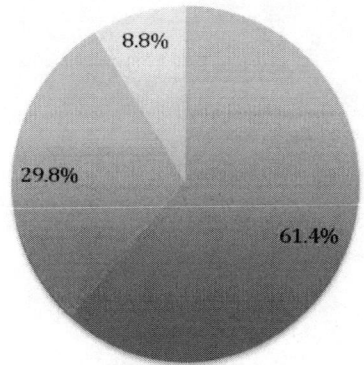

61.4% Yes
29.8% No
8.8%   I don't know

Table 1: Should Religious Teaching be Introduced in the Public Education System of the Republic of Macedonia? Response by Ethnicity[50]

	Macedonian	Albanian	Turkish	Roma	Serbian	Other
Yes	53.0%	87.1%	52.5%	46.7%	68.8%	25.0%
No	36.3%	9.1%	37.5%	40.0%	31.3%	75.0%
I don't know	10.7%	3.8%	10.0%	13.3%	0.0%	0.0%
Total	100.0%	100.0%	100.0%	100.0%	100.0%	100.0%

When asked what component of religious teaching should be emphasised in public schools, a large majority of respondents answered 'learning *about* religion', and only about one sixth of the respondents chose 'learning religion' (Figure 2). Therefore, only one sixth of the respondents called for confessional religious education: the wide majority declared themselves satisfied with a course such as the still available Introduction to Religions.

---

49   Center for Research and Policymaking, *Introducing Religious Teaching in the Public Education System of the Republic of Macedonia. A Blueprint for a Programmatic Framework*, Skopje: Center for Research and Policymaking, 2006, 4.

50   Center for Research and Policymaking, 46.

Table 2:   Should Religious Teaching be Introduced in the Public Education System
           of the Republic of Macedonia? Response by Religion[51]

	Orthodox Christian	Muslim	Catholic	Other
Yes	53.4%	79.7%	44.4%	28.6%
No	36.1%	14.8%	55.6%	71.4%
I don't know	10.5%	5.5%	0.0%	0.0%
Total	100.0%	100.0%	100.0%	100.0%

Figure 2: Which Component of Religious Teaching should be Emphasised?[52]

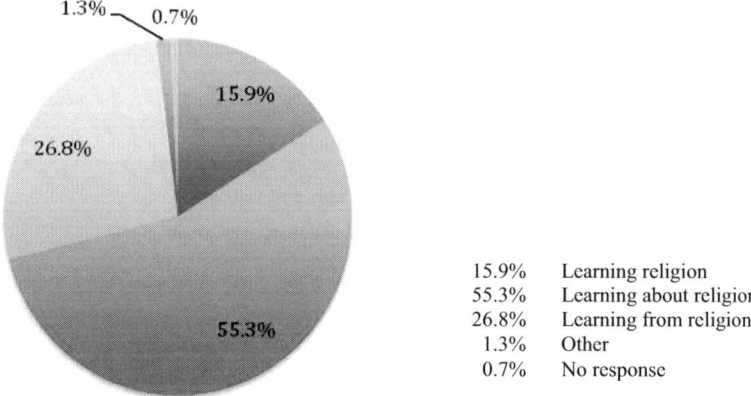

15.9%	Learning religion
55.3%	Learning about religion
26.8%	Learning from religion
1.3%	Other
0.7%	No response

Indeed, whilst anecdotal evidence confirms increasing levels of religiosity among the
population, this is not coupled with increasing observance of religious dogmas or traditions, or with a return to the church. [53] For example, Matevska in her 2011 study of
religiosity among Orthodox Macedonians, finds that the overwhelming majority of her
interviewees declare themselves religious (over 97%), but over 20% of them do not believe God created human beings and over 85% do not observe religious rituals regularly.[54]

Thus, the CRPM's survey suggests that the majority of Macedonia's citizens support
religious education but not necessarily confessional religious education. Yet, violent

51   Center for Research and Policymaking, 59.
52   Center for Research and Policymaking, 6.
53   Zoran Matevski, National and Religious Identity of Macedonian Youth after the Fall of
     Communism, in *37th World Congress of the International Institute of Sociology,* Stockholm, 3.
54   Matevska, The Relationship between the Political and Religious Elite in Contemporary Macedonian
     Society, 130–132.

reaction to the 2009 Constitutional Court ruling was not mollified by the availability of Introduction to Religions, a subject quintessentially *about* religion. Motivations for this reaction may be found in the responses to a further question posed by the CRPM.

Figure 3: What should be the Main Purpose of Introducing Religious Teaching in the Public Education System?[55]

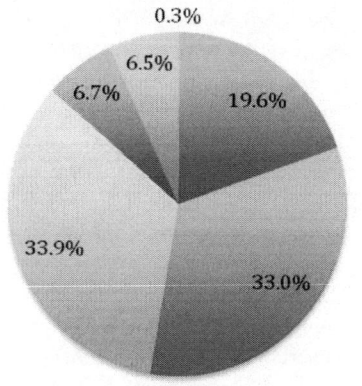

19.6% Restoring the spiritual and moral integrity of the people
33.0% Reinforcing mutual tolerance and respect for human rights
33.9% Preserving the religious communities and continuation of religious legacy and mores
6.7%   Contributing to the creation of versatile and industrious citizens that will intensify the economic development of the country
6.5%   Other

Figure 3 shows that three answers stand out among the responses to the question 'What should be the main purpose of introducing religious teaching in the public education system?' Each of these three responses provides important clues as to the new relevance of religion in the private and public life of Macedonia's citizens.

Over 19% of the respondents viewed religious education as important because of its contribution to restoring spiritual and moral integrity. As seen, this was one of the main arguments emphasised by the Macedonian Orthodox Church and by VMRO-DPMNE in their advocacy of religious education. Certainly Macedonian society was deeply trauma- tised by the end of socialism and by the decay of 'socialist morality'. Indeed, much of the argument for the introduction of Religious Education in schools centred on the ambition to fill a 'moral vacuum', provide stronger moral and ethical principles for stu- dents and protect them against drug and alcohol abuse, violence and other forms of 'moral decline' and 'deviant behaviour'.[56] Yet, this argument fails to explain the neces- sity for confessional religious education.

About one third of the respondents saw religious education as furthering inter-ethnic tolerance and respect for human rights. In fact, both parts to the 2008–2009 debate over religious education agreed on this point: both those supporting the Constitutional Court's decision and those attacking it argued that knowledge *about* religions would benefit children and encourage them to develop into tolerant and understanding citizens of a

---

55   Center for Research and Policymaking, 5.
56   Matevski et al., 143–144, 152.; Matevski, The Religious Education in the Pedagogical System in the Republic of Macedonia, 4.

multi-ethnic state.[57] They frequently pointed at the Yugoslav wars to show that religious education in schools is not essential to the transmission of virulent religious prejudice.[58] They also argued that schools may provide knowledge and information to undermine and challenge prejudices, laying the foundations for a thriving plural society. Once again, education *about* religions would suffice.

In fact, it is the majority answer that best explains the need for confessional religious education. Over a third of respondents viewed religious teaching as necessary because it contributes to the preservation of the traditions and legacy of religious communities in the country. It appears that, in contrast to a decade earlier, religion in Macedonia had come to be endowed with the function of furthering the distinctive traditions and cultures of Macedonia's communities. In Macedonia religion almost overlaps with ethnicity, especially in the case of the two largest communities, the Slav Macedonians and the Albanians. This implies a novel understanding of religion as to some extent defining the identity of Macedonia's ethnic groups. Over the last decade, therefore, religion, previously marginalised, appears to have emerged as a further cleavage, reinforcing the linguistic and ethnic divides.

This novel understanding of religion as an essential element of the identity of ethnic groups is rooted in two developments. First, encouraging identification of Macedonianness with Orthodoxy, in 2004 the state directly intervened in defence of the independent autocephalous status of the Macedonian Orthodox Church. In a rare example of concord among all political parties,[59] the Serbian Orthodox Church's representative in Macedonia and his followers were arrested charges of 'inciting religious and ethnic hatred' and sentenced to prison terms because of their proselytising activities.[60] If the state's intervention in defence of the Macedonian Orthodox Church strengthened national pride among Slav Macedonians,[61] it also marked the beginning of a new alliance of political and religious institutions in the Republic. It marked the moment when, as Matevski emphatically puts it, 'the cross and sword united'.[62] In 2004, the Macedonian president officially met the Archbishop of the Macedonian Orthodox Church for the first time. At

---

57 Goce Velickovski, Attitudes of High School Teachers to Introduction of Religious Education in the Republic of Macedonia, in *Kotor Network Conference "Religion in Schools: Problems of Pluralism in the Public Sphere"*, Kotor, 2005, 4, 5.

58 Costa Carras, Religious Identity and Religious Education in Schools, in Christina Koulouri (ed.), *Clio in the Balkans, the Politics of History Education*, Thessaloniki: Center for Democracy and Reconciliation in Southeast Europe, 2002, 365; Mirela-Luminita Murgescu, Religious Education and the View of the Others in Southeast Europe, in Christina Koulouri (ed.), *Clio in the Balkans, the Politics of History Education*, Thessaloniki: Center for Democracy and Reconciliation in Southeast Europe, 2002, 299.

59 Matevska, The Relationship between the Political and Religious Elite in Contemporary Macedonian Society, 136.

60 Quercia, Borderline Religion: The Role of Churches in Balkan Nation Building, 25.; US Depertment of State, *Macedonia. International Religious Freedom Report,* 2005.

61 Matevska, The Relationship between the Political and Religious Elite in Contemporary Macedonian Society, 136; Matevski, National and Religious Identity of Macedonian Youth after the Fall of Communism, 5.

62 Matevski, The Religious Education in the Pedagogical System in the Republic of Macedonia, 6.

the meeting, the Archbishop reportedly pressed for the introduction of religious education in schools.[63]

The new relationship between the state with the Macedonian Orthodox Church was rapidly extended to the second major religious group, the Muslims. Indeed, the state has applied rigid parallelism in its dealings with the two major religious communities. For example, when violent clashes erupted over the construction of a new Orthodox Church in Skopje city centre, the government attempted to placate debates by announcing that a new mosque would be built in the centre of Tetovo, an Albanian-majority municipality[64] –, despite the fact that, as the DUI leader Ali Ahmeti ironically pointed out, 'there are more churches and mosques in Macedonia than believers'.[65] State regard for the two major religious communities has led to accusations that, despite constitutional guarantees of secularism, the government is promoting the Islamic Community and the Orthodox Church as 'state faith communities'.[66] In fact, this parallel regard for the Christian Orthodox and Muslim religious institutions is an extension of the state's emphasis on equal respect for the Slav Macedonian and Albanian communities.

A second development contributed to the evolving relevance of religion: increasing public rhetoric on the importance of religion to the identity of ethnic communities. In particular, in the last decade frustrations with the OFA and the feeling of having lost the state to Albanians have emerged among the Slav Macedonian population. These frustrations have led to attempts on the part of the governing nationalist party to forge and convey an ancient and immemorial, pure Macedonian identity. Such identity was to replace a previous identification of Macedonian-ness with ownership of the state. Thus, religion has been tasked with providing a 'feeling of historical continuity' with an ancient, and often heavily fictionalised, past.[67] Thus, particularly since 2004, the public discourse of prominent Slav Macedonian politicians, especially those belonging to the VMRO-DPMNE, has married religion to ethnic identity. This 'overzealous religious fervour'[68] contributed to the proliferation of religious buildings and to the mushrooming of statues of prominent religious figures.[69]

Both the new relationship of the state with religious institutions and a new emphasis on religion in the construction of a Slav Macedonian identity contributed to framing a new function for religion in the Republic. After 2001, and with increasing intensity since 2004, religion emerged as a further element differentiating Slav Macedonians from Albanians. This is part of a wider drive towards the creation of a pure, ancient identity,

---

63   Ibid.
64   Risto Karajkov, Macedonia, Clashes over Religious Symbols, Again, *Osservatorio Balcani e Caucaso*, 24 February 2011; Drasko Djenovic, Macedonia: Official Discrimination Continues, *Forum 18 News*, 9 October 2009.
65   US Embassy Skopje, *Macedonia: Ahmeti Rates State of Affairs a "Four out of Ten"*, 21 August 2009.
66   Djenovic.
67   Ivekovic, Nationalism and the Political Use and Abuse of Religion: The Politicisation of Orthodoxy, Catholicism and Islam in Yugoslav Successor States, 534.
68   Karajkov.
69   Ibid.

exemplified by the VMRO-DPMNE's 'political-religious agenda'.[70] Religion was also endowed with a novel political saliency by a government applying a peculiar understanding of pluralism. This understanding limits pluralism to the provision of equal and separate rights, recognition, institutions and services to different communities.

In this light it is clear that the 2009 debate was not the struggle of a people against an 'atheist dictatorship'. It is even clearer that the decision to introduce Religious Education in schools in 2008–2009 did not reflect pedagogical concerns. Rather, it responded to a major change in the saliency of religion to Macedonian society and the political system. Above all, it reflected an ambition to redefine the major building blocks of the identity of Slav Macedonians. The failure of the 2008–2009 attempt did not spell the end of confessional religious education in Macedonia's schools.

Religious Education in Macedonia's Public Schools Today

Despite the worst predictions of the US Embassy, the 2009 'culture wars'[71] over religious education died down by the summer of the same year. Yet, in 2010–2011 the Ministry of Education introduced a new optional subject, to be offered alongside Introduction to Religions: Ethics of Religion.

Most observers interpreted this move as a further, more discreet, attempt to introduce confessional religious education in schools.[72] Certainly, Ethics of Religion is more acceptable to the public than its precursor as it is taught by a theology graduate and not by a member of the clergy.[73] Therefore, it limits the involvement of clergy members in the delivery of the curriculum. As such, it does not risk 'turning our schools into churches and mosques' as was feared in 2009.[74] Moreover, the curriculum, despite being confessional, includes information about each of the five religious communities mentioned in Macedonia's constitution: Orthodox, Muslim, Catholic, Jewish and Methodist. This validates the function of confessional religious education in providing knowledge to contribute to inter-ethnic understanding. No legal action has been brought against this subject to date.

Yet, it is still unclear why, if aiming to provide knowledge on a variety of religious beliefs and expressions without clergy involvement, Introduction to Religion would not suffice. The curricula for Introduction to Religions and Ethics of Religion are different in almost every respect (see Table 3 for a general summary of the topics) but three elements in the Ethics of Religion curriculum explain why the VMRO-DPMNE insisted on introducing this subject alongside Introduction to Religion.

---

70   Ali Ahmeti, quoted in US Embassy Skopje, *Macedonia: Ahmeti Rates State of Affairs a "Four out of Ten"*.
71   US Embassy Skopje, *Macedonia's Culture Wars*.
72   Poll Shows Macedonia Becoming More Socially Conservative, *Balkan Insight*, 26 November 2010; Djenovic.
73   Author's Interview with Mire Mladenovski, President of the History Teachers' Association, 13 September 2012.
74   Liberal Democratic MP, quoted in Macedonia Religious Classes 'Uncostitutional'.

First, as is clear from Table 3, in contrast to Introduction to Religions, over half of the Ethics of Religion curriculum is optional. Pupils are required to study one of the five optional modules for Ethics in Orthodoxy, Islam, Catholicism, Judaism or Methodism. Thus, Ethics of Religion in effect proposes again the separation of pupils along religious lines that had been so strongly criticised in 2008–2009 – despite the fact that a cursory examination of the curriculum reveals that most of the contents of the optional modules are similar if not identical. They include widely acceptable objectives such as reflecting on love for one's family, respect for older people, prevention of drug addiction, hygiene and recognition of the importance of work and education. Duplication is particularly evident in the case of the three Christian denominations, where topics and activities are often the same.[75]

Second, in contrast to Introduction to Religions, Ethics of Religion includes explicitly doctrinal elements in the optional modules. These aim to encourage students to 'adopt the basic concepts of [religious] doctrine'.[76] Encouragement of belief, rather than simply of knowledge is also evident in the objectives of lessons and in the proposed activities, which include memorising the lyrics of specific religious songs. Ethics of Religion, whist presenting elements about Orthodox, Muslim, Catholic, Jewish and Methodist doctrines in the first part of the curriculum, does not encourage students to explore the similarities between different faiths. In contrast, Introduction to Religions is designed to critically examine and compare a variety of religious expressions and beliefs, leading students to draw differences and similarities between them.

The third difference between Introduction to Religions and Ethics of Religion deeply reflects the new, fundamental function of religion in Macedonia's society. Whist Introduction to Religions considers a variety of beliefs, Ethics of Religion focuses only on indigenous confessions recognised by the Macedonian Constitution. In so doing, it reflects the new alliance between the state and some local religious communities. Ethics of Religion also emphasises the link between religion, identity and Macedonian nationality, particularly in the modules about Christian denominations. Thus, the curricula for Orthodoxy, Catholicism and Methodism underline Macedonia's Christian roots by tracing the early spread of Christianity, studying Macedonian saints in depth and using pictures of Macedonian churches. No similar effort is made in the compulsory or optional modules about Islam or Judaism.[77]

---

75 Bureau for Development of Education of the Republic of Macedonia, *Curriculum: Ethics of Religions*.
76 Bureau for Development of Education of the Republic of Macedonia, *Curriculum: Ethics of Religions*, 15.
77 Bureau for Development of Education of the Republic of Macedonia, *Curriculum: Ethics of Religions*.

Table 3: Introduction to Religion and Ethics of Religion Compared[78]

Introduction to Religion	Ethics of Religion
Defining religion (12 hours) • Religious themes • Environment • Moral function of religion	Ethics as a science of good and morality (10 hours) • Ethics • Morality
First religions (14 hours) • Animism • Totemism • Taboos • Mythology • Magic	Ethics in religion (20 hours) • Common ethical principles • Ethics and morality in Orthodox Christianity • Ethics and morality in Islam • Ethics and morality in Catholicism • Ethics and morality in Judaism • Ethics and morality in Methodism
Great world religions (36 hours) • Judaism • Christianity • Islam Impact of religions (10 hours) • Secularism • Ecumenism	Optional Modules (42 hours) Ethics in Orthodox Christian Doctrine • Theoretical foundations of Orthodox Christianity • Ethical basis of Orthodox Christianity • Orthodox Christian Morality OR Ethics in Islamic Learning • Theoretical foundations of Islam • Ethical basis of Islam • Foundations of Islamic Morality OR Ethics in Catholic Christian Doctrine • Theoretical foundations of Catholic Christianity • Ethical basis of Catholic Christianity • Catholic Christian Morality OR Ethics in Judaism • Theoretical foundations of Judaism • Ethical basis of Judaism • Morality in Judaism OR Ethics in Methodist Christian teaching • Theoretical foundations of Evangelical-Methodist Christian teaching • Ethical basis of Evangelical-Methodist Christian teaching • Morality Evangelical-Methodist Christian teaching

---

78   Bureau for Development of Education of the Republic of Macedonia, *Curriculum: Ethics of Religions*; Bureau for Development of Education of the Republic of Macedonia, *Curriculum: Introduction to Religions, 2008.*

Thus, if the function of religious education was simply, as most international observers argue, to encourage moral behaviour, provide knowledge to undermine stereotypes, encourage critical thinking and the questioning of dogmas, and to further understanding among different communities, then Introduction to Religions would suffice in Macedonia's schools.[79] Indeed, in contrast to Introduction to Religions, the curriculum for Ethics of Religion does not exploit the numerous opportunities for reflection and discussion on themes relevant to the peaceful and tolerant future of ethnic communities in Macedonia. For example, none of the modules exploits the opportunity to discuss the principles of reconciliation and forgiveness in the context of the inter-ethnic conflict in Macedonia.

Yet, this investigation of the vicissitudes of religious education since Macedonian independence has shown that religion, and religious education, has been entrusted with one further responsibility in the last decade: that of contributing to ethnic and national identity. By tracing the Ariadne's thread between religion and ethnic identity, separating children according to their denomination and encouraging the learning of religious doctrine, Ethics of Religion deeply reflects, and contributes to, the new function of religion in the plural Macedonian society.

An Atheist Dictatorship?

The 2009 Constitutional Court ruling suspending Religious Education from Macedonia's public school did not denote an 'atheist dictatorship', nor did it lead to one. Similarly, the insistence for introduction of confessional religious education did not reflect a clerical crusade for the 'desecularisation of society'[80] nor did it express a state drive to 'give youth what they don't want'.[81]

Indeed, most Macedonian citizens agree with knowledge *about* religion being part of the cultural capital transmitted by the school.[82] At the same time, they are wary of explicit church involvement in state institutions such as schools.[83]

In fact, the 2008–2009 argument over the introduction of confessional religious education in Macedonia exemplifies the deeper debate over the role of religion in defining the ambiguous identity of Macedonia's citizens at large and of members of each ethnic community in particular. The politics of difference associated with the implementation of the OFA, and the novel emphasis of Slav Macedonian political parties on the build-

---

79   Murgescu, 298; Ministry of Education and Science of the Republic of Macedonia, *Steps Towards Integrated Education,* 2010, 4.

80   Ivekovic, Nationalism and the Political Use and Abuse of Religion: The Politicisation of Orthodoxy, Catholicism and Islam in Yugoslav Successor States, 534.

81   US Embassy Skopje, *Macedonia: Implementing New Religious Freedom Law While Blurring Church-State Separation.*

82   Snezana Mirascieva, Vlado Petrovski, and Emilija Petrova Gjorgjeva, Teaching in the Religious Education in the Republic of Macedonia Today, *Procedia Social and Behavioral Sciences* 15, 2011, 1405.

83   Religious Lessons Cause Stir, *Balkan Insight*, 31 October 2008.

ing of a pure immemorial identity for each of Macedonia's ethnic communities has endowed religion with a new important role: that of custodian of communal tradition.

This understanding of religion as an important shrine for communal traditions, and consensus on the need to preserve these distinctive customs, suggests specific aims for religious education. A curriculum sustaining the new social and political function of religion needs to encourage children's identification with one particular religious faith, to transmit the contributions of religion and of religious institutions to the Macedonian state, and to convey the thread between ethnic and religious belonging. The subject Ethics of Religion, while toning down the confessional elements of its predecessors, fulfils, at least on paper, each of these aims.

Bibliography

Author's Interview with Mire Mladenovski, President of the History Teachers' Association, 13 September 2012.
Author's Interview with Ljubica Grodzanovska, journalist, 9 September 2012.
Balcan Insight:
    Macedonia Plea for Religion in Schools, *Balkan Insight*, 20 May 2009.
    Macedonia Religious Classes 'Uncostitutional', *Balkan Insight*, 15 April 2009.
    No Religion in Macedonian Schools, *Balkan Insight*, 27 August 2009.
    Poll Shows Macedonia Becoming More Socially Conservative, *Balkan Insight*, 26 November 2010.
    Religion Classes for Macedonian Pupils, *Balkan Insight*, 1 September 2008.
    Religious Lessons Cause Stir, *Balkan Insight*, 31 October 2008.
    UN: Secularism in Macedonia at Risk, *Balkan Insight*, 30 April 2009.
Buchenau, Klaus. What Went Wrong? Church-State Relations in Socialist Yugoslavia, *Nationalities Papers: The Journal of Nationalism and Ethnicity* 33:4 (2005), 547–567.
Bureau for Development of Education of the Republic of Macedonia, *Curriculum: Ethics of Religions*.
Bureau for Development of Education of the Republic of Macedonia, *Curriculum: Introduction to Religions*, 2008.
Carras, Costa. Religious Identity and Religious Education in Schools, in Christina Koulouri (ed.) *Clio in the Balkans, the Politics of History Education*, Thessaloniki: Center for Democracy and Reconciliation in Southeast Europe, 2002, 359–366
Center for Research and Policymaking, *Introducing Religious Teaching in the Public Education System of the Republic of Macedonia. A Blueprint for a Programmatic Framework*, Skopje: Center for Research and Policymaking, 2006.
Constitution of the Republic of Macedonia, 1992.
Council, Human Rights, *Report of the Special Rapporteur on Freedom of Religion or Belief, Asma Jahangir, Mission to the Former Yugoslav Republic of Macedonia*, Geneva: United Nations General Assembly, 2009.
Djenovic, Drasko, Macedonia: Official Discrimination Continues, *Forum 18 News*, 9 October 2009.
Former Yugoslav Republic of Macedonia: UN Expert Speaks out on Religious Intolerance. *UN News Centre*, 30 April 2009.

Ivekovic, Ivan, Nationalism and the Political Use and Abuse of Religion: The Politicisation of Orthodoxy, Catholicism and Islam in Yugoslav Successor States, *Social Compass* 49:4 (2002), 523–536.

Karajkov, Risto, Church, Mosque, Nato, Macedonian Parliament, *Osservatorio Balcani e Caucaso*, 14 August 2007.

Karajkov, Risto, The Government vs. the Court. *Osservatorio Balcani e Caucaso*, 24 April 2009.

Karajkov, Risto, Macedonia, Clashes over Religious Symbols, Again, *Osservatorio Balcani e Caucaso*, 24 February 2011.

Kuburić, Zoric and Christian Moe, Introduction, in Zoric Kuburić and Christian Moe *(eds), Religion and Pluralism in Education Comparative Approaches in the Western Balkans*, Novi Sad: CEIR in cooperation with the Kotor Network, 2006, 1–8.

Macedonia, Ministry of Education and Science of the Republic of, *Steps Towards Integrated Education*, 2010.

Matevska, Dushka, The Relationship between the Political and Religious Elite in Contemporary Macedonian Society, *Politics and Religion* V:1 (2011), 129–139.

Matevski, Zoran, National and Religious Identity of Macedonian Youth after the Fall of Communism, in *37th World Congress of the International Institute of Sociology,* Stockholm.

Matevski, Zoran, The Religious Education in the Pedagogical System in the Republic of Macedonia, in *Kotor Network Conference "Religion in Schools: Problems of Pluralism in the Public Sphere",* Kotor, 2005.

Matevski, Zoran, Etem Aziri and Goce Velichkovski, Introducing Religious Education in Macedonia, in Zorica Kuburić and Christian Moe (eds), *Religion and Pluralism in Education Comparative Approaches in the Western Balkans*, Novi Sad: CEIR in cooperation with the Kotor Network, 2006, 139–151.

Mirascieva, Snezana, Vlado Petrovski and Emilija Petrova Gjorgjeva, Teaching in the Religious Education in the Republic of Macedonia Today, *Procedia Social and Behavioral Sciences* 15, 2011, 1404–1409.

Murgescu, Mirela-Luminita, Religious Education and the View of the Others in Southeast Europe, in Christina Koulouri (ed.), *Clio in the Balkans, the Politics of History Education*, Thessaloniki: Center for Democracy and Reconciliation in Southeast Europe, 2002, 295–299.

Ohrid Framework Agreement, 2001.

Quercia, Paolo, Bordeline Religion: The Role of Churches in Balkan Nation Building, *CeMiSS Quarterly* II:1, 2004, 21–33.

Republic of Macedonia State Statistical Office, *Census of Population, Households and Dwellings 2002, Book X: Total Population According to Ethnic Affiliation, Mother Tongue and Religion,* Skopje: State Statistical Office, 2002.

Republic of Macedonia State Statistical Office, *Census of Population, Households and Dwellings 2002, Book XIII: Total Population, Households and Dwellings According to the Territorial Organisation of the Republic of Macedonia,* Skopje: State Statistical Office, 2002.

Stavrova, Biljana, All God's Children? *Transitions Online*, 16 January 2007.

UNICEF Country Office Skopje, *Study on Multiculturalism and Inter-Ethnic Relations in Education*, Skopje: UNICEF, 2009.

United Nations Development Programme, *People Centered Analyses Report*, Skopje: UNDP, 2008.

US Department of State, *Macedonia. International Religious Freedom Report*, 2005.

US Embassy Skopje, *Macedonia: Ahmeti Rates State of Affairs a "Four out of Ten"*, 21 August 2009.

US Embassy Skopje, *Macedonia: Implementing New Religious Freedom Law While Blurring Church-State Separation*, 18 April 2008.

US Embassy Skopje, *Macedonia's Culture Wars*, 8 May 2009.

Velickovski, Goce, Attitudes of High School Teachers to Introduction of Religious Education in the Republic of Macedonia, In *Kotor Network Conference "Religion in Schools: Problems of Pluralism in the Public Sphere"*, Kotor, 2005.

A Review of Religion in the British Education System

KELSEY SHANKS

This paper, based on a review of the existing literature, presents the evolution of mass education in the UK and locates the role of religion in its development. Exploring how religious and civic instruction communicates a code of social values. To this end, the paper will examine the legal framework and the relationship between state and religion. The study concludes with an examination of the arguments against the system. Throughout the review, particular attention is given to whether religious education involves instruction about religion or in religion, differentiating between the curricula in state-funded schools with and without faith character.

Introduction

The idea of religion playing an active role in the public sphere is, and has been for hundreds of years, a controversial one in the UK. The place of religion in the public sphere is perhaps nowhere more contested than in relation to its position within the state education system. How, and what, children are taught has the potential to shape national attitudes and influence social cohesion; therefore the function of religion in education provokes extensive debate. In the context of the UK, education and religion are historically entwined, and the very origins of mass public schooling can be found within the religious institutions of Christianity. Throughout the eighteenth century the Church clergy interpreted their Christian charitable responsibilities to include the provision of schooling for the working classes. As a consequence, instruction in basic literacy and numeracy skills were provided while enforcing religious and moral values among the population. This historical arrangement has rooted the Christian ethos in the UK school system for centuries; thus, Parker-Jenkins, Hartas and Irving maintain that "the relationship between church and state has been instrumental in the historical development of public education in England and Wales" (2005:11).

The nineteenth century saw a shift in national education policy which resulted in the Church entering into a partnership with the state. The 1870 Education Act sought to ensure that primary school education was made accessible to all working-class children. The impact of the Industrial Revolution on the British economy shifted the nation's focus, and education became viewed as an "agent of social reform" (Parker-Jenkins, Hartas and Irving, 2005:12). Subsequently, a series of laws followed to clarify the state-church relationship in the education arena. The government introduced a programme of 'free schooling' and offered financial assistance to the existing Church of England schools to help to facilitate this. Financial aid changed the way in which religious schools operated. It was accompanied by governmental involvement in curriculum and pedagogy, and stipulated the need for regular government inspections. Thus, the transition to partnership was not smooth, and religious institutions were "concerned about the implications of accepting government aid" (Parker-Jenkins, Hartas and Irving, 2005:12) owing to the accountability associated with it.

The subsequent Balfour Act of 1902 introduced local education authorities, which were given responsibility for paying teachers' salaries from state funding. A dual system of partnership between the state and Britain's churches was eventually established to provide a national system of education (Jackson, 2004). The ensuing 1944 Act clarified this system to ensure that the partnership provided an "educational system within a national legal and financial framework, locally administered, which would allow for diversity of educational aim and belief" (Pring, 2005:51). From 1944, three main categories of faith-based schools were recognised under the Education Act: voluntary schools (which are independent and self-funding), voluntary aided schools (which retain a distinctive religious character, but are supported by the government), and voluntary controlled schools (which are totally dependent on state funding). The Act acknowledged the Church's historic investment in schools, but also recognised that it was in no position to independently achieve post-war educational reconstruction. The ingenious compromise of the Education Act of 1944 was to ensure that the Churches had a statutory role in shaping religious education throughout the whole state-maintained system.

Religion in State Schools without Religious Character

The 1944 Act also made the use of Agreed Syllabuses for Religious Instruction mandatory for fully state-funded schools. It stated that each English local education authority was required to convene a Syllabus Conference which would consist of four committees, two of which represented religious constituencies: the Church of England and 'other denominations'. By the 1970s some local education authorities were interpreting the Act liberally and as such allowing representatives of non-Christian religions onto the 'other denominations' panel. But it was not until the Education Reform Act of 1988 that different interest groups were formally recognised in law and faiths other than Christianity were officially given a seat on what used to be the 'other denominations' committee at Agreed Syllabus Conferences. Many new syllabuses were subsequently introduced which included world religions other than Christianity. This was indicative of both the social changes in Britain as a consequence of immigration and the rise of religious studies as a globally orientated secular subject in institutions of higher education (Chadwick, 2001).

Increased immigration, and the transformation of Britain into a multicultural nation, changed the way in which religious education was taught in state-funded schools. Increased religious diversity in society was soon recognised by the education system, and the religious education curricula gradually evolved into a representative programme inclusive of the UK's majority religious communities. Despite retaining many features of the 1944 Act, the 1988 Education Reform Act introduced changes which sought to strengthen religious education's place in the curriculum. Most significantly, the Act replaced the term 'religious instruction', with its suggestion of deliberate ideological transmission, with the term 'religious education' and, crucially, specifically prohibited indoctrinatory teaching in completely state-funded schools. The Education Reform Act also set religious education in the context of the whole curriculum of maintained schools and, as such, the subject now had to rationalize its pedagogy and outputs on general educational grounds. The Reform Act required that any new Agreed Syllabus "shall reflect the fact that religious traditions in Great Britain are in the main Christian, whilst taking account of the teaching and practices of the other principal religions represented in Great Britain" (Education Act: 1996), be set within the wider curricular framework and, therefore, be "balanced and broadly based", promoting "the spiritual, moral, cultural, mental and physical development of pupils at the school and of society" (Education Act: 1996). Therefore, religious education in fully funded state schools should be neither indoctrination nor simply a study of religions, but, like the rest of the curriculum, should relate to the experience of pupils in such a way that it contributes to their personal development (Department of Schools, 1999). The commonly recited narrative of modern British religious education is of "confessionalism giving way to neutrality, commitment to professionalism and indoctrination to education" (Barnes, 2007:75).

Therefore, the idea that religious education should encourage observance of Christianity was no longer acceptable, and religious education developed a civic dimension. The narrow Christian focus was replaced by a multi-faith perspective which reflected the diversity of religions found in British society. Consequently, religious education in fully funded state schools aimed to encourage pupils to understand and respect the beliefs and practices of citizens from different faith communities, but still provide Christianity with a privileged status within this understanding. In support of this aim two model syllabuses were published by the School Curriculum and Assessment Authority in 1994. Produced in consultation with members of each faith group, they included material on six major religions in Britain: Christianity, Judaism, Islam, Hinduism, Buddhism and Sikhism.

Further work took place at the national level in 2003, when the Department for Education and Skills commissioned a new national framework for religious education. This framework, which aimed to clarify standards in religious education, was approved by all of the professional associations and faith communities (Gates; 2005). In addition to the world religions, the framework explicitly permits the study of non-religious philosophies, such as humanism, and emphasises how religious education can advance cultural understanding and citizenship education. The government's 'social inclusion' agenda gave religious education particular emphasis, stating it had great potential to encourage pupils' engagement with "social and moral responsibility, community involvement and political literacy" (Keast, 2005:213). Furthermore, it was highlighted as a means to tackle a lack of understanding of religions such as Islam and provide a space to analyse religious and cultural racism in the aftermath of events such as September 11 (Jackson, 2004).

Religion in State-Funded Schools with Religious Character

Meanwhile, an alternate direction for religious education unfolded within the realm of the aforementioned voluntary church schools. The majority of these schools are defined as 'voluntary aided', which means that they are supported primarily by the state, but are required to obtain an additional ten per cent of their funding from their religious community. In these schools the governing body retains control over the teaching of religious education, appointment of teachers and admissions to the school. In schools with a religious character, or 'faith schools' as they have become commonly known, religious education continues as a form of religious instruction and many faith schools are still permitted by law to teach the subject from a selective, exclusive or confessional viewpoint. As faith schools are partly funded by different religious bodies, the school ethos, principles, values, educational aims, and religious education curriculum specifically reflect the religious body and community which they serve. Yet, faith schools are obliged to allow admission to a number of students from different religions, or with no religion; as a result, some faith schools have chosen to adopt a multi-faith religious education curriculum in order to reflect the diversity of their student bodies (Keast, 2005).

With the expansion of multiculturalism came an increase in the number of religions that opened voluntary status faith schools. These schools now account for around a third of English publicly funded schools; there are just over 7000 state-funded faith schools in England, and they are no longer only Church of England schools (Paton, 2010). A number of faith schools were established by non-Christian religious communities in response to demands created by new immigrants. Schools for Irish Catholic immigrants were established as early as 1847 and for Jewish immigrants from 1853. Yet, it was not until the mid-1980s that growing pressure from newer immigrant faith groups gained momentum and demands for state funding in established independent schools were voiced. The first two state-funded Muslim schools were opened in 1998. The expansion of the state-funded faith-school sector was the conclusion of long-standing lobbying by minority faith groups to gain equality with other religious groups in the public sphere (Meer, 2007). Accordingly, the need to expand education provision in order to support diversity and pluralism within Britain became a major government focus. The role of religion in education received a great deal of attention, and government, policy makers, and educationalists debated the best way forward to support non-Christian communities within an educational setting (Gilley et al., 1994).

Church-State Relationship and Government Funding of Faith Schools

Britain's accommodation of the cultural and religious needs of its multicultural citizens has long been recognised (Spencer, 1997). As discussed in the previous section, educational policy adopted multiculturalism in state-supported schools in the 1970s and since then has evolved to fund a variety of faith schools. The multicultural stance in education also extended to the acceptance of religious practices in schools. Thus, when confronted with the issue of Muslim girls wearing the hijab in state-run schools, British educational authorities quickly reached a compromise that allowed girls to wear the head-covering as long as it conformed with the colour requirements of the school uniform (Liederman, 2000). The way in which Britain has responded to the educational needs of the Muslim community contrasts with that of other European countries, secular France in particular. Commentators have suggested that the way in which a state resolved the church-state relationship in the past influences its contemporary debate over faith schools and provides an interesting intersection at which to examine the role of religion in education.

The Church of England remains the established, or state, church in England with a legislating role in British society. Twenty-six bishops (including the two archbishops) sit in the House of Lords. Known as the Lords Spiritual, they are thought to bring a religious ethos to the secular process of law. The state's accommodation of new religious practices in Britain has been shaped by this formal religious establishment and the privileged position of the Church of England. In the first instance the establishment of a particular religion might be perceived as an obstacle to immigrant faith groups as they negotiate with the state over contested religious practices. Yet the benefits afforded to the Church of England have not served to exclude other faiths with a view to preserving the privileged position of Christianity. On the contrary, Britain's church-state model has served as an "important institutional and ideological resource" (Monsma and Soper, 1997) for faith-based communities. The close links between the Established Church and the political system in Britain provide a framework within which faith groups can seek recognition for their public needs.

The existing British church-state relationship sets forth specific avenues through which religious groups can claim resources for religious schools and social serves (Monsma and Soper, 1997). Monsma and Soper suggest that in the pursuit of public funding for schools, religious community activists fully recognise the space created for political mobilisation. If there is state funding for Christian and Jewish schools, it is only right and fair that the state also fund Muslim schools. The British government pragmatically accommodated religious minorities in the past (Weller et al., 2001); therefore, it seemed inevitable that the state would eventually also accommodate the needs of religious communities, such as Muslims, that have arrived more recently. Despite the significant debate over the issue of state funding for Muslim schools throughout the 1990s, this was, indeed, eventually the case. In addition, and critically, Muslims activists also profited from the political support of religious leaders within the British system. Religious leaders with good ties to political elites and policy makers recognised that denying benefits to Muslims called into question the very system that provided them with considerable state aid (Monsma and Soper, 1997).

Religion, Education and State Values Policy

The diversification of state-funded faith schools coincided with an overall increase in the number of faith schools in England. The British government championed this expansion. The government has justified this stance by illustrating the higher attainment record of faith schools. Students in faith-based schools obtain good academic results and faith schools are usually at the top of the Local Education Authorities' league tables. In fact, research has shown that faith schools commonly achieve considerably higher GCSE results than community schools and that students attending faith-based schools are afforded higher social capital and thus greater social mobility, (Schagen and Schagen, 2001:16). The government has attributed this achievement to the ethos of faith schools and their emphasis on the teaching of moral values. Schagen and Schagen also note that it is important to recognise that the justification for such high achievement may in fact be found in the "hidden selection that takes place" rather than in "the distinctive ethos of the school" (2001:30).

By the late 1990s it was documented by a government green paper entitled *The learning age: a renaissance for a new Britain*, that faith schools had "a good record of delivering a high quality education to their pupils" (1998:14) and they were championed by the labour government and its *Education, Education, Education* mantra. As a result, a wider range of religious schools was incorporated into the state system. A number of factors have aided the expansion of state-funded faith schools in Britain. Academic achievement and the preservation of a moral ethos, which might be more difficult to cultivate in community schools, are widely acknowledged as driving factors. So too is the provision of parental choice in support of religious pluralism and diversity. Yet it must also be recognized that the expansion is partly due to a lack of political will to dismantle the whole faith-school system.

Some scholars have questioned the government's commitment to the faith-school system. There have been suggestions that the growth in minority faith schools and the defence of religious education is not a demonstration of the government's support for religious diversity, but a by-product of the government's push to reinstate a specific Christian values-based policy in Britain. Commentators suggest that the inclusive language used to support faith schools is misleading, as support is actually directed only toward the established Church of England schools. Jivraj draws our attention to a recent speech to mark the 400th anniversary of the King James Bible by Prime Minister David Cameron. In the speech he told Church of England clergy that "Christian values would counter the country's moral collapse" (Jivraj, 2012). He also stated that the King James Bible permeates every aspect of our culture, our heritage and also our politics, and further asserted that we should not be afraid to say that we are a Christian country (Jivraj, 2012).

Continuing in this vein the Minister of Education, Michael Gove, announced plans to send a copy of the King James Bible to every school in the country. This move has been presented within a framework of community values and an increased role of religion in education; however, Jivraj suggests that what these statements demonstrate is that not all faith schools are viewed in terms of equal societal benefit and community cohesion

(Jivraj, 2013). It is a collective appreciation not of the values of all faith schools, but of those of the Church of England that drives government policy. Yet the expansion of government support for all faith schools has promoted the use of an inclusive language. Government discourse surrounding faith schools is therefore, in fact, often misleading. Hence, Jivraj states that the "holding up church schools as beacons to emulate must be understood in the context of the radicalization of Muslim schools" (Jivraj, 2013). While government minsters supported the expansion of faith schools in general, they were also sending warning signals to whole faith communities whose schools were perceived as a threat to community cohesion (Jivraj, 2013). For example, in 2006 schools were obliged to promote community cohesion. Presenting this duty, former Schools Minister Stephen Twigg described it as a "duty of faith schools, Muslim ones in particular" and warned that religious segregation in schools must not put the nation's coherence at risk (Jivraj, 2013). This stance is reflective of the post-September 11th political discourse, which called into question the ability of Muslim faith schools in Britain to promote community cohesion. Muslim faith schools have thus been warned not to foster isolation and breed extremism, while Christian faith schools are praised for exhorting moral values.

Faith Schools and Community Cohesion

The on-going role and status of all state-funded faith schools in England is negotiated through competing engagements with the policy discourse of 'community cohesion'. The most substantial criticism of the faith-school system lies in the charge that it divides communities and perpetuates a segregated sense of self-identity. In this regard, criticism is not limited to Muslim faith schools. Research linking the faith-school system with national disturbances has deepened this concern. A report on the racially motivated riots in the north of England in 2001 condemned, among other factors, "a segregated school system that has failed to challenge negative attitudes and stereotypes and that has played a marginal role in brokering cultural shifts between family, school and public life" (Ouseley Report, 2002:962). Hence, the Ouseley Report contended that segregated faith schools divide communities and foster prejudice, hostility, community fragmentation, and community conflict.

Gallagher (2004) suggests three hypotheses to explain the negative impact of faith schools in Northern Ireland, where schools are classified along strict religious lines – Protestant or Catholic. Firstly, the cultural hypothesis suggests that separatist schools enhance community divisions by introducing potentially opposing cultural environments. Relating this to the English context, we can see how the perceived freedom within the religious curriculum, and failure of government regulation, has resulted in numerous cases of faith schools teaching topics and opinion that run counter to the wider social values of the country. One of the principal arguments against faith-based schools is that they teach a specific faith doctrine which sometimes undermines state law and is often in conflict with society's 'norms'. The selective nature of some religious doctrines contradicts liberal democratic principles and, thus, emphasises the cultural difference between groups (Halstead and McLaughlin, 2005). Faith schools teaching creationism, abstinence-based sex education and homophobic propaganda have all made headlines in recent years, causing a backlash in public opinion and underscoring the potential for creating opposing cultural environments in faith schools.

However, Short (2002) states that school curricula should be regarded as a significant driver in preventing opposing environments. He suggests that faith schools in fact have the ability to enhance the development of cultural identity and social capital and therefore strengthen inter-communal ties. He goes so far as to suggest that when content is correctly managed faith schools are inherently more likely to promote tolerance in their students. Lawton and Cairns (2005) further clarify this by suggesting that "the important difference between societies and religious groups is not between religious and secularised belief systems, but between rationally maintained faith and tolerance on the one hand and fundamentalist intolerance on the other". Thus, the cultural hypothesis suggests that faith schools have a duty to evaluate how the interpretation of their religion and culture contributes towards creating open minds within their schools.

Secondly, the social hypothesis suggests that regardless of what is taught, faith schools serve to emphasise and validate group differences and hostilities, thereby encouraging mutual ignorance and suspicion. Lynne Davies (2008) concurs, writing that if pupils rarely meet those from other groups, then stereotypes are easily reinforced, and once this is combined with grievance there is little possibility to counter it. The character of faith schools has been accused of preventing not only the integration of pupils, but also of parents, who are denied the opportunity of interethnic mixing at the school gates. Davies (2008:69) draws attention to Rabbi Jonathan Romain's rejection of faith schools in the UK on this basis. He suggests that faith schools are a "recipe for social disaster" and states that "schools must build bridges, not erect barriers" (Davies, 2005). The social hypothesis is the basis for calls for amendments to the admissions and employment policies of faith schools. Commentators have suggested the need for further regulation to ensure that education in the UK provides an inclusive setting, regardless of linguistic, ethnic, religious, intellectual or physical circumstances.

Gallagher's third hypothesis suggests that separate schools are much less important than other factors to community division and that socioeconomic factors may be of greater influence in the interaction between faith schools, division and social disturbances. King (2010) agrees and proposes that socioeconomic reasons and the high concentration of religious minorities in inner city locations need further exploration. King points to the United Nations' Educational, Scientific and Cultural Organization (UNESCO) study of division, which suggests that structural reasons within societies cause divisions – divisions that are fuelled by injustice and fear, not by differences in faith (International Bureau of Education 112:2). Correspondingly, Barker and Anderson (2005) ascertain that the assumption of a causal relationship between the segregation of faith schools and social ills has resulted in faith schools becoming "scapegoats" for inner city problems. Meer (2007) concurs with this view, highlighting that the view that Islamic faith schools in the UK "are predisposed to indoctrinate and proselytise" (2007, p. 63) ignores the diversity of British Muslim schools, whose pupils are drawn from a variety of social and socio-economic backgrounds and ethnicities.

Conclusion

In the UK, faith schools have been significant in the historical development of the state education system and they continue to play an import role in ensuring a degree of diversity within it. When considering the issue from the perspective of fairness and impartiality, it is easy to assert that each faith has the right to their own schools within a pluralist society. The government has favoured the expansion of faith schools within the maintained sector, including the first Muslim, Sikh and Greek Orthodox schools. The push to support a range of faith schools is seen in the context of adding to inclusiveness and diversity and fostering social cohesion through acceptance and equality. The government's agenda assumes that diversity and extending parental choice will increase confidence in the state school system (Parker-Jenkins, Hartas and Irving 2005:188). Yet, the potential of faith schools to cause isolation and breed extremism has led to accusations that the government's agenda is biased towards the established religion. Hence, faith schools remain deeply contested spaces. Therefore, Parker-Jenkins, Hartas and Irving suggest that perhaps the government focus should not only be on the development of public faith schools, but "also on ensuring that such schools can provide an education that is socially just" by "displaying an openness about ways in which particular religious beliefs impact on the ethos of the school, admissions procedures, curriculum content, social learning and engagement with the wider community" (2005:188).

References

Annette, John (2005), Faith Schools and Communities: Communitarianism, Social Capital and Citizenship, in Roy Gardner, Jo Cairns and Denis Lawton (eds), *Faith Schools: Consensus or Conflict?* London: Routledge, 191–201.

Barker, Rachel and John Anderson (2005), Segregation or Cohesion: Church of England Schools in Bradford, in Roy Gardner, Jo Cairns and Denis Lawton (eds), *Faith Schools: Consensus or Conflict?* London: Routledge, 122–37.

Barnes, Philip (2007), Religious Education and the Misrepresentation of Religion, in Marius Felderhof, Penny Thompson and David Torevell (eds), *Inspiring Faith in Schools: Studies in Religious Education,* Farnham: Ashgate Publishing Limited, 75–86.

Brighouse, Harry (2005), Faith-Based Schools in the United Kingdom: An Unenthusiastic Defence of a Slightly Reformed Status Quo, Roy Gardner, Jo Cairns and Denis Lawton (eds), *Faith Schools: Consensus or Conflict?* London: Routledge, 83–9.

Chadwick, Priscilla (2001), The Anglican Perspective on Church Schools, *Oxford Review of Education,* 27: 474–87.

Commission on Integration and Cohesion (2007), *Our Shared Future.*

Council of Europe (2002), *The New Challenge of Intercultural Education: Religious Diversity and Dialogue in Europe,* http://www.coe.int/t/e/cultural_cooperation/education/Intercultural_education/

Davies, Lynn (2008), *Educating against Extremism,* Trentham: Stoke on Trent.

Department for Education and Skills (2001), *Schools Achieving Success.*

Gallagher, Tony (2004), *Education in Divided Societies,* Basingstoke: Palgrave.

Gates, Brian (2005), Faith Schools and Colleges of Education since 1800, in Roy Gardner, Jo
    Cairns and Denis Lawton (eds), *Faith Schools: Consensus or Conflict?* London: Routledge,
    14–35.

Gilley, Sheridan, and William Sheils (eds.), (1994), *A History of Religion in Britain*, Oxford:
    Blackwell.

Halstead, J. Mark, and Terence McLaughlin (2005), Are Faith Schools Divisive?, in Roy Gard-
    ner, Jo Cairns and Denis Lawton (eds), *Faith Schools: Consensus or Conflict?* London:
    Routledge, 61–73.

Herbert, Ian (2002), 'Apartheid' Fears over First Muslim Secondary School in State Sector,
    Independent, 2 April, 11.

Jackson, Robert (2004), *Rethinking Religious Education and Plurality: Issues in Diversity and
    Pedagogy*, London: RoutledgeFalmer.

Johnson, Helen (ed.), (2006), *Reflecting on Faith Schools*, London: Routledge.

Keast, John (2005), Faith Schools, Religious Education and Citizenship, in Roy Gardner, Jo
    Cairns and Denis Lawton (eds), *Faith Schools: Consensus or Conflict?* London: Routledge,
    213–21.

King, Carolyn (2010), Faith Schools in Pluralistic Britain: Debate, Discussion, and Considera-
    tions, *Journal of Contemporary Religion*, 25:2, 281–299.

Levin, Lynndy (2005), Through the Looking Glass: Religion, Identity and Citizenship in a Plu-
    ral Culture: From the Viewpoint of the Modern Orthodox Jewish School, in Roy Gardner, Jo
    Cairns and Denis Lawton (eds), *Faith Schools: Consensus or Conflict?* London: Routledge,
    138–44.

Mason, Marilyn (2005), "Religion and Schools – A Fresh Way Forward? A Rights-Based Ap-
    proach to Diversity in Schools, in Roy Gardner, Jo Cairns and Denis Lawton (eds), *Faith
    Schools: Consensus or Conflict?* London: Routledge, 74–82.

Meer, Nasar (2007), Muslim schools in Britain: Challenging mobilisations or logical develop-
    ments?, *Asia Pacific Journal of Education*, 27:1, 55–71.

Modood, Tariq (1992), On Not Being White in Britain: Discrimination, Diversity and Com-
    monality, in Mal Leicester and Monica Taylor (eds), *Ethics, Ethnicity and Education*, Lon-
    don: Kogan Page, 72–87.

Molokotos-Liederman, Lina (2000), Religious Diversity in Schools: the Muslim Headscarf
    Controversy and Beyond, *Social Compass*, 47:3, 367–381.

Monsma, Stephen V., and J. Christopher Soper (2009), *The Challenge of Pluralism: Church
    and State in Five Democracies,* 2nd ed., Lanham, MD: Roman and Littlefield.

Murphy, Alan, Learning Together (2005), in Roy Gardner, Jo Cairns and Denis Lawton (eds),
    Faith Schools: Consensus or Conflict? London: Routledge, 113–21.

Ofsted (2007), *Making Sense of Religion: A report on religious education in schools and the
    impact of locally agreed syllabuses*, London.

Ouseley Report (2002), *Community Pride not Prejudice: Making Diversity Work in Bradford*,
    Bradford: Bradford City Council.

Parker-Jenkins, Marie (2005), Dimitra Hartas and Barrie A. Irving, *In Good Faith: Schools,
    Religion and Public Funding*, Aldershot: Ashgate Publishing Limited.

Paton, Graeme (2010), Coalition pledge on faith schools, *Telegraph*, 20 May.

Pring, Richard (2005), Faith Schools: Can They be Justified? in Roy Gardner, Jo Cairns and
    Denis Lawton (eds), *Faith Schools: Consensus or Conflict?* London: Routledge, 51–60.

Schagen, Sandie and Ian Schagen (2001), Faith Schools and Specialist Schools, *Education
    Journal*, 62, 30–1.

Schagen, Sandie et al. (2002), *The Impact of Specialist and Faith Schools on Performance*,
    Slough: National Foundation for Educational Research.

The National Curriculum Handbook Department for Education and Employment (1999), https://ww w.education.gov.uk/publications/eOrderingDownload/QCA-99-457.pdf.

Weller, Paul (2009), How participation changes things: 'inter-faith', 'multi-faith', and a new public imaginary, in Adam Dinham, Robert Furbey and Vivien Lowndes (eds), *Faith in the Public Realm*, Bristol: Policy Press, 63–81.

Teaching About Religion in a Spirit of Laïcité
The Case of France

ANNE FRANÇOISE WEBER

Teaching about religion in France is strongly influenced by the principle of *laïcité*[1] as laid down in the French Constitution: "France shall be an indivisible, secular (*laïque*), democratic and social republic."[2] The strict separation between church and state is a long-term result of the French Revolution and was finally implemented by law in 1905. Education was at the heart of the lengthy emancipation process of the new republic from the Catholic Church, so it is not surprising that the teaching of religion, or even teaching *about* religion, was banned at the end of the nineteenth century.

Jules Ferry, minister for state education at the beginning of the 1880s and father of the modern French state school, promoted laws first to make primary schooling free and, a few months later, to make it compulsory and laic. In 1886, another law laid down that the primary school teachers had to be lay persons, so as to diminish the influence of clerics and nuns on the children. Notwithstanding this, Ferry also ruled that one day a week (apart from Sunday) should be free to allow families the opportunity to take care of their children's religious education. In other words, his measures were not directed against religion as such, but against the influence of the church on primary school, a public institution most important for the implementation of a new social order.[3]

Today, the constitution of the Fifth Republic not only states that the republic is secular (*laïque*), but also that "the state has the duty to organise public free and secular education at all levels". Again, as the Code of Education shows, this stance is not anti-religion. The Code states that children and young people will receive an education "that accords all faiths equal respect" and that the state ensures the students' freedom of worship and freedom of religious instruction. Therefore, the day off is maintained to give parents the chance to ensure their children's religious instruction outside the school. Primary school teachers still have to be lay persons.[4]

Although the principle of *laïcité* seems so crucial for French national identity, there is one important exception: the case of Alsace-Moselle. This region consists of three of the 96 French departments and about 5% of the population (excluding the overseas territories). Located on the left bank of the River Rhine, the region has a complicated history, passing back and forth between France and Germany several times. Following the Franco-Prussian War of 1870–71, Alsace-Moselle was part of Germany when the

---

1   In this article, I prefer using the word *laïcité,* which has a uniquely French connotation, instead of the English word laicism
2   Constitution of the Fifth Republic, http://www.assemblee-nationale.fr/english/8ab.asp
3   For an historical overview, see Baubérot (2004), Portier (2011) and Bedouelle/Casta (1998).
4   Code de l'Education, Art. L 141.

French public school system was consolidated and the law of separation between the church and the state was passed. Therefore, the concordat concluded in 1801 between Napoleon Bonaparte and the Catholic Church as well as the subsequent arrangements with Protestant and Jewish religious authorities survived in Alsace-Moselle, as did the Falloux Law of 1850, which provided for religious education in public schools. When the territory was returned to France in 1918, some local law remained in force, among it the parts concerning the cooperation between religious authorities and the state as well as those governing religious education. The special case of Alsace-Moselle will be treated at the end of this article; first, we shall trace the history of teaching about religion in France, how it is practised and what the difficulties are.

A Need for Knowledge About Religions

Despite the strong *laïcité* framework,[5] religion has found its way back into French schools even outside Alsace-Moselle. In the 1980s, concerns arose about a lack of religious culture among students. A survey showed for example that only a small percentage of the French were able to name the four Evangelists.[6] Teachers complained about the difficulties of studying historical events such as the crusades or reading works by Blaise Pascal, Jean Racine, Victor Hugo or Voltaire with students who lacked a basic knowledge of religion.

The Ministry of National Education therefore commissioned Philippe Joutard, a historian and school inspector, to write a report on teaching about religion. In this report, Joutard strongly recommended teaching more about religion in history, geography and literature classes to avoid losing a part of the collective memory.[7] In a follow-up conference, there was a consensus not to create an additional course, taught by a specialist, but to incorporate knowledge about religion in existing school subjects. The history curriculum for secondary schools was changed accordingly. But, apparently, implementation did not go very far.

In the aftermath of the terrorist attacks of September 11, 2001, students expressed a huge need for more information about religions and fundamentalism. The Ministry of National Education asked Régis Debray, a philosopher and counsellor to several French presidents, to evaluate current practice and develop some proposals for amelioration. His report, published in 2002, again called for the teaching about religion, claiming that "fact of religion (*le fait religieux*)" is part of most civilisations and that its study could give an awareness of place and time to students who nowadays live more and more in a "prison of the present".[8] He evaluated what had been done since the curriculum review in the 1990s and stated that despite some progress in the matter there were still tensions on both sides. The defenders of *laïcité* were afraid of proselytisation and of encouraging

---

5   For a strong stand on the essential importance of *laïcité* in public school, see for example Menasseyre (2003).
6   See Estivalèzes (2003) 189, n. 4
7   See Joutard (1989).
8   Debray (2002) 6.

communitarianism if religion were a topic in school; the churches and believers were afraid that if teachers adopted an attitude of relativism it would deny their faith and feelings.

Debray also opposed introducing a separate school subject, primarily because the school syllabus was already very demanding, but also to avoid a situation in which, in the absence of qualified public school teachers, external instructors could be asked to teach this subject. A large part of his report deals with the question of what kind of *laïcité* would be suitable for French public schools. It concludes that schools would prove themselves even more laicistic by combatting religious analphabetism with an impartial and neutral teaching staff. Schools had the duty to understand the "fact of religion", and could no longer act as though it were not their concern.

In his report, Debray also briefly mentioned the case of Alsace-Moselle and used it to demonstrate that the demand for knowledge about religion was not a demand for religion at school, as many students in Alsace-Moselle had asked to be exempted from religious education courses – the rate is as high as one third in primary school and about 86% in the final years of secondary school (*lycée*).[9] Debray recommended small changes to the curricula, and, more importantly, a new module in the training of future primary school teachers[10] titled "the philosophy of *laïcité* and history of religions". Furthermore, he suggested the creation of an institute focused on ensuring a better transmission between university studies of religion and teachers' in-service training on the topic.[11] Most of Debray's recommendations were put into practice, although a few years later he criticised that certain *académies* (regional school authorities) were very slow in implementing the modules. In 2011, he concluded that the question was no longer *if* teaching about religion was legitimate, but *how* to do it and how to do it better.[12]

France was agitated during these years by on-going conflicts about the possibility of Muslim girls wearing a head scarf in school – another commission again examined the question of *laïcité* and in 2004 a new law on *laïcité* in school was passed. It prohibited wearing ostensibly religious signs, but stated at the same time that schools should not be places of uniformity and anonymity that ignored the "fact of religion".[13] One year later, a report related to a new educational law highlighted the importance of teaching about

---

9   Gillig (2012) gives these figures for the school year 2011/2012: in elementary school 63.7% of the students took religious education, in *collège* 31.2% and in *lycée* 13.8%.

10   This training currently takes place at the IUFM (*instituts universitaires de formation des maîtres*); due to important changes in the French university system, these institutes might be transformed or even replaced in the next few years.

11   The *Institut européen en sciences des religions* was founded in 2002 as a part of the *École pratique des hautes études* in Paris.

12   Debray (2011).

13   Law 2004–228 of March 15, 2004. This brief overview cannot deal with the situation of French private schools, most of which are Catholic, although there are some Jewish and Protestant schools; recently a few Muslim private schools have also been established. During the 1980s, the question of public subsidies for private schools, which are free to offer religious education, was hotly debated in France.

religion as "transmission of knowledge and references to the fact of religion and its history".[14]

Religion in the Curricula

In France, curricula are issued by the Ministry for National Education, which also appoints teachers. It is worth looking at how these declarations about teaching the fact of religion in a spirit of *laïcité* have been included in curricula. This applied not only to the detailed subject-related curricula, but also to a text called the common foundation (*socle commun*) for primary school and the first years of secondary school (*collège*). This common foundation, established in 2005, defines what every student should know at the end of his compulsory schooling.[15] It embraces for example knowledge about different historical periods, including some religious aspects, and knowledge of major antique texts such as – listed in this order – the Iliad and Odyssey, texts on the foundation of Rome and the Bible. Most explicit is the point: "Understand the unity and complexity of the world", which includes studying the fact of religion in France, Europe and the world in an "*esprit de laïcité* that respects conscience and conviction". *Laïcité*, as a principle students are supposed to know, appears again, in the paragraph on social and civic competences.

With regard to individual subjects, religion appears most explicitly in the history curricula. For example, Islam is taught in the second class of secondary school (*cinquième*), under the title "The beginnings of Islam". The first lines of the first paragraph in the curriculum are revealing here: "Muslims are treated in the context of the conquest and the first Arab Empires (…)". Thereby, Islam is considered as a political rather than a religious phenomenon. The prophet Muhammad is not even mentioned here; only later is there a recommendation to use basic texts from the Koran, the Hadith or the Sunna to talk about Muhammad.[16] An interesting topic was the treatment of the Mediterranean basin in the twelfth century as part of the curriculum for the *seconde*, the tenth school year. Here, the Christian West, the Byzantine Empire and the Islamic World were studied under the title "Crossroads of three civilizations"– but this topic was dropped with the revision of the curricula in 2010 and replaced by a topic on medieval Christianity, which brought back a Eurocentric focus.[17] It is notable that religions other than the big monotheistic ones are barely mentioned in the curricula.

In general, the curricula treat religion as a historical rather than a contemporary phenomenon. For historical reasons, ethical problems are dealt with as part of moral instruction: when he abolished religious education in public schools, Jules Ferry introduced moral and civic instruction to put "in children's souls the basic, solid foundations of simple morality".[18] Throughout the ensuing decades, despite name changes and

---

14 République Française (2005) 37.
15 Ministry of National Education (2006).
16 Ministry of National Education (2008).
17 Ministry of National Education (2010), 4.
18 Ferry (1883).

sometimes the loss of the moral component, the subject alway retained the idea of an education for citizens. In 2008, moral instruction was re-introduced in primary school with the aim of teaching respect for universal values and common rules as well as promoting the exercise of individual liberty. A covering circular by the Minister of National Education explained that the principles of neutrality and *laïcité* had to be strictly applied in this matter, especially with regard to the political and religious domain: "Knowledge of the fact of religion in particular implies no debate about religious obligations or questions related to belief." [19] Avoiding such debates seems to be a difficult task when teaching six-to-ten-year-old children.

The Practice: Vague Textbooks and Insecure Teachers

Several studies show that presenting the fact of religion in textbooks in a neutral and child-adapted way is not an easy task.[20] Some textbooks fall into religious language, calling Abraham "the father of the Israelites" or classifying Judaism, Christianity and Islam as the "religions of the Book", as if other religions did not have sacred books. The choice of words is never innocuous in this matter: by always calling God "Allah" in the context of Islam, textbooks make Islam even more foreign to non-Muslim students than necessary. Textbooks that give the subtitle "Jesus Christ" to an image of the crucifixion are not neutral, as Jesus is Christ only to the Christians. In 2005, one important textbook publisher decided to remove the face of the prophet Muhammad from its textbook illustration, a move that generated a lot of protest. In general, critics deplore the fact that the textbooks do not highlight mutual influences between religions and do not encourage direct comparisons; rather, they seem to treat the sources, especially the Koran, literally, instead of placing them in their historical context.

Concerning the acceptance of teaching about religion, a European study shows that students in France are reasonably convinced that this has its place in school.[21] At the same time, a majority of students think that religion should not be a separate subject; this means that the practice chosen in the 1980s and confirmed by the Debray report is accepted among those primarily affected.[22] With regard to the teachers supposed to impart this material, it seems that they do not feel at ease with this task. A small survey of teachers-to-be shows that those interviewed do know the essentials about *laïcité* and the laws concerning religious teaching in school. They are also able to name the basic facts about Judaism, Christianity and Islam. But none of them felt properly prepared to teach

---

19 Ministry of National Education (2011).
20 For the following, see Dussère et al. (2012), Nouilhat (2011), Harang (2007), Becquelin et al. (2003) and Nasr (2001). Whereas the curricula are coming directly from the Ministry of Education, it does usually not intervene on the content of the textbooks, which are just obliged to follow the curriculum and not to contain any hate speech or other message contrary to the mission of education. It is the teachers of every school who choose in subject-specific councils the textbooks for their school.
21 Willaime (2009) 436.
22 Körs (2009) 272.

this to their students. They find that teaching about religion is a delicate matter and they are afraid of the fears parents and children could have concerning this topic.[23]

In 2003, a survey of 400 school teachers in Alsace revealed that most of them wish to have more information on Islam and that they have difficulties teaching this topic. The notion of the fact of religion does not seem very clear to many of them. They complain about facing students who are either not interested in this topic or feel overly concerned. Some teachers deplore the fact that in Alsace-Moselle, in agreement with the religious authorities, one hour a week is already allotted to religious instruction;[24] they fear religious authorities could try to influence their laic principles regarding teaching about religion. A small minority of the teachers quoted in this study still disapprove of any teaching about religion as in their view it contradicts *laïcité*.[25]

Religious Education as a Source of Political Conflict – The Case of Alsace-Moselle

The fact that, according to the aforementioned study, some teachers are still opposed to teaching about religion in school shows that some still understand *laïcité* to mean the refusal to have anything to do with religion in the public space. But this is no longer a national consensus. During his term as president, Nicolas Sarkozy promoted a concept of "positive *laïcité*" that called for a more open state attitude towards religion and religious communities.[26] With the election of a socialist president in 2012, defenders of an extreme *laïcité* felt encouraged, as François Hollande had insisted in his election programme on the separation of religion and state and suggested entrenching the fundamental law on *laïcité* of 1905 in the constitution. Although Hollande had not even mentioned Alsace-Moselle in his initial comments, subsequently he had to assure the religious leaders in this region that he would not touch their particular status and would even be prepared to include it in the constitution (although this might be difficult from a juridical point of view). Politicians to the left of the socialist party, such as Jean-Luc Melenchon, keep on pressing for the abolition of this special status.[27]

Even in Alsace-Moselle this status is no longer uniformly accepted. One point of dissent is the staff giving religious instruction. It was first supposed to be done by teachers who would volunteer for it, but as their number has decreased these lessons are increasingly given by religious instructors sent by religious institutions. In primary schools, religious instructors cannot be given permanent teacher status. With regard to secondary schools, a state diploma for religion teachers was introduced in 2000, shocking defenders of strict *laïcité*. They also protested against the procedure of exemption from religious instruction practised in primary schools in Alsace-Moselle from 2008 to 2012. In June 2012, two teacher unions and one parent federation launched a campaign

---

23   Nabor (2012).

24   This was fixed by a ministerial decree of 3 September 1974, see Gillig (2012) 305.

25   Comerro / Dieterich (2004).

26   He used this expression for example in a discourse in Rome in December 2007, see Sarkozy (2007)

27   See Fortier (2012) and Gorce (2012). In April 2013, Hollande created an observatory for the *laïcité*, a project already put forward by Jacques Chirac.

to facilitate this exemption: they critised the distribution of a form that asked parents to choose between Catholic, Protestant and Jewish religious instruction or to ask for another form to have their child exempted from religious teaching. The campaign asked for the schools to immediately include moral instruction (the replacement course for these children) as a fourth possibility on the first form, thereby demonstrating that this choice is as normal as the others are.[28] This had also been the recommendation of the Commission on *laïcité* in 2003, and was finally put into practice at the beginning of the 2012–2013 school year.[29] The Commission also suggested the introduction of Islamic religious instruction in Alsace-Moselle, a project that has not yet been realised.[30] Nevertheless, in some secondary schools the strong presence of Muslim students and the awareness of a need for interreligious encounter has encouraged Protestant and Catholic religious instructors to draw up a subject called cultural and religious initiation (*éveil culturel et religieux*), which takes different religions into account.[31] This step has to be approved by the religious authorities and every school director concerned.

Conclusion

Considering students' ongoing need for information about religion and the sensitivity of this topic for believers, atheists and defenders of a strict *laïcité*, there will certainly be more debates on the place of religion in French public schools. The maintenance of the special status of Alsace-Moselle will depend on whether initiatives such as the "cultural and religious initiation", or possible future Muslim religious instruction, will provide convincing answers to the questions raised in these debates. As the official documents quoted in this article show, the *laïcité* of the French Republic and its schools remains an important political and social issue.

Bibliography

Baubérot, Jean, 2004: *Laïcité, 1905–2005, entre passion et raison*, Paris: Seuil.
Bedouelle, Guy and Jean-Paul Costa, 1998: *Les laïcités à la française*, Paris: Presses Universitaires de France.
Becquelin, Geneviève et al., 2003: *Table ronde: L'enseignement du fait religieux à l'école*, Paris: Collection "les Actes de la DESCO", Scéren, CRDP de l'académie de Versailles.
Comerro, Viviane and Françoise Dieterich, 2004: *Bilan d'un sondage sur l'enseignement du fait religieux*, AC/Essentiel Alsace, 16, 4–9.

---

28 See Marck (2012). Gillig (2012), 307 quotes a letter from the director of the regional *académie* admonishing school directors in 2008 not to encourage demands for exemption from religious instruction.
29 UNSA Bas-Rhin (2012).
30 Commission Stasi (2003) 51.
31 Gillig (2012) 309.

Commission Stasi, (Commission de réflexion sur l'application du principe de laïcité dans la république), 2003: *Rapport au Président de la République*, Paris: La Documentation française.

Debray, Régis, 2002: *L'enseignement du fait religieux dans l'École laïque* (Report to the Minister of National Education), Paris: Odile Jacob.

Debray, Régis, 2011: *Dix ans après le rapport Debray*, Enseigner les faits religieux dans une école laïque, Paris, http://eduscol.education.fr/cid56291/enseigner-les-faits-religieux-semina ire-2011.html.

Dussère, Pierre et al., 2012: *Dossier septembre 2012 de l'Observatoire des Programmes de Manuels scolaires*, http://ens-religions.formiris.org/?WebZoneID=260&ArticleID=3674.

Estivalèzes, Mireille, 2003: *Teaching about religion in the French education system, Prospects*, XXXII, 2, 179–190.

Ferry, Jules, 1883: *Lettre adressée aux instituteurs* – 17 November 1883, www.vie-publique. fr/documents-vp/lettre_ferry.shtml.

Fortier, Jacques, 2012: *Le débat autour du Concordat anime la campagne en Alsace*, Le Monde, 1 June 2012.

Gillig, Jean-Marie, 2012: *Bilinguisme et religion à l'école: La question scolaire en Alsace de 1918 à nos jours*, Strasbourg: La Nuée Bleue.

Gorce, Bernard, 2012: *Sur la laïcité, les clivages sont nombreux en France*, La Croix, 10 December 2012, http://www.la-croix.com/Actualite/S-informer/France/Sur-la-laicite-les-clivages -sont-nombreux-a-gauche-_EG_-2012-12-10-886126.

Harang, Charles-Edouard, 2007: *Les manuels scolaires et le fait religieux*, http://hist-geo.spip. ac-rouen.fr/spip.php?article5104.

Joutard, Philippe, 1989: *Rapport de la mission de réflexion sur l'enseignement de l'histoire, la géographie et les sciences sociales*, Paris: La Documentation française.

Jozsa, Dan-Paul, Thorsten Knauth and Wolfram Weisse (eds), 2009: *Religionsunterricht, Dialog und Konflikt. Analysen im Kontext Europas*, Münster: Waxmann.

Körs, Anna, 2009: *Jugend und Religion in Europa. Einstellungen zu Religion in Lebenswelt, Schule und Gesellschaft im Vergleich acht europäischer Länder*, in Jozsa, Dan-Paul, Thorsten Knauth and Wolfram Weisse (eds), 2009: *Religionsunterricht, Dialog und Konflikt. Analysen im Kontext Europas*, Münster: Waxmann, 241–286.

Marck, Luc: *Enseignement religieux: Initiative pour une "dispense publique"*, Lalsace.fr, 26 June 2012, http://www.lalsace.fr/actualite/2012/06/26/initiative-pour-une-dispense-publique

Menasseyre, Christiane, 2003: *Laïcité et enseignement du fait religieux*, L'enseignement du fait religieux, Paris: Collection "les Actes de la DESCO", Scéren, CRDP de l'académie de Versailles.

Ministry of National Education, 2006: *Le socle commun de connaissances et de compétences, Decrét du 11 juillet 2006*, Paris, http://eduscol.education.fr/cid45625/presentation-socle. html.

Ministry of National Education, 2008: *Programmes de l'enseignement d'histoire-géographie-éducation civique, classe de cinquième*, Bulletin officiel spécial n° 6 du 28 août 2008.

Ministry of National Education, 2010: *Programmes de l'enseignement d'histoire et de géographie en classe de seconde générale et technologique en classe de seconde*, Bulletin officiel spécial n° 4 du 29 avril 2010.

Ministry of National Education, 2011: *Circulaire n° 2011-131 du 25 août 2011 relative à l'instruction morale à l'école primaire*, Bulletin officiel n°31 du 1er septembre 2011.

Nabor, Cédric, 2012: *Enseigner le fait religieux à l'école élémentaire*, Mémoire de Master, IUFM Outreau, http://dumas.ccsd.cnrs.fr/dumas-00735786.

Nasr, Marlène, 2001: *Les Arabes et L'Islam vus par les manuels scolaires français*, Paris: Éditions Khartala.

Nouilhat, René, 2011: *Quel enseignement des religions à l'École?* Le Plus du Nouvel Observateur, 4 November 2011, http://leplus.nouvelobs.com/contribution/210458-quel-enseignement-des-religions-a-l-ecole.html.

Portier, Philippe, 2011: *Ecole et religion en France (XIXe-XXe siècles)*, Enseigner les faits religieux dans une école laïque, Paris, http://eduscol.education.fr/cid56291/enseigner-les-faits-religieux-seminaire-2011.html.

République Française, 2005: *Rapport annexé à la loi n°2005-380 d'orientation et de programme pour l'avenir de l'école du 23 avril 2005*, http://eduscol.education.fr/cid47390/textes-reference.html.

Sarkozy, Nicolas, 2007: *Allocution de M. le Président de la République dans la salle de la signature du Palais de Latran*, 2007, http://www.lemonde.fr/politique/article/2007/12/21/discours-du-president-de-la-republique-dans-la-salle-de-la-signature-du-palais-du-latran_992 170_823448.html.

UNSA Bas-Rhin, 2012: *Alsace: le recteur "revoit sa copie" sur la demande de dispense de l'enseignement religieux*, http://ud-67.unsa.org/post/2012/10/10/Alsace-%3A-le-recteur-%C2%AB-revoit-sa-copie-%C2%BB-sur-la-demande-de-dispense-d-enseignement-religieux.

Willaime, Jean-Paul, 2009: *Religion im Klassenzimmer. Die Herausforderung einer europäischen "laïcité d'intelligence" und die Ergebnisse des REDCO-Projekts*, in Jozsa, Dan-Paul, Thorsten Knauth and Wolfram Weisse (eds), 2009: *Religionsunterricht, Dialog und Konflikt. Analysen im Kontext Europas*, Münster: Waxmann, 435–440.

Teaching Religion in Germany

KARL SCHMITT

Germany, a leader in the Protestant Reformation, has been a multi-denominational country since the sixteenth century. After more than a century of religious civil war, an elaborate system for peacefully regulating conflicts was introduced. One of the main elements of this system was denominational segregation by territory: within the German Empire, the respective regional sovereign was entitled to determine the denomination of his subjects (*cuius regio eius religio*). As a consequence, Germany consisted of regions in which inhabitants were either exclusively Catholic or exclusively Protestant.[1]

In the twentieth century, major changes occurred: industrialization, millions of refugees from former German territories, anti-religious policies of the communist government in East Germany and massive immigration from southern and eastern Europe, Turkey and the Arab countries transformed the traditional religious landscape. Today, Germany is no longer an almost exclusively Christian country.[2] The Protestant (31 %)[3] and the Catholic (30 %) churches have lost ground, Orthodox churches (2 %) have a presence and Muslims (6 %) far outnumber Jews (0.2 %) and are now the third largest religious group. Almost one third of the population (31 %) is not affiliated with any religious community.

Unsurprisingly, entirely homogenous Catholic or Protestant regions no longer exist. However, some of the traditional strongholds persist, mostly in the countryside, though less so in the big cities, which are the most secular areas in Germany. In the formerly predominantly Protestant cities of Berlin, Bremen, and Hamburg, Christians, irrespective of their denomination, are now a minority group. In addition, four decades of communist rule in the German Democratic Republic have left their mark: only one out of four East Germans is a member of a religious community,[4] the lowest proportion in Europe, similar only to the Czech Republic.

---

1 The only exception was the small minority of the Jews, who were tolerated in the individual German states, but gained full citizen rights only during the nineteenth century.
2 Figures for 2010. See Statistisches Jahrbuch der Bundesrepublik Deutschland 2012, Wiesbaden 2012, 65. Religionswissenschaftlicher Medien- und Informationsdienst (REMID) – www.remid.de/statistik, 2 November 2012.
3 EKD + 'Freikirchen'.
4 In the absence of immigration from Turkey and the Arab world, there are very few Muslims in eastern Germany.

Church and State: Legal provisions

As in most modern democracies, the German Constitution incorporates the principle of religious freedom. It guarantees freedom of belief and conscience, freedom to profess a religious or philosophical creed, and the undisturbed practice of religion (Art. 4 Fed-Const). Likewise, religious freedom is guaranteed in a "negative" sense: no person can be required to profess a religious creed or be compelled to perform any religious act or to take a religious oath. Enjoyment of civil and political rights is independent of religious affiliation (Art. 140 FedConst/Art. 136 WRV).

In addition to the religious freedom of individuals, the German Constitution guarantees corporate religious freedom, i.e. the freedom to form "religious societies" as well as the independence of these societies to regulate and administer their own affairs, in particular to confer their offices without interference of the state (Art. 140 FedConst/Art. 137 WRV). Notwithstanding its neutrality with regard to religion, the state may confer the special status of "corporation under public law" to particular religious societies,[5] which are, in consequence, entitled to levy taxes. In practice, the internal revenue service of the state collects these taxes on behalf of the religious societies.

This is but one example of the specifically German understanding of the principle of separation of state and church. As opposed to the French and American traditions, the German constitution requires cooperation between the state and religious organizations in a wide range of matters of common interest (*res mixtae*). Religious societies are permitted to provide religious services and pastoral work in the armed forces, hospitals and prisons (Art. 140 FedConst/Art. 141 WRV). The most comprehensive field of cooperation is the educational system. Traditionally, many state-run German universities have faculties of theology.[6] The government employs the teaching staff as civil servants and pays their salaries, but the appointment of professors and the courses of study require the approval of the churches.

Within the field of education one of the most important matters of common interest is religious education.[7] According to the German Constitution, religious education is part of the regular curriculum in state schools. It is to be "taught in accordance with the tenets of the religious community concerned" (Art. 7 para. 3 FedConst).

---

5   The competence to confer the status of corporation resides not in the federal government, but in the individual states. So far, various Christian denominations, Jewish religious organizations, Jehovah's Witnesses, Mormons, etc., but no Muslim religious organizations, have been registered as corporations under public law.

6   Six universities have both a Protestant and a Catholic faculty; thirteen other universities have departments of Protestant theology, and another six have departments of Catholic theology. For a recent overview, see Wissenschaftsrat, *Recommendations on the Advancement of Theology and Sciences Concerned with Religions at German Universities*, Berlin 2010 (Drs. 9678-10), 14–30.

7   See Hermann Avenarius, "Die öffentliche Schule als Einrichtung der Bildung und Erziehung", in idem (ed.), *Schulrecht*, 8th edition, Cologne/Kronach: Carl Link, 2010, 108–138.

The main elements of the legal provisions governing religious education follow from these clauses. (a) Religious education is compulsory in state schools[8] at all levels. In the German school system religion is, on principle, a compulsory subject for almost all students. However, parents decide whether their children under the age of 14 receive religious education; after14[9] students decide for themselves. Likewise, teachers are under no obligation to teach religion against their will. (b) That religious education has to be taught "in accordance with the tenets of the religious community concerned" determines its character. It is not religious instruction, i.e. teaching *about* religion or *about* religions, but rather an introduction to the content of the faith. (c) In order to accomplish this task, teachers have to fulfil specific criteria. They have to be members of the religious community whose creed they teach. Religion has to be taught separately to members of each community. Religious education classes thus have to be homogeneous in respect of the community being taught, i.e. they are segregated along religious lines.

In the German federal system, not the Federal government, but the individual states in the federation, i.e., Bavaria, Berlin, Brandenburg, Hesse, etc., have jurisdiction in matters of religion and education. The above-mentioned provisions of the Federal Constitution are thus not applied by the Federal government directly, but are binding norms in respect of legislation and administration in the individual states. Within the limits set by the provisions of the Federal Constitution, each one of the sixteen states is free to organize its school system and to implement the rules governing religious affairs.

German federalism is particularly relevant to religious education owing to the fact that the Federal Constitution allows for an exception to the federal rules summarized above by stipulating that these are not applicable in any state in which state law provided otherwise on 1 January 1949 (Art. 141 FedConst). This provision, referred to as the "Bremen clause", applies in three states: Bremen, Berlin and Brandenburg. Another state, Hamburg, while not claiming to be subject to the Bremen clause, has its own policy with regard to religious education. For practical purposes, we may summarize the legal situation as follows: the majority of the German states implement the mono-denominational model implied in the general provisions (Art. 7) of the Federal Constitution; four states do not, instead they practise models that deviate from the general provisions.

---

8   More than 90 % of the respective age groups are enrolled in the state school system. Attendance at private schools varies according to the type of school: 2 % in primary and 10 % in secondary schools. The majority of private schools are run by Christian churches.

9   In Bavaria and in the Saarland, students can opt out only at the age of 18.

Institutions and Agents of Religious Education[10]

The rule: Mono-denominational religious education (Art. 7 para. 3 FedConst)

Twelve[11] of the 16 states of the Federal Republic of Germany, accounting for more than 90 % of the German population, organize religious education along the lines laid down by Article 7 of the Federal Constitution. This model of cooperation between the state and individual religious communities implies a division of tasks. The state provides school organization and rooms, trains and employs teachers, sets general standards for teaching, supervises the school system, including religious education, and is responsible for funding.[12] The religious communities determine the religious education curricula, define the religious standards the teachers have to meet[13] and control the content of teacher training in state or private institutions.[14]

Religious education is taught when a minimum number[15] of students per class are members of a particular community. For students who are not members of any religious community and for those who have opted out of religious education, most states have introduced the substitute (compulsory) subject of ethics or (practical) philosophy. The actual attendance in religious education and in the substitute subjects varies considerably across states. In western Germany, a majority of more than three quarters of the students attend either Protestant or Catholic religious education.[16] The ratio of those opting out is low[17] and is largely compensated for by students with no or another religious affiliation who do attend the religion classes of the two major Christian denominations.[18] Attendance in ethics or (practical) philosophy classes ranges from 10 to 15 %. The situation in the eastern states, formerly part of the German Democratic Republic, is

---

10 See Martin Rothgangel/Bernd Schroeder (ed.), *Evangelischer Religionsunterricht in den Ländern der Bundesrepublik Deutschland*, Leipzig (Evangelische Verlagsanstalt) 2009; unless otherwise noted, figures in this section are taken from this volume. For an overview, see Michael Meyer-Blanck, Formen des Religionsunterrichts in den Ländern der Bundesrepublik Deutschland, in Martin Rothgangel et al. (eds), *Religionspädagogisches Kompendium*, 7th edition, Göttingen: Vandenhoeck & Ruprecht, 2012, 160–174.

11 Baden-Württemberg, Bavaria, Hesse, Lower Saxony, Mecklenburg-West Pomerania, North Rhine-Westphalia, Rhineland-Palatinate, Saarland, Saxony, Saxony-Anhalt, Schleswig-Holstein and Thuringia.

12 The global costs of religious education (all states taken together) are estimated at EUR 1.5 billion per year.

13 In order to get the permission (*nihil obstat*) to teach religious education in school, Protestant teachers need the *vocatio* and Catholics need the *missio canonica* of their church officials. In some cases, church personnel, who are remunerated by the state, teach religion in school.

14 Teachers of religious education are trained in theological faculties at state universities and in state teacher training colleges (Baden-Württemberg). In addition, there are institutions operated by the Christian churches. The private College of Jewish Studies in Heidelberg trains Jewish religious education teachers.

15 The minimum number ranges from five (Saarland) to 12 students (Brandenburg).

16 North Rhine-Westphalia: 33 % in Protestant and 47 % in Catholic religious education.

17 North Rhine-Westphalia: 4 % of Protestants and 3 % of Catholics; Bavaria: 8 % of Protestants.

18 North Rhine-Westphalia: 6 % in Protestant and 6 % in Catholic religious education; Bavaria: 8 % in Protestant religious education. The religious communities decide whether to admit students who are not members.

quite different. Only a minority of students attend religious education classes and about two thirds ethics.[19]

A prerequisite for cooperation between the state and religious communities in the field of education is that the latter have an organizational structure which enables them to fulfil the tasks implied in the partnership, in particular to define what their religious doctrine is and who is a member of the community and who is not. This prerequisite does not pose a problem for the Christian churches, the small Christian denominations and the Jewish community. All of them have a clear hierarchical structure and are officially acknowledged as religious societies by the states.[20]

The Muslim community, however, is composed almost exclusively of immigrants deeply divided by country of origin and theological creed and amorphous in terms of organization. Thus, except for the Alevis,[21] whose categorization as Muslim is controversial, none of the Muslim groups, let alone the Muslim community as a whole, has as yet been officially recognized by any of the states. The problem is pressing, though, as there are 700,000 Muslims of school age, who, according to the decisions of state and federal courts, have the right to religious education in school. Moreover, in the meantime, religious education is taking place in Koran schools, some of them attached to mosques run by fundamentalist sects who are suspected of instilling radical Islamism. Yet, most initiatives[22] to introduce Muslim religious education in schools have failed, as the Muslim community does not have a generally accepted representative who can serve as a reliable partner for the states.

In summer 2012, however, North Rhine-Westphalia became the first state to establish Muslim religious education in German schools in accordance with Art. 7 of the Federal Constitution. North Rhine-Westphalia, the state with the largest population (18

---

19 Thuringia, which has the highest proportion of church members among the eastern German states (24 % Protestant and 8 % Catholic), also has the highest attendance in religious education classes: in primary schools Protestants (Catholics): 28 (8) %, in middle schools: 23 (7) % and in gymnasia 32 (9) %. Cf. Michael Wermke, Religion unterrichten in Thüringen, in Rothgangel/Schroeder (n. 10 above), 361–377, 365. The attendance in religious education is somewhat lower in Saxony. But in both Thuringia and Saxony religious education attracts many young people from non-Christian families. In Leipzig about two thirds of the students attending Protestant religious education in secondary schools in 1994 and in 2003 were reportedly not baptized. Helmut Hanisch, Religion unterrichten in Sachsen, in Rothgangel/Schroeder (n. 10 above), 327–345, 334; idem et al. (eds), *Religionsunterricht im Freistaat Sachsen*, Leipzig: Evangelische Verlagsanstalt, 2012. Freistaat Sachsen, *Statistischer Bericht, Allgemeinbildende Schulen im Freistaat Sachsen, Grundschulen/Mittelschulen/Gymnasien Schuljahr 2011/12*, B I 3–5 – j/11, Dresden, 2012.

20 Until 2011, the state of North Rhine-Westphalia acknowledged six religious societies as partners in religious education: the Catholic Church, the Protestant Church, the Orthodox Church (Greek, Russian, Serbian and Romanian), the Syrian-Orthodox Church, the Jewish Synagogue organization and the Alevi organization.

21 Alevi religious education is offered in seven states: Baden-Württemberg, Bavaria, Berlin, Hesse, Lower Saxony, North Rhine-Westphalia and Saarland.

22 For many years now, pilot projects with this goal have been launched in Baden-Württemberg, Bavaria, Lower Saxony and Rhineland-Palatinate. Cf. Wolfgang Bock (ed.), *Islamischer Religionsunterricht?*, 2nd edition, Tübingen: Mohr Siebeck, 2007; Deutsche Islam Konferenz (ed.), *Islamischer Religionsunterricht in Deutschland. Perspektiven und Herausforderungen, Dokumentation der Tagung 13.–14. Februar 2011*.

million), currently has about 300,000 Muslims[23] in its school system (about 10 % of all students) and a long history of tackling the problem.[24] In the 1980s religious instruction in the Turkish language was introduced in primary schools and extended to Grades 5 to 10 in the 1990s. Islamic Instruction in Turkish, Arabic, Bosnian and German has been gradually introduced since 1999, beginning in primary school. For all of the above-mentioned courses the curricula were drawn up by the Ministry of Education in consultation with Muslim organizations and individual experts, i.e. without solving the crucial problem of a responsible Muslim counterpart.

The solution finally adopted in the new school law approved by the parliament of North Rhine-Westphalia in December 2011 had been elaborated in discussions of the *Deutsche Islam Konferenz*.[25] There is still not, as yet, a single organizational structure which can serve as a religious society. But an agreement between the Ministry of Education and the *Muslim Coordination Council*[26] created an Advisory Board that functions as a substitute for a religious society. This Advisory Board is composed of eight members (who have to be Muslims), four of which are appointed by the Ministry of Education; the other four represent the member organizations of the Muslim Coordination Council. The Advisory Board has two tasks: to develop and to approve a curriculum for Muslim religious education and to select teachers for the new subject.

Muslim religious education in North Rhine-Westphalia, which started in about 40 schools in the 2012–13 school year, is in an initial phase, since there is no curriculum as yet. It is, however, very controversial. As a matter of principle critics deny that the Advisory Board is the equivalent of a religious society and can function as a legitimate counterpart of the Ministry of Education. But there are practical objections as well. The statutes[27] of the Board provide that religious education teachers have to produce a certificate of good conduct in order to be appointed. This certificate has to be signed by a mosque which belongs to one of the four organizations represented in the Board. The Ministry of Education claims that the organizations represent 80 % of the mosques in North Rhine-Westphalia; critics assert that they represent only 20 %. Moreover, the regular training of teachers for Muslim religious education has only just begun.[28] Obvi-

---

23   Ten percent of the Muslim youth hold a German passport, 63 % a Turkish passport and 27 % a passport of another country.

24   Ulrich Pfaff, Zur Situation des Islamunterrichts in Nordrhein-Westfalen, in Bock (n. 22 above), 135–148.

25   Cf. Heinrich de Wall, Verfassungsrechtliche Rahmenbedingungen eines islamischen Religionsunterrichts, Unterarbeitsgruppe der AG 2 (DIK) 2008. The *Deutsche Islam Konferenz* was established by the Federal Minister of the Interior in 2006 as a forum for dialogue and coordination. Initially, the concept of an Advisory Board was advocated in the context of Islamic studies. Cf. Wissenschaftsrat (n. 6 above), 74–77.

26   The *Muslim Coordination Council* is an umbrella organization of four associations: Zentralrat der Muslime in Deutschland, DITIB, Verbund der islamischen Kulturzentren and the Islamrat für die Bundesrepublik Deutschland. The majority of Muslims living in Germany are not members of any religious association.

27   Lehrerlaubnisordnung, 1 September 2012.

28   The Centre for Islamic Theology at the University of Münster established the BA programme in Islamic Religious Education at the beginning of the 2012–13 winter semester. The University of Osnabrück has introduced a Masters programme in the same field.

ously, there is a long way to go before religious education can function in German schools on a generally accepted legitimate basis for all religious groups.

The exceptions to the rule: Bremen, Berlin, Brandenburg and Hamburg[29]

The four states which do not comply with the rule of mono-denominational religious education have one feature in common: they are predominantly Protestant regions, currently with a high proportion, if not a majority, of non-Christian inhabitants. Three of them, Bremen, Berlin and Hamburg, are big cities, where secularization progressed furthest in the last century; Brandenburg was largely de-Christianized during four decades of communist rule. Thus, the importance of religion in these states, in which Catholics in particular have always been and still are a tiny minority, is generally comparatively low.

BREMEN,[30] the state for which the exception of the German Constitution (Art. 141) was explicitly introduced, has a long tradition of a non-denominational religious instruction. Art. 32 of the Bremen constitution calls for the teaching of "Biblical History on a general Christian basis without reference to the creed of the churches". This type of religious instruction originated in the liberal-Protestant climate of a city that was tired of confessional rivalry between Lutherans and Calvinists. The Bible was considered to be an important document of humanity, able to foster positive ethical attitudes in the youth. At present, Biblical History seeks to convey information on a broad spectrum of religious phenomena and tries to promote a dialogue between religions. It is a compulsory subject for all students, irrespective of religious affiliation. The religious communities offer religious education classes to their members outside school hours on a voluntary basis.

Although the "Bremen clause" applies to BERLIN[31] as well, the state follows a different model. Religious education is not a regular part of the syllabus in Berlin schools, as opposed to "ethics", which is a compulsory subject for all students. However, religious communities may offer, under their own auspices, two hours of religious education per week in rooms of the school, taught by their own personnel.[32] Parents have to register their children. The state of Berlin reimburses most of the communities' teaching costs. Since very little cooperation between the state and religious communities is needed in Berlin, the threshold for access to religious education in school is comparatively low. Thus, the Islamic Federation Berlin, even though suspected of fundamentalism, succeeded in enforcing, by way of the courts, access to state schools. General attendance at

---

29 See Avenarius (n. 7 above) and Meyer-Blanck (n. 10 above).
30 Cf. Jürgen Lott/Anita Schröder-Klein, Religion unterrichten in Bremen, in Rothgangel/Schroeder (n. 11 above), 111–128.
31 Cf. Ulrike Häusler, Religion unterrichten in Berlin, in Rothgangel/Schroeder (n. 10 above), 65–94.
32 Seven communities teach religion in Berlin schools: the Protestant Church, Catholic Church, Jewish community, Islamic Federation Berlin, Alevi association, Humanistic association and Buddhist association.

Karl Schmitt

religious education is high: more than half of the youth, at least in the lower grades, participate,[33] a remarkable proportion given its voluntary character.[34]

When BRANDENBURG[35] was (re)constituted in 1990 in the wake of German reunification, it was the only one of the former east German states not to (re)establish religious education. Instead, taking into account the minority status of Christians,[36] Brandenburg developed a new, compulsory subject that combined an introduction to the traditions of philosophical ethics with information about religion (Lebensgestaltung–Ethik–Religionskunde – LER). The churches and parents' organizations objected to this measure. The conflict resulted in a compromise in 2002[37]: the parents (and from the age of 14: the students) can opt out of LER if they prefer religious education. The latter subject has to be taught if at least 12 students in a class demand it. In the 2006–07 school year Protestant religious education was taught in about half of the state schools, mostly by church personnel. Attendance is increasing, as is the number of private schools with a Christian background.

The situation in HAMBURG[38] is unique in many respects. *De iure* Hamburg complies with the rule of mono-denominational religious education as provided for by the Federal Constitution; *de facto*, however, religious instruction is interreligious. With the highest proportion of foreigners of all German states, the religious composition of Hamburg's population is very plural by German standards: 33 % Protestant, 10 % Catholic, 10 % Muslim, 7 % smaller communities and 40 % with no religious affiliation. After World War II, Catholics built up their own private school system in the city, renouncing their claim to denominational religious education in the public school system. The Protestant Church decided to develop an interreligious subject labelled "religious education for all". Under the umbrella of the Protestant Church, Christian denominations (except Catholics) and non-Christian religious communities (Muslim, Alevi, Jewish, Buddhist and Bahai) cooperate in creating common curricula, common school materials and common programmes for teacher training intended to foster interreligious learning as a basic element of education in a multi-cultural society.[39] 'Religious education for all' is a compulsory subject in all Hamburg schools and is officially provided under the auspices of the Protestant church.

---

33 Distribution: Protestant 26 %, Humanistic 14 %, Catholic 8 %, Islamic Federation 1.5 % and other less than 1 %.

34 Despite satisfactory attendance, many Protestants and Catholics resent what they consider to be the lower status of religious education in school. Attempts to introduce regular religious education (Art. 7 FedConst) by way of a referendum failed in 2009.

35 Karin Borck/Henning Schluss, Religion unterrichten in Brandenburg, in Rothgangel/Schroeder (n. 10 above), 95–110.

36 20 % Protestant, 3.5 % Catholic.

37 The compromise was suggested in the ruling of the Federal Constitutional Court in 2001 (BVerfGE 104, 305). The Court did not rule on the question of whether the Bremen Clause is applicable in Brandenburg or not.

38 See Folkert Doedens/Wolfram Weisse, Religion unterrichten in Hamburg, in Rothgangel/Schroeder (n. 10 above), 129–156.

39 Folkert Doedens/Wolfram Weisse (eds), *Religionsunterricht für alle. Hamburger Perspektive zur Religionsdidaktik*, Münster, etc.: Waxmann, 1997, 59.

Curricula of Religious Education

Since each of the 16 German states autonomous in its in organizing its educational system, and since in most states quite a few religious communities are allowed to give religious education, there is a multitude of religious education curricula in Germany. The following observations concentrate on two states as representative of two models: North Rhine-Westphalia, where, according to the mono-denominational model, each individual religious community is responsible for its own curriculum, and Hamburg, where there is one single, nominally Protestant, but in effect interreligious curriculum for all students.[40] In North Rhine-Westphalia, there are five curricula: Catholic, Protestant, Orthodox, Syrian-Orthodox and Alevi.[41]

Recently, curricula in German schools have undergone a process of standardization. At present, there is a consensus among school administrators and academic educationists that curricula should define intended learning results in two dimensions: student competences and the subject matter to which the competences refer. To facilitate a standardized evaluation of learning results, this applies to all subjects and at all levels of the school system. Thus, all religious education curricula have to describe the goals they pursue in terms of religious competences and religious subject matter – and they do.[42]

Surprisingly, the religious competences enumerated in the curricula under review are very similar, not only for the mono-denominational curricula of North Rhine Westphalia, but also for the interreligious curriculum of Hamburg. Regardless of denomination – Catholic, Protestant, (Syrian) Orthodox or Alevi – and also regardless of the type of curriculum, they all seek the same competences: the students should learn to perceive, to understand, to interpret, and to describe religious phenomena; they should acquire the capability to systematically analyse religious texts and other media; they should learn to develop their own answers to religious questions, and to advocate their own opinions and views in dialogue with adherents of other religious creeds. There are only minor differences between the curricula: the Hamburg curriculum places greater emphasis on the ability to handle a dialogue between different or even opposing religious belief systems. On the other hand, it minimizes the competence to act (*Handlungskompetenz*) by reducing it to oral and written expression (*Gestaltungskompetenz*).

---

40 Freie und Hansestadt Hamburg, Behörde für Schule und Berufsbildung, *Bildungsplan. Gymnasium, Sekundarstufe I. Religion*, Hamburg 2011.

41 Ministerium für Schule und Weiterbildung Nordrhein-Westfalen, Kernlehrpläne Sekundarstufe I, Gymnasium. Katholische Religionslehre (11 May 2011), Evangelische Religionslehre (11 May 2011), Orthodoxe Religionslehre (6 April 2011), Syrisch-Orthodoxe Religionslehre (6 April 2011), Alevitische Religionslehre (3 February 2012). The Orthodox and Syrian-Orthodox curricula are almost identical, except for provisions regarding holidays, language, etc. No curricula have yet been introduced for Jewish and for Muslim religious education.

42 For the implications of the "output turn" on curriculum theory and practice, see Martin Rothgangel, Religiöse Kompetenzen und Bildungsstandards Religion, in idem et al. (eds) (n. 10 above), 325–337; Friedhelm Kraft, Lehrpläne/Kerncurricula, in ibid., 310–323.

By contrast, the mono-denominational curricula refer more or less explicitly[43] to the ability to practise religion in all its dimensions.

The almost unanimous description of intended competences hides the fundamental difference between the mono-denominational curricula (represented here by North Rhine-Westphalia) and the interreligious curriculum (Hamburg): whether Catholic, Protestant, Orthodox, Alevi or another, the aim of the mono-denominational curriculum is to enable the student to adopt the creed of his own denomination, participate in its religious life and identify with it, all of which is, at most, a by-product of an interreligious curriculum. However, neither adherence to a creed, nor religious practice, nor religious identity can be explicit goals of religious education in German schools, since only the acquisition of particular competences is a legitimate object of evaluation.

The subject matter to be studied in religious education classes reflects the actual goals of different types of curricula much better than the intended competences do. The mono-denominational Christian curricula focus on the characteristics of the particular church (see Table 1). Whereas the Protestant and Catholic curricula present a much broader perspective of Christian visions for individual and social life, diaspora denominations like the (Syrian) Orthodox and die Alevi communities tend to concentrate very much on their canonical texts and on the language, liturgy, and history of their church. By contrast, the interreligious curriculum of Hamburg deals with general themes like the nature of man, creation, justice, God, faith and science, friendship and love and life and death, mainly by comparing the perspectives of various creeds. All curricula familiarize students with basic facts about the world's major religions. None of the curricula directly addresses political matters or political controversies.[44]

Finally, a word of caution: the curricula drawn up by school administrators and academic educationists do not necessarily reflect what is actually taught in the class room. Goals and subject matter are only loosely defined in curricula. Teachers are expected not so much to execute precise prescriptions as to follow general directions, taking the students' situation and interests into account. Thus, curricula should be read as indicators for the aims of religious education rather than as descriptions of its actual effects.

---

43 The *Protestant* curriculum wants "to make it possible to use different ways of religious experience and religious practice or to refuse to do so" (p. 14). The *Catholic* curriculum states that the competence to act refers to activities beyond the realm of the school: "cultivating one's religiosity, … participation in church and society on the basis of religious and ethical insights" (p. 15). "The competences aimed at include value judgements, attitudes and behaviour which are not susceptible to direct evaluation. Religious education should enable the faith of the students, but should neither presuppose nor require it. As a consequence, performance evaluation has to be practised regardless of the student's decision to believe or not to believe" (p. 32). The aim of the *Alevi* curriculum is to "support the development of an Alevi identity in a non-Alevi environment" (p. 9) and to "enable active participation in the Alevi community and in society" (p. 14).

44 The interreligious curriculum of Hamburg is an exception inasmuch as it provides for general discussions of social justice and ecology.

Table 1: Religious Education Curricula in North Rhine-Westphalia: Subject Matters

Catholic	Protestant	(Syrian) Orthodox	Alevi
1. Human life in freedom and responsibility	1. Finding one's own identity	1. Bible and tradition	1. God and man in Alevi creed
2. Speaking about God and with God	2. Christian faith as guidance for life	2. Prayer and liturgy	2. Alevi creed and Alevi rituals
3. The Bible as document of belief in God	3. Striving for justice and human dignity	3. Holidays in the church calendar	3. Alevi guidance for life
4. Jesus the Christ	4. The church and other religious communities	4. The church in history and the present	4. Alevi holidays and feasts
5. The church as a community of followers	5. Dialogue of religions and ideologies	5. The creed of the church	5. History of the Alevi community
6. The major religions	6. Religious phenomena in everyday life and culture	6. Dialogue with other Christians and other religions	6. Other religions
		7. Responsible behaviour under God	
		8. The language of the church	

Grades 5 to 10, gymnasium – 2012–2013 school year

The Effectiveness of Teaching: Empirical Evidence

It is a common place that religion as a belief system, as social behaviour, and in particular as a social institution has a political dimension. Thus unsurprisingly, religious education was and is assumed to affect not only religious convictions and practice, but also political attitudes and behaviour.[45] Whether this is the case is an empirical question. Does religious education function in Germany as an agent of political socialization? Does it contribute to instilling the values needed in a democratic political culture? Does it promote social consensus or disagreement? What is the effect of different types of religious education?

There is a considerable body of empirical studies on the religious and political attitudes of German youth, both at the national level and at the level of international comparison. Two recent projects focus on aspects most relevant to this article: (i) Religion

---

45   The extreme position is to view the main function of religious education as political. Leftist German educationists in the 1970s and 1980s, borrowing Marx's view of religion as the opium of the people, considered religious education to be an instrument of political indoctrination and wanted to redefine the subject as part of progressive social studies. Cf. e.g. Folkert Rickers, Die politische Aufgabe der Religionspädagogik, in idem (ed.), *Religion und politische Bildung*, Stuttgart, etc.: Calwer Verlag, 1973, 9–32.

and Life Perspectives[46] analyses religious attitudes of about 10,000 youth between the ages of 16 and 18 in eight European countries,[47] Turkey and Israel from 2000 onwards; (ii) Religion in Education: A contribution to dialogue or a factor of conflict in transforming societies of European countries,[48] financed by the EU Commission and conducted in 2008 among about 8,000 youth (between the ages of 13 and 19) in eight European countries.[49]

However, neither project tells us much about religious education. We learn that the level of xenophobia varies considerably by the religious community of the respondents.[50] About three quarters of the Jewish respondents display xenophobic attitudes, whereas less than half of the Christian respondents do. Muslim youth rank in between; two thirds agree with xenophobic statements. The least xenophobic group are those with no religious affiliation. However, the effect of religion depends on the context. Muslims living as a minority in one of the countries of Western Europe are much less xenophobic than Muslims living in Turkey.

We learn that German students consider religious plurality to be normal.[51] Many of them spend most of their leisure time with fellow students from different communities. They report, however, that the majority of their close friends have the same religious convictions as themselves. We also learn that religiosity is correlated with respect for differences. It appears that the greater the importance German students attach to religion in their own lives, the greater their respect for students with different convictions, the greater their interest in dialogue on controversial religious subjects and the greater their belief that even people who follow religions with strict rules can live peacefully together. In sum, we learn much about what students think, e.g. on questions such as whether religion improves understanding between social groups. Regrettably, we do not learn about the effects of teaching religion on political attitudes and behaviour, whether the type of religious education determines the ways in which religious groups interact, or whether it is relevant or not for attitudes like xenophobia and tolerance.

Nevertheless, there is some useful evidence on how the students and the public at large perceive religious education. First, generally speaking, religious education has a positive image in German schools. A majority of students and the public consider religious education to be a necessary subject in state schools.[52] Only one out of five stu-

---

46 See Hans-Georg Ziebertz et al. (eds), *Youth in Europe II*, Berlin, etc.: Lit-Verlag, 2009; idem, *Youth in Europe III*, Berlin, etc.: Lit-Verlag, 2009.

47 The German sample of about 1,900 respondents is not representative of the youth of that age group.

48 See Dan-Paul Jozsa et al. (eds), *Religionsunterricht, Dialog und Konflikt*, Münster, etc.: Waxmann, 2009.

49 Most of the German sample (3,500 respondents) was drawn from Hamburg and North Rhine-Westphalia.

50 Zehavit Gross/Hans-Georg Ziebertz, Religion and Xenophobia, in Ziebertz et al. (eds), *Youth in Europe III* (n. 46 above), 181–198.

51 Dan-Paul Jozsa et al., Religion in der Schule. Eine Vergleichsstudie zwischen Hamburg und Nordrhein-Westfalen, in idem (n. 48 above), 199–240.

52 Jozsa (n. 51 above), 218ff.; Anna Körs, Jugend und Religion in Europa, in Jozsa et al. (eds) (n. 48, above), 241–286. ALLBUS data show that since the 1990s a constant proportion of one quarter is opposed to religious education in state schools. In Saxony, Protestant religious education is one of the three most popular subjects in school. Cf. Hanisch (n. 19 above).

dents (one out of four people in general) thinks that religious education should not be part of the curriculum. In addition, about one third of the students interviewed in North Rhine-Westphalia and Hamburg and about one half of West Germans advocate setting aside time in all schools for prayers, contemplation and meditation.

Second, the dominant expectation is that religious education should impart know-ledge about religion.[53] Except for Muslim students,[54] three quarters of the students inter-viewed wanted religious education to give information about the major religions rather than introducing them to the faith of their own community. The understanding of the German public at large seems to be more comprehensive: 90 % expect religious educa-tion to contribute to tolerance and understanding, 78 % expect it to convey Christian values and to foster social commitment, and 72 % want it to help the students find their own religious identity.[55]

Third, there is, among students, no general preference for either the mono-denomi-national or the interreligious model of religious education. The preference for one or other model depends very much on the context. Students prefer the model they are fa-miliar with: 63 % of the students in North Rhine-Westphalia prefer the mono-denomi-national religious education they are used to, and, as a consequence, have an above-average desire to be introduced to the faith of their community; by contrast 73 % of the students in Hamburg favour the interreligious model and want information about re-ligions rather than an introduction to faith. What might be seen as a conformist tendency holds true in a European comparison as well. In Spain, Russia and Estonia, where the mono-denominational model is practised, it is widely approved; by contrast in England, the Netherlands, and Norway, countries with interreligious religious education, the op-posite is the case.[56]

Fourth, schools are only of secondary importance compared to other agents of reli-gious socialization. Even with regard to information about religion, religious education in schools ranks behind the family.[57] This applies all the more so in respect of integra-tion into religious communities: students report that the influence of their family is much greater. However, for the growing number of students brought up in non-religious families, school, even apart from religious education, is the first place where they en-counter religion.

---

53 Hans-Georg Ziebertz, Germany. Belief in the idea of a higher reality, in Ziebertz et al. (eds), *Youth in Europe II* (n. 46 above), 58–80, 70f.; idem et al., Religiosity of youth in Europe – a comparative analysis, in ibid., 246–265, 251f.; Leo van der Tuin, Do pupils get the religious education they want?, in Ziebertz et al., *Youth in Europe III* (n. 46 above), 105–118.

54 About half of the Muslim students in Germany want religious education to introduce them to Islam. Most Muslims in England and Spain expect the same. Cf. Körs (n. 52 above), 269, and Dan-Paul Jozsa, Ansichten muslimischer Jugendlicher zu Religion und Schule, in idem et al. (eds) (n. 48 above), 287–318.

55 Study commissioned from Emnid by the German Protestant churches (EKD) in 2001. Cf. Körs (n. 52 above), 270.

56 Even France conforms to this pattern. The majority of French students reject any kind of religious education and thus agree with its absence in French schools.

57 Cf. Jozsa (n. 54 above), 292.

Religious Education: A source of political conflict?

There is a long history of religious conflict and confrontation in Germany. In 1648, after more than a century of religious war, Catholics, Lutherans and Calvinists agreed to a system of peaceful coexistence between the major denominations in Germany. However, when the German nation state was founded in the late nineteenth century under the leadership of Protestant Prussia, antagonisms between the denominations were revived. But the basis of these hostilities vanished with the fall of the monarchy; the Weimar Republic was conceived of as a secular state, neutral in religious matters, but open to cooperation with all religious communities. Denominational religious education in state schools, introduced under the Weimar constitution and continued under the constitution of the Federal Republic, is a crucial element in this system designed to pacify sectarian strife.

The system has been very successful. At present, rivalries and hostilities between Protestants and Catholics are much less acute, even to the point of disappearing altogether. Conflicts between the denominations are no longer susceptible to mass mobilization for political purposes. This holds true for religious education as well. In disputes over religious education conflict is not between Catholics and Protestants, but between the two Christian denominations on the one hand and a state government on the other. This was the case in Brandenburg in the 1990s and in Berlin ten years later. Protestants and Catholics together tried to introduce denominational religious education in accordance with Art. 7 (FedConst). This attempt failed in Berlin, because, unable to attract wider support for their minority position, Christians lost a referendum. In Brandenburg, as neither side could get its way, the Federal Constitutional Court helped to find a compromise.

However, conflicts over religious education are not a minor matter of shrinking minorities at the eastern fringe of the country, but a matter of principle. This is demonstrated by another minority: the four million Muslim immigrants. Because most of them do not hold German passports, they are not in a position to initiate a referendum. But they have succeeded in putting religious education back on the political agenda. For the last two decades, Muslim organizations have been claiming the right to Islamic religious education in accordance with Art. 7 (FedConst), asking to be integrated into the German system on equal footing with other religious communities. In principle, German authorities acknowledge the right of Muslim youth to Islamic religious education in state schools, but so far practical problems have prevented the implementation.

Introducing Islamic religious education is not only the proper answer to a legal obligation; it is also the only solution that is adequate for the German concept of a secular state. "A liberal and secular state lives from prerequisites that it cannot guarantee by itself."[58] The state relies on the ethos of its citizens, which it cannot produce. A state that creates its own civil religion legitimizes itself and will end as a totalitarian system.

---

58 Ernst-Wolfgang Böckenförde, *Staat, Gesellschaft, Freiheit. Studien zur Staatstheorie und zum Verfassungsrecht*, Frankfurt a.M.: Suhrkamp, 1976, 60.

By contrast, a liberal and secular state, which respects its own limitations by guaranteeing religious freedom, leaves civil religion to civil society. Civil society, by necessity, provides a plurality of civil religions: Christians, Muslims, Jews and other creeds have their own versions of the general consensus on values.

In order to assume this role in a secular state, religions, in turn, need to be qualified to operate in the public sphere: "Religion is compatible with a secular state only when it is able to communicate, when it is willing to be questioned on its premises and when it is able to give answers ... Thus, the liberal state has a vital interest that the competence to communicate religious convictions is maintained."[59] The Christian denominations took many centuries to acquire this competence to communicate. It was the theological faculties in state universities and it was, at the level of the rank and file members, religious education in public schools which contributed most to the process of "civilizing religion by education"[60]. There is no reason to interrupt this process.

---

59 Hermann Pius Siller, Das konfessionelle Element in der öffentlichen Schule, *Essener Gespräche zum Thema Staat und Kirche*, vol. 32, Münster: Aschendorff, 1998, 123–134, 129.

60 Rolf Schieder, Die politische Dimension des Religionsunterrichts, in Siegfried Frech/Ingo Juchler (eds), *Dialoge wagen. Zum Verhältnis von politischer Bildung und Religion*, Schwalbach: Wochenschau Verlag, 2009, 145.

Madrasa Education in Afghanistan
Between Reform and Militancy

RÜDIGER BLUMÖR

Since 9/11, *madrasas*, religious education institutions, have been linked to international terrorism.[1] They are suspected of fostering fundamentalist views and training Taliban fighters. This has led to misconceptions about madrasa education in general and its role in Afghanistan in particular. The following is an attempt to correct misconceptions about the role of madrasas. The roots of militancy and violence against schools will be explored as well as the efforts by the Afghan Ministry of Education to reform Islamic education. The education policy of the Taliban movement during their rule between 1996 and 2001, and their resurgence after 2001, a largely unexplored world, is also dealt with. Although we have a rudimentary knowledge of the mindset and attitudes of the Taliban movement towards education, we are as yet unable to fit together the pieces of the jigsaw to make a complete picture.

Religious Education in Afghanistan

Religious education in Afghanistan has a history going back centuries. During the Ghaznavid Empire (10th–12th century) and the Timurid Empire (15th century), madrasas contributed to the cultural blossoming of urban centres (Ghazni, Herat) along the Silk Route. But by the nineteenth century, "intellectual and cultural stagnation" (Olesen 1995) had set in, and there were no internationally recognised madrasas in Afghanistan until the twentieth century.

The first attempts to bring madrasas under state control were made during the reign of Abdur Rahman in the late nineteenth century, and for the first time a madrasa was established for the education of administrative staff. Ever since the first moves to introduce western-oriented education under King Amanullah (1919–29) and the slow development of an education administration, the focus of discussion has been on the state control of religious education and the role of Islam in education. But in the 60 years covering the reigns of Amanullah, Habibullah II (1929), Nadir Shah (1930–33) and Zaher Shah (1933–73) and rule of Mohammad Daud Khan (1973–78) there were never more than 25 madrasas under state control. The government had no influence over most of the country's madrasas. The number of madrasas only increased with the jihad against the People's Democratic Party of Afghanistan and the Russian intervention in Afghanistan in 1979.

---

1   Malik, Jamil (ed.) (2008), *Madrasas in South Asia*, has the provocative sub-title *Teaching Terrorism?* Unfortunately, Afghanistan is not included as a case study.

Since then, religious education has fulfilled various functions. The educational facilities teach children and young people the basic laws and doctrines of Islam and train *mullahs* (clerics with no higher religious education), the religious scholars (*ulema*) and legal scholars. In the Afghan context, religious education is generally synonymous with Islamic education. Out of an estimated population of 30 million, 80% are Sunni Muslims and 19% are Shia Muslims.

Religious education at state schools is organised either within the curriculum as Islamic studies or at special educational institutions. There are at least three different established institutions for Islamic education: mosque schools, madrasas and Koran schools (*Darul Huffaz*). The terminology varies depending on level of schooling. The *Darul Uloom* caters for Grades 1–14, *Madaris-e Thanawi* for secondary Grades 7–12 and *Madaris-e Aali* for Grades 7–14. A summary of Islamic educational institutions can be found in Table 1.

Madrasas teach an Islamic system of values with specific norms and rules of conduct accepted in Afghan society. Contrary to common perception, poverty and a lack of alternative educational opportunities are not the only reasons why families send their children to madrasas. Many prosperous families also opt for a madrasa because they seek a religious education for their children; moreover, madrasas represent a value in themselves (Borchgrevink 2010).

The majority of madrasas in Afghanistan are in the Deobandi tradition. The Deobandis developed from the Sunni Hanafis in British India during the nineteenth century as an anti-colonial reaction to non-Muslim rulers. The first madrasa was founded in Deoband in the Indian state of Uttar Pradesh in 1867. Today the Darul Uloom Deoband is the second-largest theological centre in the Islamic world after the Al-Azhar in Cairo. The Deobandis strive for a purist reform Islam that seeks to maintain the purity and correctness of religious practice and faith. On various religious issues they adopt orthodox and even radical positions. Although the Taliban movement is based on the Deobandi school of thought, the Deobandis for their part do not identify with the policies of the Taliban. The Deobandis and their madrasas are principally a religious education movement that serves to strengthen religious lifestyles and piety. Strong anti-Western opinions dating back to the Deobandis' active participation in the anti-colonial struggle against the British persist to this day. By the time of the movement's centenary in 1967 there were around 9,000 Deobandi madrasas in South Asia (Hartung and Reifeld 2006). Ever since the founding of the Darul Uloom Deoband in India, relations with Afghanistan have always been relatively close, with students going to study in Deoband and with Afghan governments over the decades relying on Deobandi expertise to help set up state madrasas (Olesen 1995). Having links to the Deoband School does not in itself represent a militant position or mindset. Many madrasas are rather to be viewed as apolitical, with neither political orientation nor proximity to any militant group, and see their sole purpose in providing religious education (Borchgrevink 2010).

Many private madrasas have network-like links to Deoband madrasas in Pakistan. Many of these madrasas developed only during the Afghan jihad in the 1980s and as a result became radicalised. The politicisation of religious education is particularly noticeable in what is now a broad spectrum of political and ideological orientations.[2] For Abdulbaqi (2008) the sectarianism of Afghan madrasas is potentially a major risk. The politicisation of religious education under Taliban rule is a case in point.

Table 1: Islamic Educational Institutions in Afghanistan

	Mosque school	Traditional madrasa	*Darul Huffaz*	Government madrasa
Pupils/age	Boys/4–20 Girls/4–12	Boys/10–20	Mainly boys /10–20	Boys and girls who have completed grade 6
Teachers	*Imam* or *talib*	*Mullah*	*Qari*	Religious scholars or qualified teachers
Admission	Open to all children	Open to all boys	Open to all boys (some girls' schools)	Entrance exam
Administration	*Imam*/Ministry of Haj and Religious Affairs	*Maulawi* or *mullah*	*Qari*/Ministry of Education	Ministry of Education
Graduation/ leaving certificate	No leaving certificate	Graduation ceremony	No leaving certificate, but title of *qari*	Ministry of Education
Core content	Fundamentals of Islam	Koran, *hadiths, sira, fiqh, tafsir,* Arabic, Persian literature, logic, etc.	Koran	New curriculum
Financing	Municipality, no fees, parents buy books	Municipality, no fees, parents buy books	Municipality and Ministry of Education, no fees	Ministry of Education, no fees, books provided

Source: Karlsson and Mansory (2007)

---

2   The influence of Saudi Arabia and the Gulf States on the foundation and maintenance of madrasas in Afghanistan has not yet been the subject of any systematic study (oral conversation with C. Schetter). For further information, see Borchgrevink (2010).

Education Policy under Taliban Rule (1996–2001)

The origins of the Taliban date back to Islamic resistance to the rule of the Russian-supported communist People's Democratic Party of Afghanistan and the experience of the mainly young refugees in the refugee camps and madrasas in Pakistan. Most of the leading Taliban (Elias 2002, Rashid 2001) attended madrasas in Pakistan and Afghanistan; very few attended state schools. Some of them were also in charge of or taught in madrasas. Rashid (2001) reports on the Darul Uloom Haqqania, a madrasa in Khyber Pakhtunkhwa, formerly North Western Frontier Province in Pakistan. It was run by Samu ul-Haq, a close associate of Mullah Omar, and in the 1990s was one of the principal training centres for the Taliban leadership. At least eight Taliban cabinet ministers and numerous provincial governors, military commanders, judges and other Taliban officials completed their education there. The ideological basis of the Darul Uloom Haqqania is an extreme form of Deobandism.

Even before Taliban rule, the number of children enrolled in primary and secondary schools nationwide fell from 1.2 million in 1980 to under 1 million in 1990. Numbers at primary school level[3] then rose again slightly under Taliban rule, from 622,000 in 1990 to 875,605 in 1999. The increase refers only to boys, however, as the number of girls attending primary schools fell dramatically from 212,000 in 1990 to 64,000 in 1999 (Samady 2001). The Taliban closed most of the girls' schools in the towns and cities and forbade female teachers from practising their profession. The Taliban's justification was that such measures ensured that girls and women received the care that tradition demanded. They believed that women and girls were not safe in public. But the harsh restrictions were rooted not so much in the religious ideology of the Taliban as in a cultural clash between two different value systems and ways of life: "... the long-standing clash of values between luxury-loving urbanites and the puritanical rural villagers." (Barfield 2010).

In rural areas non-governmental organisations succeeded in running girls' schools, sometimes with the permission of the local Taliban, as home schools. The Swedish Committee for Afghanistan in 2000 maintained a network of around 600 mixed schools (all of them in rural areas) with 170,000 pupils, of whom 21% were girls (Samedy 2001, Karlsson and Mansory 2007). In December 1998 UNICEF reported that the country's school system was on the brink of collapse, since nine out of ten girls and two out of three boys did not attend school (Rashid 2001).

The Taliban made few, if any, efforts to control or develop the public education system; on the contrary, they closed girls' schools, particularly in the cities. At the same time, they expanded Islamic education and in so doing continued the initiatives begun under the Rabbani Government (1992–96). By the early 1990s there was already a move afoot to promote madrasas, introduce secular subjects such as foreign languages, mathematics and natural sciences into the madrasa curriculum and increase the number of hours of religious teaching in state schools. Immediately prior to and then during the Taliban rule, the number of madrasas rose from 314 in the early 1990s to more than

---

3   No figures available for secondary schools.

1,000 in 2001, with over 100,000 pupils (Naumann 2009). The proportion of religious teaching in the curriculum at state schools rose to around 50%.

The Taliban continued the Islamisation of the education system introduced under the Rabbani Government. However, they did not implement the teaching of secular subjects (in particular English, mathematics and natural sciences) in madrasas as there were not enough qualified teachers in these subjects. By the second half of the 1990s, just two teacher training colleges were still functioning. Moreover, female teachers were no longer able to practise and qualified teachers often chose to abandon the profession in view of the constant threats and demands made by the Taliban (Giustozzi 2010b).

Under Taliban rule, if not before, the suspicion grew in the West that madrasas were a breeding ground for militancy. As far as the West was concerned, the demand for religious education reflected a return to a stage of civilising development it regarded as obsolete. Madrasas were described as "medieval outposts" (Haqqani 2002) in order to brand the Taliban as an antiquated phenomenon.

Reform Efforts since 2001

After the fall of the Taliban in 2001, the new government and its Ministry of Education systematically promoted Islamic education to the best of its ability. It is an intrinsic part of the national educational strategy, the National Education Strategic Plan (NESP II) and the national priority programme Education for All.[4]

According to figures published by the Ministry of Education for the year 2010, a total of 171,546 school students (13% girls) were enrolled at 626 Islamic educational facilities (madrasas catering for a variety of educational needs) with 5,041 teachers (3.5% female). This represented approximately 3% of all children enrolled in school. It is not known how many madrasas are not registered by the Ministry of Education and therefore not included in these figures. One gets some idea of the total number of madrasas by considering that almost every mosque in the country has a mosque school attached to it that teaches religious studies. In 2009 the Ministry of Haj and Religious Affairs assumed responsibility for the administration of over 1,200 madrasas with more than 210,000 pupils (21% girls). It is not known whether the figure reflects overlapping in school administration or whether it includes additional madrasas with additional pupils.

For Islamic education a special curriculum was developed that includes languages (English), mathematics and natural sciences. Despite signs of an acceptance of mathematics and natural sciences in Islamic educational institutions, religious and non-religious courses are kept isolated from one another in the curriculum. In an analysis of the curriculum, Malik (2011) notes a Salafist orientation that does not reflect the traditions

---

4   Priority areas of the educational reform, which is receiving massive support from the international community, include the quantitative development of basic and vocational education, curriculum development, teacher education and improving the administration of education. A comprehensive appraisal of efforts to date was conducted in 2012 (Ministry of Education 2012). Islamic education received little attention.

of Islam in Afghanistan. In 2009 a national conference on reforming religious education rejected the curriculum. Nevertheless it remains today the only binding directive issued by the Ministry of Education. The rejection of the curriculum by Afghan legal and religious scholars would appear to be an expression of their repudiation of attempts by the Ministry of Education to take control of Islamic educational institutions.

Throughout its long tradition in Afghanistan, Islamic education has always enjoyed popular support. Religious education continues to be held in high esteem by the Afghan people, who support Islamic educational institutions through monetary and material donations. Islamic educational institutions provide free education and in some cases free board and lodging, which ensures access to education for children from poorer sectors of the population.

Violence against Schools and the Return of the Taliban

At no time in Afghanistan's history has school attendance been higher than it is today. The steady increase in the number of boys and girls attending state schools since 2002 is perceived by the Afghan government and the international community as an Afghan success story. While fewer than one million children were enrolled at schools in 2002, by 2011 that number had risen to over eight million; but that still means that over 40% of school-age children do not attend school. The international community promoted access to education with considerable goodwill and made a significant contribution to legitimising the Ministry of Education and the Afghan government.

However, this development was clouded from 2005 onwards by a tangible reverse trend. The resurgence of the Taliban movement brought with it an increase in violence against schools, teachers and pupils. In the wake of sporadic media reports, a study published by Human Rights Watch in April 2007 made reference to the increasing violence aimed at schools. On behalf of the Ministry of Education and the World Bank, CARE published a further study in 2009 that attracted international attention (Glad 2009). Finally, one year later, UNESCO published the comparative study *Education under Attack*, which highlighted 32 case studies, Afghanistan among them. If little was previously known about this topic, international public opinion was now at least informed of the worldwide phenomenon of violence against schools and of its magnitude in Afghanistan.

The Afghan Ministry of Education recorded a total of 1,153 violent attacks on schools, teaching staff and pupils between January 2006 and December 2008. These included fire and bomb attacks,[5] attacks with grenades, "night letters" (death threats) and murders. A total of 103 head teachers and staff and 110 schoolchildren were killed between January 2006 and April 2008; by June 2009, 695 schools had been forced to close. The provinces of Helmand, Kandahar and Zabul in the south and the provinces bordering Pakistan recorded the highest number of school closures.

---

5   Most of these are carried out using improvised explosive devices (IEDs). These include vehicle-borne and body-borne IEDs.

Surveys of the populations affected (Glad 2009) revealed that the Taliban and criminal groups were held responsible for these acts of violence in roughly equal measure. In addition, Glad (2009) reported that schools were also damaged by military operations of the Afghan military and the NATO-led International Security Assistance Force (ISAF), an allegation confirmed by UNAMA (2012). Such incidents are generally described as collateral damage (ibid.).

Glad (2009) offers some suggestions for the motives for Taliban violence against schools: 40% of the schools attacked were girls' schools, 28% boys' schools and 32% mixed schools. Taking into account the overall number of girls' and boys' schools, Glad concludes that 40% of violent attacks targeted 19% of all schools (i.e. the girls' schools): "… a clear sign that girls' education is deliberately under fire" (Glad 2009, 33). Moreover, according to Glad's analysis, more state schools came under attack than private schools or those supported by non-governmental organisations. Glad gives no details of attacks on madrasas. The study published by Human Rights Watch also gives reason to suppose that state schools are seen as being representative of the government, symbolic of the state and therefore a target for attack by the Taliban movement.[6] Staff and head teachers, both male and female, are accused by the Taliban of collaborating with the government. In "night letters" they are urged to abandon their profession and leave the school. The code of conduct (*layha*) introduced by the Taliban movement in 2006 specifically justifies the closure and possible demolition of government-run schools as well as punishments for teaching staff at these schools: "… If a teacher or mullah continues to instruct contrary to the principles of Islam, the district commander or group leader must kill him" (cited in Clark 2011, 14). Giustozzi and Franco (2011) consider that the growing violence against schools, staff and pupils represents a clear sign of the resurgence of the Taliban movement since 2001.

Since about mid-2010 there has been a counter-development as far as acts of violence are concerned. On the one hand, violence rose steadily from 2007 to 2011 as measured in civilian deaths. The United Nations Assistance Mission in Afghanistan (UNAMA 2012) registered a total of 3,021 civilian deaths in 2011, an increase of 8% compared to 2010 (2,790 deaths) and an increase of 25% compared to 2009 (2,412 deaths). In total, 11,864 civilians have been killed as a result of violent attacks since 2007. UNAMA holds first and foremost the Taliban movement responsible for the escalation in violence. It is thought the movement was responsible for 77% of civilian deaths (2,332) in 2011. It made more frequent use of improvised explosive devices (IEDs), carried out more suicide attacks involving civilian victims and more targeted attacks on civilians. It terms of suicide attacks alone, a dramatic rise of 80% was noted from 2010 to 2011.

On the other hand, this trend has been accompanied by a dramatic decline in violence against schools. UNAMA (2012) reports a total of just 28 confirmed attacks on schools, teachers and pupils in 2011.[7] The UN confirmed (ibid.) an almost equal number of inci-

---

6 Seen as representative of the communist government, schools had already been targets of the *mujahedeen* in the 1980s. (Dadfar 1999, 87)

7 Only time will tell whether this is a short-term decline in violence against schools or a long-term trend.

dents (24) in which schools were damaged as a result of military operations conducted by the Afghan military or the ISAF. Before considering the reasons for this reduction in violence against schools, it is useful to briefly examine issues surrounding the educational background of suicide bombers in Afghanistan. This gives rise to a hitherto unexplained peculiarity. Furthermore, a spotlight is turned on madrasas, necessitating a brief discussion of the relationship between education and militancy.

Schools as Battlefield: The Case of Andar District

In 2006, the Taliban took control of Andar district in Ghazni province, southeast of Kabul. They appointed their own governor, a district chief and an education officer. They allowed schools to remain open. However, schools were frequently closed whenever the Taliban's local power was threatened (Reuter and Younus 2009). In spring 2012, it was again reported that the Taliban were forcibly closing schools in Ghazni province. Residents of Andar district rebelled and took up arms against the insurgents. The Taliban lost control of substantial parts of one of their strongholds. The government and national and international media called it a popular uprising and a spontaneous struggle of local villagers for the right to education (see Foschini 2012). However, is it really the popular uprising it was initially taken to be?

Early in 2012, the government announced a ban on motorcycles, as it had done several times before. A comprehensive attempt to reduce the number of unregistered motorbikes in circulation may sound strange. But motorbikes are one of the insurgents' main means of transport. In April, the Taliban responded to the motorcycle ban by ordering the closure of all schools in the province. Andar was one of the most severely affected districts. Armed confrontation erupted between the inhabitants of a cluster of villages south of the district centre and the insurgents. The Taliban were able neither to resolve the revolt diplomatically nor to suppress it militarily.

In recent years, despite barely existent government control, schools in Andar district were reopened due to the exertions of the local communities. After years of insurgent attacks on school buildings and personnel, locals succeeded in convincing the Taliban of the need for education. The Taliban who decided to allow schools to re-open a couple of years ago are for the most part the same as those who today are moving in the opposite direction, thereby risking the loss of the communities' support. What is the reason for this hard-line attitude towards communities?

The cluster of villages where the fighting erupted has a history of Hezb-e-Islami presence, and clashes between armed members of this organization and the Taliban started immediately after the school ban. The development in Andar soon caught the attention of the government. Local powerbrokers linked to Hezb-e-Islami, like the former governor and a former member of parliament, both from the area, returned to try and reassert their influence in Andar after years of Taliban hegemony had forced them to remain in Kabul. Hezb-e-Islami networks were instrumental in extending the anti-Taliban uprising. These networks were able to operate because fighting broke out between disgruntled youth members of Hezb-e-Islami who had joined the Taliban and the mainstream Taliban (Habib 2012; Giustozzi and Franco 2013). The Andar uprising seems to be a conflict between Taliban and renegades of Hezb-e-Islami origin, which may explain the hard line attitude behind Taliban attempts to put down the rebellion militarily and target the civilians involved. The closure of schools exacerbated existing grievances of the local communities, which the renegades tapped into. Schools again became a battlefield.

Madrasas and Militancy

The phenomenon of suicide attacks has developed in Afghanistan over the last decade. Until Ahmad Shah Massoud, the leader of the Northern Alliance, was murdered during a staged interview by two suicide bombers from the al-Qaida terrorist network on 9 September 2001, suicide attacks were still largely unknown on Afghan soil, despite decades of civil war. When the frequency of suicide bombings started increasing after 2005, the notion that Afghans were behind the attacks was initially disputed by most Afghan observers. In a study devoted to suicide attacks in Afghanistan, UNAMA (2007) noted for the first time that suicide bombings had increased dramatically after 2005 and were almost commonplace. They had become part of the military strategy of the Taliban movement.

From the viewpoint of the bomber, successful suicide attacks require a properly functioning organisational structure for recruitment, preparation and implementation. It is possible that the Taliban movement only achieved this stage of operations following its resurgence from 2005 onwards (Giustozzi 2007).

In contrast to other regions of the world, Afghanistan's suicide bombers are pre-dominantly young people who in most cases did not attend government schools, but were educated at madrasas in the Afghan-Pakistan border region (UNAMA 2007). These findings are remarkable in as far as comparative studies conducted in other conflict situations have not established any significant correlation between educational achievement and terrorism (Berrebi 2007) or have produced results that suggest the contrary (Krüger and Malechova 2003). According to these studies, the perpetrators of terrorist attacks have a relatively high level of education. Pedahzur (2005) notes that almost 90% of the 183 suicide bombers of the Palestinian intifada of 1993–2004 had either attended or graduated from secondary school or university. No one as yet has put forward an explanation for these differences. It is conceivable that the Afghan theatre[8] – in contrast to that of the Middle East – is more appropriate for the deployment of less-educated suicide bombers.

In her analysis of the relationship between madrasas and militancy, Fair (2008) also comes to the conclusion that suicide bombers are educated at madrasas in Pakistan and perpetrate their deeds in Afghanistan. The Taliban movement specifically targets Pakistani madrasas, which provide a continuous supply of recruits. In a comparative study conducted in Pakistan, Rahman (2008) shows that pupils in madrasas have a consistent and significantly greater propensity to militant attitudes than their colleagues in state and private schools. Rahman surveyed 488 tenth-grade pupils at state and private schools and madrasas on their attitudes to the Kashmir conflict, violent and peaceful conflict resolution and the treatment of minorities and women. However, the study does not prove unequivocally that madrasas produce intolerant young people, or that parents choose madrasas for their children because madrasas convey a world view that matches

---

8   For a definition of suicide bombing and the concept of terrorism as communication or theatre see UNAMA (2007), Pedahzur (2005). Brian Jenkins was the first to use the phrase "terrorism as theatre" and explained it as follows: "… terrorist attacks are often carefully choreographed to attract the attention of the electronic media and the international press" (cited in UNAMA, 2007, 24).

or is similar to their own. In fact both are possible: madrasas help develop specific moral concepts and parents who share these concepts choose madrasas for their children.

In their study of the relationship between education and militancy in Pakistan, Winthrop and Graff (2010) come to the conclusion that madrasas are not the principal reason for the recent rise in militancy. The government is unable to meet the high demand for education in Pakistan. The resulting education supply gap is filled in part by private schools rather than madrasas. Winthrop and Graff blame the increased risk of conflict to some extent on the failure of the Pakistani government to close the education supply gap by providing high-quality education.

The transnational links between the Taliban movement in Afghanistan and madrasas in Pakistan play a role in the recruitment of suicide bombers. Afghan madrasas are generally part of a transnational network (Borchgrevink 2010). Since Afghanistan has no internationally recognised Islamic education institutions, young people often travel to neighbouring countries (Iran, Pakistan) to attend a higher Islamic educational establishment. On returning they teach at a madrasa in Afghanistan or set up a madrasa of their own. They remain in contact with their school and teachers abroad. Any attempts on the part of the Afghan government to reform religious education often encounter difficulties on account of these personal relationships and informal links. Part of the strategy of the Ministry of Education involves efforts to establish control of transnational networks through the registration of Islamic education institutions and recognition of school qualifications gained abroad. The greatest resistance is posed by the Taliban movement, which is closely integrated into international networks and has a refuge in Pakistan. Their military operations and civilian activities depend on the proper functioning of their transnational networks.

The refugee camps in the border area between Afghanistan and Pakistan were centres of resistance against Soviet intervention. Every one of the approximately 300 refugee camps was under the control of a mujahideen party. The official policy of the Pakistani government under Zia-ul-Haq (1977–88) was to ensure that madrasas were set up in all refugee camps to prepare children and young people for a life of resistance to Soviet occupation. In addition to religious education, many madrasas also provided military training. These madrasas saw themselves as a kind of talent pool for the mujahideen. Pupils were taught to regard the jihad as a lifelong mission against all infidels. The camps became hotbeds of militant political Islam. With the disintegration of family and tribal units as a result of displacement or flight, many pupils found in madrasas an ersatz family with all the characteristics of a closed community. At the same time, the madrasas in the refugee camps became catalysts for a change in cultural values. For, the war in Afghanistan brought about a fusion of the values and norms of the traditional tribal society of the Pashtuns[9] with the mindset of Islamism. The Taliban movement grew out of "Pashtun Islam" (Schetter 2002).

---

9   *Pashtunwali* is the basis of a Pashtun's ethnic identity. It is an unwritten ethical and legal code that
    forms the basis of tribal order and governs Pashtun coexistence.

Support included comprehensive military aid for the mujahideen parties, with the USA as the biggest international donor[10], and humanitarian aid for refugees. Given the scale of the protracted refugee situation[11], international support went far beyond emergency aid measures and led to long-term programmes, including in the education sector (Ekananayake 2004, Munsch 2005). In the context of the Reagan Doctrine, which declared that anti-communist insurgencies worldwide should receive international support, promoting education gave rise to some unusual developments. On behalf of USAID, for example, the University of Nebraska developed textbooks for use in Afghan refugee schools in Pakistan which featured loaded content and topics that glorified the jihad. Even the mathematics books were geared to the jihad (Jones 2011, Rugh 2012). Under Taliban rule (1996–2001) these very textbooks were approved by the Taliban with minor modifications. The textbooks were printed in Peshawar and distributed in Afghanistan. After the fall of the Taliban government, new textbooks were developed with UNICEF support, but these were not approved by the Afghan Ministry of Education. Instead, the Nebraska books were re-issued. In the absence of a new print run, it was initially impossible to provide any textbooks for pupils in the 2002–2003 school year.[12]

Micro Education Policies of the Taliban Movement

In order to explain violence against schools it is essential to understand local structures of power and coercion. The decades of progressive fragmentation in Afghanistan (Rubin 1996) became evident once again after the collapse of the Taliban regime. Rural regions have again slipped from state control. As Schetter (2007) demonstrates, local power structures range from occasional self-defence forces and public order units at village and tribal level to highly professional militias, gangs, criminal organisations and militant opposition groups. The Taliban movement is an example of the latter. Although reasons for affiliating with the movement vary, depending on the local context, it has mainly to do with maintaining local autonomy and establishing security and justice. Recently the provision of social services has played an increasingly important role. A key aspect of this is the control of educational institutions.

When the state is weak and its authority largely limited to towns and cities, in villages the school is perhaps the only state presence. Since the social order in towns and cities, and even more so in the villages, is built around personal networks, there is a tendency for any educational system based on achievement and merit to be systematically undermined. Village populations remain dependent clients in a patronage network in

---

10 US aid for the mujahideen parties is conservatively estimated at US$2 billion (Maley 2009, 66).

11 Over four million Afghans spent some time in Pakistan and a further three million in Iran. Two million Afghans are still registered as refugees in Pakistan, with a further one million in Iran. Schetter (2012) notes that the situation of Afghan migrants ("transmigrants") is much more complex than the term "refugee" implies.

12 For more on the controversy over the Nebraska school textbooks, see Coulson (2004). The debate reflects the aftereffects of 9/11. Militant madrasas – not just in Afghanistan – were perceived by the USA as a threat to their national security (see Blanchard 2006).

which services are provided as favours through connections. Maladministration in the educational system is experienced directly by disadvantaged pupils and parents as injustice and discrimination. Their expectations of a better life remain unfulfilled. Such educational shortcomings and dashed expectations are a good entry point for the Taliban. The battle for the schools is therefore also an expression of the intensified conflict between urban and rural areas.

The Islamic Taliban movement is now "by far the most powerful, best organised and most influential group" (Ruttig 2011, 32) in the Afghan insurgency.[13] The Taliban movement can be described as a network of networks. The common denominator is the recognition of Mullah Omar as leader. The networks in the four southern provinces of Kandahar, Helmand, Uruzgan and Zabul form the movement's core (Quetta Shura Taliban), but the militant networks of the Haqqani, Mansur and Khalis clans in eastern Afghanistan are also affiliated to the Taliban movement. The Islamic Party of Afghanistan (*Hizb-i Islami*) led by Hekmatyar is not affiliated, although it has declared armed opposition to the Karzai government and NATO.

Given the resurgence of the Taliban movement in recent years, Schetter and Klußmann (2011) ask "to what extent being Talib has not already developed into a lifestyle that opposes all outside intervention – whether in the form of military presence, destruction of opium poppy fields or building schools for girls" (21). This is reason enough for an analysis of the way in which the Afghan Taliban movement views education in general and its attitude towards education in Afghanistan's state schools in particular.

In their study Giustozzi and Franco (2011) offer an insight into the world of the Taliban movement and a mindset that has hitherto not been revealed.[14] The authors paint a differentiated picture of educational thinking – shaped of course by a primarily religious self-image – that fundamentally rejects western-oriented education, while at the same time recruiting pupils from secondary school (see below), and promoting various forms of religious education.

With regard to the decline in violence against schools, teachers and pupils, Giustozzi and Franco (2011) note firstly that there has been a shift in the Taliban movement's strategy towards the educational requirements of the population and in line with their demands (western-oriented as well as religious education). In short, the Taliban movement has taken up the battle to win people's hearts and minds. Whether this reveals a fundamental change in attitude towards education or whether it is simply a tactical manoeuvre beyond repression, violence and terror remains to be seen. The revised version of the code of conduct (layha*)* of the Taliban movement of 2010 contains no justification of violence against schools (Clark 2011). Two years later, in 2012, the most recent version of the layha refers to education as a right as defined by the Taliban (Giustozzi and Franco 2013). It includes a focus on Islamic subjects such as Quran-e

---

13 For Dorronsoro (2009) the Taliban represent the most powerful and effective "guerrilla movement" in Afghan history.

14 The study draws on 82 interviews, 32 with Taliban commanders, in ten provinces (including Kunduz and Takhar). It is unusual in that it makes the interviews with Taliban commanders the starting point and object of the analysis.

sharif, fiqh, hadith and Arabic. Girls' education is accepted on condition that girls are taught by female teachers and separately from boys. There are rules for the punishment of students and teachers if they violate Islam and jihad, which may include the dismissal of teachers, closure of schools and killing of teachers and students. The layha does not provide specific details; interpretation is left to local Taliban authorities.

Negotiations on the reopening of schools are part of everyday life in the communities affected. Concessions are expected from all partners in the negotiations (Taliban, local elite, education administration and schools). They may be more cosmetic in nature, such as the terminology used for institutions (madrasa rather than school) or they may concern more fundamental aspects, such as the appointment of teachers to monitor Islamic standards and values (e.g. the content and images used in school textbooks). Whether Taliban demands are recognised depends largely on who chooses the monitors and on the community's standards and values. Giustozzi and Franco (2011) also describe in detail concessions on teaching and learning objectives and syllabuses. The importance of the syllabuses is often overestimated, since their implementation has less to do with their actual quality than with the qualifications of the teaching staff. If a school has no mathematics teacher, then there are either no mathematics lessons or the lesson is conducted by an unqualified member of staff, with all the repercussions this entails for teaching quality and pupils' knowledge. In Afghanistan three out of four teachers still lack the required teaching qualifications. In such circumstances even the best curriculum is of little value.

The reopening of state schools, including those in areas controlled by the Taliban movement, is the result of negotiations between local elites and the Taliban at local level. The concessions (on both sides) depend primarily on local circumstances and the local balance of power, in particular the mindset and attitudes of local elites to state and religious education. In other words, in communities in which local elites prefer a religious education to a western-oriented one, the Taliban movement is likely to have greater success in implementing its demands.

Madrasas are a vital link for the Taliban movement when it comes to recruiting new activists. Around two thirds of the mullahs and possibly an even greater percentage of teaching staff at madrasas in the northern provinces have attended madrasas in Pakistan. There is evidence of a regular exchange between madrasas in Afghanistan and Pakistan. "The madrasas (in Afghanistan) seem to be the main source of grassroots recruitment." (Giustozzi and Reuter 2011). Giustozzi and Franco (2011) also report that the Taliban movement has just started systematically recruiting secondary schools pupils.

Giustozzi (2012) reports Taliban "shadow governments" with shadow governors in 33 provinces and in around 180 districts in 2010. In only one province in Afghanistan (Panjshir) does the Taliban movement not have a shadow governor.[15] There have been reports of activities involving education commissions in four provinces (Ghazni, Paktika, Kunar and Kunduz). In Chahar Dara, a district in Kunduz province, the Taliban movement more or less completely controlled security, justice and school administra-

---

15   Ruttig (2011) maintains the Taliban movement has "the structures of a parallel government" in all 34 provinces (32).

tion from 2009 to 2010. The state curricula remained in place and English and natural sciences were taught. Boys' schools remained open and girls' schools were closed, as in the 1990s. A few non-governmental organisations, such as the Swedish Committee for Afghanistan, were allowed to support schools.

In 2007 the Taliban movement announced the establishment of its own madrasas in six provinces (Kandahar, Zabul, Uruzgan, Helmand, Nimroz and Farah). For this US$1 million was provided, according to reports in the media. It is thought these funds were used to print the aforementioned textbooks used at the time of Taliban rule

Setting up education commissions in local shadow governments, ensuring these operate effectively and establishing and maintaining its own madrasas requires a great deal of energy and resources on the part of the Taliban. It needs long-term plans to set up and strengthen madrasas. The Taliban movement is able to integrate an education commission into its quasi-governmental parallel structures and in so doing take (partial) control of state and religious schools. This development gives some idea of the potential of the Taliban movement in the educational sector, while simultaneously demonstrating the need for popular support if it is to implement its ideas. While there is reason to believe that the Taliban movement has learned from its aggressive strategy towards schools, it is not yet clear to what extent it has gained legitimacy from this change in strategy. To the extent the Taliban movement is hostile to state schools, it no longer has much sympathy among the population (Giustozzi 2012). But it is able to implement its ideas through coercive measures and present these to the population as an alternative or even as the only educational option. In the view of Giustozzi (2012), the Taliban movement is in a position to establish a local monopoly of violence. Education plays an important role in legitimisation. But it remains to be seen whether this monopoly of violence can be maintained or even developed in the long term.

As yet nothing has been published on violence against vocational schools or higher educational institutions. In his study on militancy at universities in Afghanistan, Giustozzi (2010a) reports on sympathisers among university students for the various groups in the Afghan insurgency. The litmus test for the Taliban movement will be vocational and university education.[16] Put simply, the question is whether the Taliban can imagine producing engineers and doctors consistent with their educational ideology. What concessions are they willing to make?

By establishing shadow governments, the Taliban movement is now in a position to challenge the government in the civil domain. On the one hand, there is the weak Karzai government with its claim to modernisation; on the other, the Taliban movement and its self-professed furtherance of the Islamic Emirate of Afghanistan. But which one will provide the better educational services in the view of the people?

---

16 In the 1960s and 1970s the University in Kabul was one of the centres of a growing Islamist movement made up primarily of university professors and the militant Muslim Youth with their own *shura* (council) (Roy 1990). The Islamists were committed to an Islamic legitimation of statehood. Prominent Islamists such as Rabbani and Sayyaf were professors in the Faculty of Theology at the University in Kabul. Rabbani was president of the shura from 1972 and Sayyaf was his deputy. Hekmatyar was a student at the University in Kabul and in 1975 became First Secretary for the Muslim Youth. Later all three were leaders of various mujahedeen parties.

Since 9/11, the militant Islam of the Taliban movement has taken up the fight against every external influence. It symbolises the fight against the modern world, the western state model and the West in general. In day-to-day life there has been a return to local value systems and norms, with the result that radical, tribal and very moderate mindsets exist alongside one another.

On the one hand, the version of Islam practised by the Taliban lays claim to immutability; the Taliban see Islam as a final and perfect revelation. But social change is taking place so rapidly that the gulf between religious dogma and reality is growing ever wider. Not even the Taliban have been left unmarked by the crisis in religion. Their radicalism is perhaps also an expression of their refusal to separate religious life from everyday social routines. Their vision and practical implementation of education reflects both this crisis and this radicalism.

Bibliography

Abdulbaqi, Misbah (2008), Madrassahs in Afghanistan: Evolution and its Future, in *Policy Perspectives*, Special Issue Afghanistan

Barfield, Thomas (2010), *Afghanistan. A Cultural and Political History*, Princeton

Berrebi, Claude (2007), Evidence about the Link between Education, Poverty, and Terrorism among Palestinians, in *Peace Economics, Peace Science, and Public Policy*, 13:1, 1–38

Blanchard, Christopher M. (2006), *Islamic Religious Schools, Madrasas: Background*, Congress Research Service Report for Congress, Order Code RS21654

Borchgrevink, Kaja (2010), *Beyond Borders: Diversity and Transnational Links in Afghanistan Religious Education*, Peace Research Institute Oslo (PRIO) Paper, Oslo

Clark, Kate (2011), *The Layha: Calling the Taleban to Account*, Afghanistan Analyst Network Thematic Report 6/2011

Coulson, Andrew (2004), Education and Indoctrination in the Muslim World. Is there a Problem? What Can We Do about it?, in *Policy Analysis*, No. 511

Dadfar, Azam (1999), Psychosozialer Hintergrund des Krieges in Afghanistan, in Conrad Schetter and Almut Wieland-Karimi (eds.), *Afghanistan in Geschichte und Gegenwart*, Frankfurt, 79–108

Dorronsoro, Gilles (2009), *The Taliban's Winning Strategy in Afghanistan*, Carnegie Endowment for International Peace, Washington DC

Ekanayake, S.B. (2004), *Education in the Doldrums. Afghan Tragedy*, Peshawar, second edition

Elias, Barbara (2002), *The Taliban Biography. Documents on the Structure and Leadership of the Taliban 1996–2002*, The National Security Archive, Electronic Briefing Book No. 295

Fair, C. Christine (2008), *The Madrasah Challenge. Militancy and Religious Education in Pakistan*, Washington

Foschini, Fabrizio (2012), *The Battle for Schools in Ghazni – or, Schools as Battlefield*, The Afghanistan Analyst Network

Giustozzi, Antonio and Claudio Franco (2013), *The Taleban and the Schools*, Afghanistan Analyst Network, forthcoming

Giustozzi, Antonio (2012), Hearts, Minds, and the Barrel of a Gun. The Taliban's Shadow Government, in *Prism 3*, 2, 71–80

Giustozzi, Antonio and Claudio Franco (2011), *The Battle for the Schools. The Taleban and State Education*, Afghanistan Analyst Network Thematic Report 8/2011

Giustozzi, Antonio and Christoph Reuter (2011), *The Insurgents of the Afghan North*, Afghanistan Analyst Network Thematic Report 4/2011

Giustozzi, Antonio (2010a), *Between Patronage and Rebellion. Student Politics in Afghanistan*, Afghanistan Research and Evaluation Unit Briefing Paper Series

Giustozzi, Antonio (2010b), *Nation–Building is not for All. The Politics of Education in Afghanistan*, Afghanistan Analyst Network Thematic Report 02/2010

Giustozzi, Antonio (2007), *Koran, Kalashnikov and Laptop. The Neo-Taliban Insurgency in Afghanistan*, London

Glad, Marit (2009), *Knowledge under Fire: Attacks on Education in Afghanistan*, CARE

Habib, Emal (2012), *Who fights whom in the Andar Uprising (Part 1), The Andar Uprising – Has the Tide Already Turned? (Part 2)*, The Afghanistan Analyst Network

Hartung, Jan-Peter and Helmut Reifeld (2006), *Islamic Education, Diversity, and National Identity*, New Delhi

Haqqani, Husain (2002), Islam's Medieval Outposts, in *Foreign Policy*

Jones, Adele M.E. (2011), The Politics of "Peace" Curricula in Afghanistan, in Heribert Weiland, Kerstin Priwitzer and Joschka Philipps (eds.), *Education in Fragile Contexts. Government Practices and Challenges*, Freiburg i. Br.

Karlsson, Pia and Amir Mansory (2007), *An Afghan Dilemma: Education, Gender and Globalisation in an Islamic Context*, Stockholm

Krueger, Alan B. and Jitka Maleckova (2003), Education, Poverty, and Terrorism: Is there a Causal Connection? in *Journal of Economic Perspectives* 17:4, 119–144

Maley, William (2009), *The Afghanistan Wars*, New York, second edition

Malik, Jamal (2008) (ed.), *Madrasas in South Asia. Teaching Terror?* London and New York

Malik, Jamal (2011), *Madrasa-Reform in Afghanistan*, GIZ, unpublished manuscript

Ministry of Education (2012), *Education Joint Sector Review*, 1391/2012. Main Report, Kabul

Munsch, Holger (2005), Case Study: Basic Education for Afghan Refugees (1990–2004), in *Basic Education for Refugees and Displaced Populations*, Deutsche Gesellschaft für Technische Zusammenarbeit, Eschborn

Naumann, Craig C (2009), *Books, Bullets, and Burqas. Anatomy of a Crisis – Educational Development, Society, and the State in Afghanistan*, Milton Keynes

Olesen, Asta (1995), *Islam and Politics in Afghanistan*, Surrey

Pedahzur, Ami (2005), *Suicide Terrorism*, Cambridge

Rahman, Tariq (2008); Madrasas: The Potential for Violence in Pakistan? in Jamil Malik (ed.), *Madrasas in South Asia. Teaching Terror?* London and New York, 61–84

Rashid, Ahmed (2001), *Taliban. Afghanistans Gotteskrieger und der Dschihad*, Munich, third edition

Reuter, Christoph, Borhan Younus (2009), The Return of the Taliban in Andar District, in Antonio Giustozzi (ed.), *Decoding the New Taliban*, New York, p. 101–118

Roy, Olivier (1990), *Islam and Resistance in Afghanistan*, Cambridge, second edition

Rubin, Barnett R. (1996), *The Fragmentation of Afghanistan*, Lahore

Rugh, Andrea B. (2012), *International Development in Practice. Education Assistance in Egypt, Pakistan, and Afghanistan*, New York

Ruttig, Thomas (2011), Elastisch und stabil: Organisationsstrukturen und Ideologie der afghanischen Taliban, in Conrad Schetter and Jörgen Klußmann (eds.), *Der Taliban-Komplex. Zwischen Aufstandsbekämpfung und Militäreinsatz*, Frankfurt, 31–55

Samady, Saif R. (2001), *Education and Afghan Society in the Twentieth Century*, UNESCO Paris

Schetter, Conrad (2012), Translocal Lives. Patterns of Migration in Afghanistan, in: *Crossroads Asia* Working Paper Series, No. 2

Schetter, Conrad and Jörgen Klußmann (2011), Introduction, in Conrad Schetter and Jörgen Klußmann (eds.), *Der Taliban-Komplex. Zwischen Aufstandsbekämpfung und Militäreinsatz*, Frankfurt, 9–28

Schetter, Conrad (2007), Lokale Macht- und Gewaltstrukturen in Afghanistan, in *Aus Politik und Zeitgeschichte*, 39, 3–10

Schetter, Conrad (2002), Paschtunwali oder Islam? Kultureller Wertewandel im Afghanistan-krieg, in *Interkulturell,* 3/4, 82–109

United Nations Assistance Mission to Afghanistan (UNAMA) (2007), *Suicide Attacks in Afghanistan (2001–2007),* Kabul

United Nations Assistance Mission to Afghanistan (UNAMA) (2012), *Annual Report 2011. Protection of Civilians in Armed Conflict*, Kabul

Winthrop, Rebecca and Corinne Graff (2010), *Beyond Madrasas. Assessing the Links between Education and Militancy in Pakistan*, Center for Universal Education at Brookings, Working Paper 2

Policies and Politics of Teaching Religion in India

SHREYA PARIKH

At the time of India's independence, the policies governing the relationship between religion and the state were never defined; it was hoped that they would evolve in the post-independence period. Hence, India started out as an independent state whose attitude to religion was neutral. Jawaharlal Nehru, the first prime minister of independent India, set out to create a nation-state along the lines of modernization theory: by modernizing through economic transformation primordial sentiments would be erased in a long run. This theory was popular among the elites of Third World who came to power when their countries gained independence and sought to build an over-arching sentiment of nationalism for the new nation-state that had emerged when the colonizers departed. This sentiment was to link identity at the individual level with the state, which was to be developed though bureaucratic rationality and developments in science and technology.

The lack of a policy governing the relationship between the state and religion in India led to the birth of nationalist movements, especially under the rule of Bharat Janta Party (BJP) and the influence of Shiv Sena, which represented the Hindu nationalist agenda. These parties filled the void created by the need to voice religious opinion in a political domain. 'Saffronisation' of Indian history took place under the right-wing Hindu nationalists, who rewrote high-school history textbooks.[1] In the provinces governed by the BJP, schools were set up with the aim of promoting the Hindu nationalist agenda. Policies governing the role of religion in education were defined under British rule and these clauses were included in the Indian constitution with little or no amendment. These policies remain vague and leave room for various misinterpretations. This paper discusses the implementation and the political implications of these policies regarding religious education as indicated by the Constitution of India at the central and provincial level. I shall then take Gujarat, a province that has been under BJP rule since 1995, as a case study to demonstrate that the current central government has no control over education about religion. I shall analyse how this has led to the absence of a dichotomy between religious education and religion in education and, hence, incited controversies regarding the presentation of education in religion and education about religion.

---

1   Mushirul Hasan, The BJP's intellectual agenda: Textbooks and imagined history, *South Asia: Journal of South Asian Studies*, 25:3, 200.

The Constitution and the Teaching of Religion

Historically, religion has underpinned civilization's development in India. Religion was a way of life, and people did not consciously separate the transmission of knowledge from religion. Historically, the Brahmins (i.e. religious priests, who belong to the highest caste in Hinduism) were responsible for education and imparting knowledge. Hence, the dichotomy between education and religion did not exist. The British East India Company established itself in India in eighteenth century and subsequently took charge of the administration of Greater India. This period saw the development of state neutrality towards religion in that it did not interfere in the transmission of religious education if the core curriculum followed by the school or institution was secular in nature. Hence, the school or the institution was free to teach the religion of its choice in addition to the state-regulated curriculum, provided that religious education was not forced. This view of neutrality is still policy in post-colonial India and continues to govern policies regarding the contemporary system of education.

The British came to India as traders. But they were increasingly involved in the administration of larger populations of native Indians through the land they won by war or arbitration of conflicts between states. Hence, they built schools mostly to create Indian bureaucrats who could facilitate their administration. Contrary to the popular myth, the British had no intention of spreading Christianity, and the East India Company tried to revive the Islamic and Hindu learning by helping to establish *madrassas* and centres for Hindu scripture studies until the late eighteenth century.[2] But in the early nineteenth century, following the first wave of the Industrial Revolution, Britain experienced renewed interest in Christianity. In 1793 the House of Commons in Britain passed a resolution saying:

> "It is the peculiar and bounden duty of the British legislature to promote by all just and prudent means the interest and happiness of the inhabitants of the British Dominions in India; and that for these ends such forces ought to be adopted as may gradually tend to their advancement in useful knowledge and to their religious and moral improvement."[3]

The neglect of education led the Company to tolerate missionaries. Subsequently, the aforementioned clause was supplemented by the following:

> "In the furtherance of the above objects sufficient facilities shall be afforded by law to persons desirous of going to, or remaining in, India for the purpose of accomplishing those benevolent designs."[4]

The need for 'religious and moral improvement' mentioned in the first clause indicates the belief that Christianity was superior to Hinduism and Islam, which, it was claimed, were full of superstition. This was used to increase the number of missionary schools, which began to compete with the Company-run schools. The Company-run schools

---

2   Malikail, Joseph S., State Policies on Religious and Moral Education in India 1765–1858, *Paedagogica Historica: International Journal of the History of Education*, 13:2, 454; http://dx.doi.org/10.1080/00 30923730130206.

3   Malikail, Joseph S., 456.

4   Malikail, Joseph S., 460.

used a modern and enlightened approach without reference to the Bible, unlike the missionary schools, and, hence, were more popular among the growing number of Indians who looked on this education as a source of social mobility. This produced an Indian elite class that lost its native religious beliefs, which the missionaries argued posed a serious threat to Indian development since it produced knowledge that was not bound by any religious principles. Threatened by the popularity of the Company-run schools, the missionaries asked the Company to leave the task of education to them: instead of investing in its own educational system, the Company should give grants to the missionaries. The Company, which at this point was already looking to lower its public expenditures, accepted this alliance.

This system of education developed during the Industrial Revolution, which led to the birth of a class structure based on capital. Hence, conversion to Christianity became popular especially amongst the lower classes in the Indian caste system, who saw Christianity as a way to enter the British bureaucracy. Religion became a form of social mobility for this population. This concept of accessing white-collar jobs through the blind pursuit of westernized education continued to mentally colonize India, a form of pseudo-colonization. 'Enlightened' education competed with the traditional idea of the importance of spiritual pursuits or *dharma*.

Today, India, according to its Constitution, is a secular country. Its position on the question of the role of religion in education, like the question on the role of religion within other public institutions, has been one of neutrality. India's attitude towards religious education is best reflected in Article 28 of the Constitution:[5]

1. No religious instruction shall be provided in any educational institution wholly maintained out of State funds.

2. Nothing in clause 1 shall apply to an educational institution which is administered by the State but has been established under any endowment or trust which requires that religious instruction shall be imparted in such institution.

3. No person attending any educational institution recognized by the State or receiving aid out of State funds shall be required to take part in any religious instruction that may be imparted in any such institution or to attend any religious worship that may be conducted in such institution or in any premises attached thereto unless such person, or if such person is a minor, his guardian has given his consent thereto.

These three clauses in Article 28 should be read in conjunction with Article 30, which states:[6]

1. All minorities whether based on religion or language shall have the right to establish and administer educational institutions of their choice.

---

5   Malikail, Joseph S., S. 446.
6   Malikail, Joseph S., 446.

2. The State shall not, in granting aid to educational institutions, discriminate against any educational institution on the ground that it is under the management of a minority, whether based on religion or language.

These clauses do not define the term 'religious education' and there is no real policy on education about religion in schools. Moreover, the state cannot police the content of books used for religious education; nor are there any independent institutions to oversee this task. Hence, the objectivity of the curriculum remains debated, along with the process of recruitment of teachers for teaching subjects related to religion.

Politics of Teaching Religion in India

Today, India is the world's most populous democracy. India has succeeded in presenting itself as a state in spite of the existence of multiple nations. Through the chaos of multiple languages and cultures runs the thread of Indian identity. This indicates that the state of India has established a certain legitimacy among its people through a set of shared values that the state disseminates through its institutions, education being one of them.

India as a state is governed by laws and India as a nation is governed by norms. The norms are derived from popular culture, or the Hindu culture that binds social behaviour and defines roles for individuals within a community. Hinduism developed as a way of thought, a development which can be traced back to the Indus Valley civilization that flourished in the region in the Neolithic.[7] The Hindu way of thought has had and continues to have a direct effect on the social and political environment of India. Despite the waves of conversions to Islam and Christianity during the Mughal Empire and British Empire, respectively, popular culture retains a Hindu flavour.

By religion the Indian population is 80.5% Hindu, 13.4% Muslim and 2.3% Christian.[8] To be able to understand the anthropological context of India, it is important to see Hinduism as a culture, as a mould that defines both the methodology of thought at the individual or microlevel and the social norms governing society at the macrolevel. Be it mosques that look like temples, or Hindu women praying at Sheikh Nizamuddin's tomb in Delhi or churches in South India that host gospels that sing to Bollywood beats: Hindu culture is the mould for the different religions that India has absorbed.

The dichotomy between religion and education was defined and crystallized during British rule in India, the period which saw the introduction of the British educational system so as to create the bureaucracy needed to run the administration in the wake of the Industrial Revolution. This introduction was preceded by the introduction of capitalism as India's trade with Britain and Europe grew. Hence, this period brought not

---

7   Flood, Gavin, History of Hinduism, *BBC News*, 24 August 2009, web, 9 November 2012 http://ww w.bbc.co.uk/religion/religions/hinduism/history/history_1.shtml.

8   Central Intelligence Agency, The World Factbook, *Central Intelligence Agency*. United States of America, web, 6 November 2012, https://www.cia.gov/library/publications/the-world-factbook/ge os/in.html.

only the top-down process of religion-state dichotomy, but also a shift from the pursuit of spiritual goals to the pursuit of material goals as the end of education.

Jawaharlal Nehru, in the post-independence period, followed modernization theory, which attempted to define religion as an obstacle to progress – a Marxist thought that was popular among the elites that governed in the newly independent states in the Third World. In the wake of the violence that followed the partitioning of Greater India between India and Pakistan, talk about religion in politics was a sensitive issue. Hence, Nehru attempted to avoid defining the relationship between the state and religion by emphasizing ideas about legality, economic development and rationality. The scholars in this period were hopeful that with time primordial sentiments like religion, caste and sect would diminish as India entered the brave new world.[9] Yet, religion in India has traditionally defined human relations and the rules governing their interaction, i.e. was essentially social rather than individual. This is still true today, especially as the implementation of the secular idea has been a top-down process and the ideological spread of secularism has not been underpinned by building institutions that administer the implementation and supervision of secular principles.

The lack of institutions is observed in education in both urban and rural India. The absence of policies governing education in religion and about religion has resulted in a lack of structure and uniformity in this field in urban and rural areas. Furthermore, since the provision of education falls largely within the remit of the provinces, the nature of teaching religion continues to be defined by the party in power in a specific province. To provide some idea of the politics of teaching religion in India, I shall take the case of Gujarat, a province located in the west of India.

Politics of Teaching Religion: The case of Gujarat

Gujarat is a province with a population of around 60,383,628 (2011 census). Around 42.6% of the total population is urban and 57.4% rural.[10] About 9% of this population is Muslim (2001 census of India). The state has been under the rule of BJP since 1995, a party that later split under Keshubahi Patel, who formed Gujarat Parivartan Party (GPP). Hence, the major opposition parties in Gujarat are also derivatives of BJP and push the Hindu agenda.[11] This has led the Congress Party, the current ruling party in India, to put forward a centre-right agenda to win votes in Gujarat instead of sticking to the secularist agenda that it has promoted since it was founded. Gujarat has also been prone to communal riots between Hindus and Muslims, the most recent being in 2002.[12] This has

9   Mitra, Subrata Kumar, Desecularising the State: Religion and Politics in India after Independence, *Comparative Studies in Society and History*, 33:4, 774.
10   State Profile, *Gujarat State Portal*, State of Gujarat, web, 13 December 2012.
11   Desai, Darshan, Modi's Bete Noire, Keshubhai, Projects Himself as the Alternative, *The Hindu*, 6 November 2012, web, 13 December 2012.
12   Biswas, Soutik, India Godhra Train Blaze Verdict: 31 Convicted, *BBC News*, 22 February 2011, web, 13 December 2012.

led religion to become a topic of debate in Gujarat, making it impossible for the government to pursue objective policies on religion.

The government of Gujarat has its own separately designed curriculum for education, which is overseen by the Education Department. The Gujarat Secondary and High Secondary Education Board is responsible for examinations and certifications, while the Gujarat State School Textbook Board administers the content of the curriculum.[13] The government does not make any provision for education about or in religion through these institutions, nor are there any provisions to set up institutions to administer and make recommendations regarding policies on education. Yet, BJP has tried to promote its Hindu nationalist agenda through history textbooks, over whose content it has direct control. Ideological manipulation through a biased presentation of history leaves no space for analytical introspection. This should be considered in the context of the Indian education system, which encourages students to memorize the information presented in textbooks rather than question the content.[14] One of the anti-minority statements present in the social science textbook reads as follows:

> "Making full use of Muslim fanaticism, Osama Bin Laden organized die-hard Muslims and founded the International Jihad Organization in the name of the Jehedi movement."[15]

The growth of cities and the urban middle class in India has not necessarily led to secularism replacing the religious nature of the institutions, since in most cases caste continues to play a leading role in commercial and professional interactions. Gujarat has seen an increase in urbanization, yet the growth in urbanism among the inhabitants remains low. Here urbanization can be defined as the structure of creating an urban arrangement through economic development and modernization, and urbanism as a "qualitative change in people's outlook, behavioural patterns, and the organizational networks which they create and participate in", according to Saad E.M. Ibrahim.[16] Religious identities continue to play an important role in the dynamics of formal and informal relations in the population in spite of the spread of urbanization in Gujarat. This can be demonstrated in the case of educational institutions and their nature at an urban level.

Public schools run by the local municipality, missionary schools, semi-private and private schools are the main categories of schools in the urban and semi-urban parts of Gujarat. The rhetoric of education in every municipal school depends on the popular religion or caste in the region. For example, the municipal schools in the Muslim majority areas tend to have a rather pro-Islam rhetoric to balance the Hindu nationalist agenda propagated in textbooks. They have lessons in Urdu or Arabic and teachers are attached to specific mosques in the region. On the other hand, municipal schools in Hindu ma-

---

13 Gujarat State Board for School Textbooks, Education Department, Government of Gujarat, n.d., web, 13 December 2012.

14 A, Deepa, *India Together: Gujarat's Textbooks: Full of Biases and Errors*, 19 February 2007, web, 13 December 2012.

15 *Social Studies Text Book: Standard 5 and Standard 9*, Government of Gujarat, n.p.n.d., n. pag.; *India Together: Gujarat's Textbooks: Full of Biases and Errors*, 19 February 2007, web, 13 December 2012.

16 Ibrahim, Saad Eddin, Over-Urbanization and Under-Urbanism: The Case of the Arab World, *International Journal of Middle East Studies*, 6:1, 29–45.

jority areas tend to emphasize the learning of Sanskrit, with classes preceded by prayer assemblies and yoga sessions. Missionary schools, on the other hand, are important for presenting the Christian minority agenda. Established in India at the time of British rule, they became linked with upward social mobility for the elites of post-independence India. This view still persists, with parents of Hindu or Muslim affiliation opting to send their children to these schools in spite of the rumours that these schools attempt to brainwash and convert their students. Admission to missionary schools is competitive or through payment of special 'donation' fees, whereby an exception is made for Christian students. The school day starts with prayers that begin with 'Oh Lord' and end with 'Amen'. Catechism is offered to the Christian students for about two hours every week, in which time the non-Christian students take a class on ethics called Moral Science. Instead of being analytical, the books used in this class preach morals based on the Biblical idea of 'good and evil', where anecdotes and fables are recounted from the Bible to substantiate the importance of 'God' and 'good' morals. The idea of non-belief is not accommodated in the class, and atheism is taboo. Semi-private and private schools are usually affiliated to a religious institution or a body linked to a certain caste or sect. For example, Vishwa Bharati schools, which are found all over India, advocate a strong Hindi culture through Hindu nationalist agenda to attract and recruit Hindu students. SGVP International, a boarding school, has been established in Ahmedabad by an institution run by the followers of Shri Swaminarayan, viz. Shri Swaminarayan Gurukul, which describes itself as an educational, socio-spiritual and non-profit organization.[17] Built on temple premises, the walls in the school are inscribed with quotations from religious texts. The school curriculum includes instruction in religious texts and practices, and education is moral-based rather than analytical and objective. In all of the afore-mentioned types of schools, religion is taught as absolute fact. It has also been observed that parents tend to enrol their children in schools that are affiliated to their religious background so that a "correct culture" is passed on to their children through socialization. This has increased the popularity of caste and sect-based schools in urban areas.

Education in rural India, especially in remote parts, is still governed by religious bodies. The dichotomy between religion and education still does not exist in the general consciousness of the people. Government efforts to promote a more secular form of education have been in vain, as the imposition of curricula designed for education in urban areas means the emphasis is on skills necessary for an urban lifestyle. This has led to an increase in importance of *madrassas* and *gurukuls* (Hindu schools) in local education. Based on the author's observations, education in rural and remote areas of Gujarat remains informal. Few or no formal institutions exist in rural areas; in most cases the popular centres for education are religious bodies. For example, in Dinara, a remote village with a majority Muslim population in Kutch district of Gujarat, the local mosque is responsible for providing education though a *madrassa*. The same is the case for villages and towns with a Hindu majority, like Dwarka for example, where education is provided through *gurukuls* and institutions linked to a certain Hindu temple. The formal institutions, when in place, adapt to the local religious rhetoric, ostensibly to

---

17   Shree Swaminarayan Gurukul, Rajkot - SGVP Ahmedabad, web, 13 December 2012.

give people an incentive for education, but mostly with an eye to winning votes at the local level. The teachers are appointed locally; few of them have any teaching qualifications. Hence, they tend to pass on popular stereotypes and prevailing misunderstandings about 'others'.

Accordingly, in the absence of national or provincial policies on teaching religion, education in religion has become synonymous with creating a religious environment based on religious rhetoric.

Conclusion

Post-independent India refrained from defining the relationship between religion and state so as not to aggravate the sensitive question of religion in the wake of the partition of Greater India and the violence associated with it. Now, after a long delay, India as a state has the ability to raise the issue without triggering violence. But it should also be understood that India faces the pressures of globalization, of having to keep the domestic economy growing at the pace of the global economy. As a result, the government has a preference for short-term policies with an eye to immediate economic growth rather than long-term policies that require large investments in the near term. This also applies to the question of religious teachings in India. With a limited budget, the government is forced to take a quantitative approach – how many people are being educated to enter the market economy – rather than a qualitative approach such as the creation of institutions to monitor educational curricula and make policy recommendations. In the capitalist economy, education increasingly focuses on providing skills suitable for the global market economy. Opposition to a curriculum based on Indian philosophical thought, or 'Indianizing' the curriculum, emphasizes the need to globalize in order to be able to compete on an international scale.

I would like to conclude by saying that education, especially in developing countries with divided societies, such as India, Morocco and Lebanon, needs to be rebalanced so as not to answer solely to the needs of the globalized capitalist economy, but also to base itself on an objective internal analysis and the resolution of the social and political problems unique to its people.

What We Know – and What We Don't
An Epilogue

THEODOR HANF

The sheer diversity of countries and religions revealed in our case studies should give anyone in search of generalisations cause for circumspection and reticence. The choice of our case studies is another reason for caution. Countries with majority Muslim populations are overrepresented, as are culturally segmented societies. There are good reasons for this: in both instances not only is great importance attached to religious instruction, but it also has great political relevance. Such cases are useful for identifying problems; on the other hand they seldom lend themselves to generalisations. Any general statements in the following comments refer primarily to our selected cases or others with similar properties.

In the light of the above, what do we know about the *Policies and Politics of Teaching Religion*?

The first point may seem almost banal; it is, however, anything but: in all of the countries in the study religion is taught in school, including state schools, with the exception of France. And even in the country that introduced *laicité* there is now an intense discussion about the need to impart knowledge about religion in some form or other so as to avoid a rupture in the country's cultural heritage. In most other cases it is taken for granted that religion is taught in school. Political controversy is rare about whether, and far more common about how it is taught. Who determines what should be taught? Who draws up the curriculum and who trains the teachers? Where such questions trigger political disputes, it is obvious that the political actors are convinced, implicitly, if not explicitly, that religious instruction has an impact on society and on the political system.

A second finding is that not only the political class, but also broad sections of the population appear to share this conviction. Religious instruction often serves to politically mobilize people. While politicians sit and debate the matter, ordinary people frequently take to the streets. Although now less common in liberal western states, in many predominantly Muslim countries conflicts about religious instruction are closely linked with the fundamental conflict about the character of the state: how religious and how secular should it be? This question is currently the crux of the political debate in many Muslim states, where the question of power cannot be separated from questions about the power of religion, who teaches it and how it should be taught.

A third observation holds primarily for states with cultural and religious diversity: that the significance of the role played by religious communities affects not only religious instruction, but education at large. Communities not only run schools and universities, but defend their right to do so tooth and nail. It is obvious that communities view schools as important agents for preserving the community's identity. Clearly, the question of coexistence between different communities cannot be separated from the question of how schools coexist with each other, alongside each other and often against each other, expressed primarily in the curricular arrangements that these schools apply and what they teach.

These three findings of our case studies raise the question of whether modern-day social science gives religious instruction and the political function of education in general the credit they deserve for facilitating an understanding of social conflicts and possibilities of their peaceful regulation. The body of relevant literature is modest and needs to be broadened and in particular deepened.

This need becomes all the more urgent when we review our case studies in the light of what we do not know, or know only partially. This exercise raises in particular three questions.

First, what do we actually know about the effectiveness of religious instruction? The interest in and commitment to such instruction on the part of political and religious actors appears to be based on a firm belief in its powers of socialisation. There is no robust empirical evidence to support this belief. Research findings on political socialisation advise caution. Political attitudes of young people may well be partially influenced by the contents of school textbooks and what the teacher says and repeats. They are also, perhaps more strongly, impacted by agents of socialisation that compete with the school, such as family, media and peer groups, and in particular by what young people perceive as their interests. Were this not the case, there would never have been any revolts by the young – something schools tend not to talk about. Doubts about the influence of political socialisation in school may, by analogy, apply to the influence of religious instruction. The well-known slogan, "Show me the school and I'll show you the pupils", is not empirically verified. The question of whether whoever "owns" religious instruction can decisively shape the religious convictions of the young still needs to be tested. Crucial in this regard is the extent to which what schools do, in religious instruction as well as in other emotive areas, agrees with what agencies other than the school do or runs counter to it.

The second question addresses in particular culturally and religiously divided societies: What is more conducive to peaceful coexistence: segment-specific schools or schools that integrate different groups? There is some evidence for the view that pupils of integrated schools are more tolerant of other groups than are pupils of group-specific schools. But no one can say with any certainty whether this can be attributed to the schools or to parents who send their children to integrated schools because they are already more tolerant than average. It is rare to find "integrated" religious instruction, i.e. instruction about the multiplicity of religions – instruction in comparative religion, as it were, rather than instruction in one religion – and these rare cases tend to occur in private rather than state schools. It would not be surprising to learn that pupils who received integrated instruction are more understanding of and tolerant towards other religions than other pupils. Once again, it is necessary to examine whether this attitude can be attributed to school instruction or to the social selection of these pupils, in other words: to their upbringing.

Given the strength of the religious communities in most of our case studies, it cannot be assumed that they would be prepared to forgo their own schools, let alone instruction in their own religion. This raises a third question: Is it conceivable that in separate religious instruction schoolchildren can be taught about other religions in a way that promotes mutual understanding? There is very little on this point in the literature. An interesting comparison in this respect is the teaching of history in former enemy states such as Germany, France and the Czech Republic. After many years of work, commissions of historians have persuaded the relevant authorities to agree that all statements about the respective other country in school textbooks of the country in question must be approved by this country's historians. Is something similar not possible in respect of textbooks for religious instruction?

This question oversteps the mark of reasonable research demands and takes us into the field of educational experiments beyond the boundaries of our case studies. But if this promotes a better understanding of other religions within and between states, it is surely permissible to push the envelope in this way. It remains to be seen whether religious authorities prove to be more or less amenable to crossing bridges than historians.

Authors

Rüdiger Blumör
Chief Planner Education, G.I.Z., Eschborn

Annalena Di Giovanni
Researcher, American University of Beirut

Muhammad Faour
Senior Associate, Carnegie Middle East Center, Beirut

Giuditta Fontana
Senior Researcher, King's College, London

Theodor Hanf
Professor, University of Freiburg and American University of Beirut

Karim El Mufti
Professor, La Sagesse and Arab University, Beirut

Hisham Nashabe
President, Makassed University, Beirut

Shreya Parikh
Researcher, American University of Beirut

Karl Schmitt
Professor, University of Jena

Kelsey Shanks
Research Fellow, University of York

Anne Françoise Weber
Journalist, Cairo

Studien zu Ethnizität, Religion und Demokratie

THEODOR HANF UND JAKOB RÖSEL (HRSG.)

In dieser Reihe sind bisher folgende Bände erschienen:

Gudrun Krämer, Gottes Staat als Republik. Reflexionen zeitgenössischer Muslime zu Islam, Menschenrechten und Demokratie. Band 1. 1999, 362 Seiten. ISBN 978-3-7890-6416-6

Theodor Hanf (ed.), Dealing with Difference. Religion, ethnicity, and politics: comparing cases and concepts. Band 2. 1999, 456 Seiten. ISBN 978-3-7890-6243-8

Theodor Hanf / Ghia Nodia, Georgia Lurching to Democracy. From agnostic tolerance to pious Jacobinism: societal change and peoples' reactions. Band 3. 2000, 156 Seiten. ISBN 978-3-7890-7010-5

Theodor Hanf / Nawaf Salam (eds.), Lebanon in Limbo. Postwar society and state in an uncertain regional environment. Band 4. 2003, 228 Seiten. ISBN 978-3-8329-0310-7

Julia Eckert, Partizipation und die Politik der Gewalt. Hindunationalismus und Demokratie in Indien. Band 5. 2004, 278 Seiten. ISBN 978-3-8329-0861-4

Ann Frotscher, Banden- und Bürgerkrieg in Karachi. Die Ethnisierung von Politik am Beispiel der Mohajir. Band 6. 2005, 288 Seiten. ISBN 978-3-8329-1100-3

Katharina Hofer, Implications of a Global Religious Movement for Local Political Spheres. Evangelicalism in Kenya and Uganda. Band 7. 2006, 274 Seiten. ISBN 978-3-8329-1741-8

Anne Françoise Weber, Le Cèdre islamo-chrétien. Des Libanais à la recherche de l'unité national. Band 8. 2007, 255 Seiten. ISBN 978-3-8329-3102-5

Andreas Baumer, Kommunismus in Spanien. Die Partido Comunista de España – Widerstand, Krise und Anpassung (1970–2006). Band 9. 2008, 445 Seiten. ISBN 978-3-8329-3266-4

Jakob Rösel / Pierre Gottschlich, Indien im neuen Jahrhundert. Demokratischer Wandel, ökonomischer Aufstieg und außenpolitische Chancen. Band 10. 2008, 196 Seiten. ISBN 978-3-8329-3267-1

Beatrice Schlee, Die Macht der Vergangenheit. Demokratisierung und politischer Wandel in einer spanischen Kleinstadt. Band 11. 2008, 668 Seiten. ISBN 978-3-8329-3274-9

Theodor Hanf (ed.), The Political Function of Education in Deeply Divided Countries. Band 12. 2011, 338 Seiten. ISBN 978-3-8329-6805-2

Helga Dickow, Religion and Attitudes towards Life in South Africa. Pentecostals, charismatics and reborns. Band 13, 2012, 211 Seiten. ISBN 978-3-8329-7049-9

Pierre Gottschlich, Die indische Diaspora in den Vereinigten Staaten von Amerika. Band 14. 2012, 244 Seiten. ISBN 978-3-8329-7146-9

Marcel M. Baumann, Kirchliche Beiträge zur nachhaltigen Friedenskonsolidierung in Post-Konflikt-Gesellschaften. Eine Literaturstudie. Band 15. 2013, 132 Seiten. ISBN 978-3-8487-0169-8

Titel mit verwandter Thematik außerhalb dieser Reihe:

Yves Bizeul, Gemeinschaften mit Eigenschaften? Die Identität der deutschen und französischen Gemeinschaften und ihre Sozialisationspraktiken. 1993, 312 Seiten. ISBN 978-3-7890-2811-3

Helga Dickow, Das Regenbogenvolk. Die Entstehung einer neuen civil religion in Südafrika. 1996, 288 Seiten. ISBN 978-3-7890-4610-0

Theodor Hanf / Hans N. Weiler / Helga Dickow Hrsg.), Entwicklung als Beruf: Festschrift für Peter Molt. 2009, 541 Seiten. ISBN 978-3-8329-4967-9

Eugen Lemberg, Anthropologie der ideologischen Systeme. 1987, 168 Seiten. ISBN 978-3-7890-1144-3

Peter Molt / Helga Dickow (Hrsg.), Kulturen und Konflikte im Vergleich / Comparing Cultures and Conflicts. Festschrift für Theodor Hanf. 2007, 946 Seiten. ISBN 978-3-8329-2400-3

Jakob Rösel, Der Bürgerkrieg auf Sri Lanka. Der Tamilenkonflikt: Aufstieg und Niedergang eines singhalesischen Staates. 1997, 445 Seiten. ISBN 978-3-7890-4611-7